THE INTERNATIONAL WINE AND FOOD SOCIETY'S GUIDE TO

Poultry & Game

Other Books in the Series

Single-subject Cookery Books

BAKERY, CAKES
AND SIMPLE CONFECTIONERY
Maria Floris

CHEESE AND CHEESE COOKERY
T. A. Layton

CLASSIC SAUCES
AND THEIR PREPARATION
Raymond Oliver

EGGS
Margaret Sherman

HERBS, SPICES AND
FLAVOURINGS
Tom Stobart

MEAT
Ambrose Heath

SOUPS
Robin Howe

Regional Cookery Books

FAR EASTERN COOKERY
Robin Howe

THE FRENCH AT TABLE
Raymond Oliver

GERMAN COOKERY
Hans Karl Adam

SPANISH COOKERY
Mary Hillgarth

Wine Books

THE COMMONSENSE OF WINE
André L. Simon

GODS, MEN AND WINE
William Younger

THE WINES OF BORDEAUX
Edmund Penning-Rowsell

THE WINES OF BURGUNDY
H. W. Yoxall

Titles in Preparation

TRADITIONAL BRITISH COOKERY
Malpas Pearse

FISH
Jane Grigson

REGIONAL FRENCH COOKERY
Odette Kahn

THE GAZETTEER OF WINES
André L. Simon

REGIONAL ITALIAN COOKERY
Robin Howe

JEWISH COOKERY
Madeleine Masson

SCANDINAVIAN COOKERY
Tore Wretman

SWEET PUDDINGS AND DESSERTS
Margaret Sherman

A brochure is available from David & Charles, South Devon House, Newton Abbot, Devon.

THE INTERNATIONAL WINE AND FOOD SOCIETY'S GUIDE TO

Poultry & Game

Robin Howe

with colour photographs by Kenneth Swain
and line drawings by Ian Garrard

THE INTERNATIONAL WINE AND FOOD PUBLISHING COMPANY

DAVID & CHARLES

A publication of
The International Wine and Food Publishing Company
Marble Arch House, 44 Edgware Road, London, W2

© Robin Howe, 1970

This book was designed and produced by
Rainbird Reference Books Limited
Marble Arch House, 44 Edgware Road, London, W2

Editor: Robin Howe
House Editor: Mimi Franks
Designer: Judith Allan
Indexer: Dorothy Frame

ISBN 0 7153 4812 4

Printed in Great Britain by
A. Wheaton & Co., Exeter. Devon

Contents

Also by the same author

Balkan Cooking

A Cook's Tour

Cooking from the Commonwealth

A Dictionary of Gastronomy (with André L. Simon)

Far Eastern Cookery

French Cooking

German Cooking

Greek Cooking

Italian Cooking

Making your own Preserves

Rice Cooking

Russian Cooking

Soups

Sultan's Pleasure (with Pauline Espir)

Acknowledgements

I would like to express my most sincere thanks to James Carlton Shy Jr., a good friend from the United States, for all the willing help he gave me while I was writing this book. He is both a keen hunting man and an ardent cook.

Also to Major Hugh B. C. Pollard who has in his day written a great deal on sport, both in the field and in the kitchen. One of his books is an old favourite of mine, *The Sportman's Cookery Book*. I have read it again and again as readers of this book will discover, for the Major had much to say on the subject of game, how to shoot and very much how to cook it.

Errata

page 115   in line 9 the cross reference should read (see page 205)

page 174   in line 23 the cross reference should read (see page 204)

Colour Plates

All of the dishes shown in the colour plates were prepared by the author in her kitchen.

Foreword

We are pleased to think that we are part of the Free World; not that we can do just as we please, but that we can say what we like. In the feather and fur world, the free have to find their own food and they must expect to be shot at dawn any day, once the breeding season is over. The others are hand-fed, but not free; they never are shot, but they are sure to be killed and eaten at any time of the year, unless they are clever enough to give us eggs.

In gastronomy, as we all know, the quality and quantity of the food eaten by cattle, poultry and game makes all the difference to what cook and chef can do for us. Many a well-fed tame rabbit has been enjoyed by people who were by no means fools, and who were convinced that they were eating chicken; they were given the white meat only, of course, and none of the tell-tale bones. But no hare could ever pass for chicken, goose or gander. That is where all game, feather and fur alike, score over the hand-fed poultry and guinea pigs. Most of the food upon which they feed is as wild as they are themselves; tougher they may be, but with a greater flavour and smell from their diet of grasses, leaves, flowers and even roots. This is why the flesh of game has a more distinctive as well as a more obvious taste than the flesh of poultry or tame rabbits. This is also why, in gastronomy, there are one hundred different recipes for cooking chicken and a hundred for dealing with hens' eggs, but less than a dozen recipes for cooking a young grouse and a single one to deal with plovers' eggs.

If we were to consider the partnership of wine and poultry as distinct from the partnership of wine with game, we would inevitably come to a similar conclusion, that there is a far greater variety of wine with poultry, increased still further by the sauces and garnishings given in different recipes. There is a very much more limited choice of wines to partner game, since the chief gastronomic asset of game, in the opinion of most gastronomes, is their distinctive gamey flavour.

Personally I like to think that the greater has been the time and skill given by the cook, the finer, hence also the more costly, should the wine be. If, for instance, left-overs of chicken were to be served at lunch, such as creamed chicken or *coquilles de volaille*, a good but unpretentious white Graves would do; a planked broiler in the right or 'proper Bostonian' fashion would deserve a Corton Charlemagne; a boiled chicken with rice, a good Riesling, Alsace or Hock; a *coq au vin* a fair claret, one of the *bourgeois supérieurs* of 1955 or 1959. It is not possible to name a particular wine that one believes would be best with all sorts of different dishes, since it is obvious that the best wine must be first of all the wine which you happen to have by you; in the second place, the wine that you have both the means and the chance to get hold of at the time; and last, but by no means least, the wine which you happen to like best. We all have different finger prints and we also have different taste buds; we cannot do anything about our finger prints but we can, sometimes, and as often as possible, give our taste buds what they like.

Game is rather easier to partner with wine because its more highly developed flavour has a more obvious affinity with red burgundy than any other red wine, but whilst I would be content to drink a genuine young beaujolais with venison, I would be glad to pay a somewhat fancy price for a bottle of 1955 *Les Amoureuses* (Chambolle-Musigny) to drink with the plain roasted, not blue but pink, first young grouse of the season.

General Instructions for Poultry

By poultry is understood all edible domestic birds except squabs, which are classed as game. Included in poultry is fowl in all its forms, including duck, goose and turkey. Poultry is highly priced meat for it costs more per pound than animal meat on account of the large proportion of waste, i.e., the carcass, bones and inedible parts.

Poultry, classified as white meat, is more easily digested than most butcher's meat because the fibres are shorter and the flesh is not marbled with fat. In poultry the fat is found beneath the skin and around the intestines. The most digestible portion of the bird is the white meat of the breast and wings. As with all white meat, it should always be well cooked.

Within the last thirty years the practice of choosing poultry according to the season has become obsolete. All poultry, even turkey, is available throughout the year.

Increasing competition and consumption have caused better rearing methods and this has come to mean that we are seldom offered an ancient or inferior bird as a roasting, quality chicken. Some may say that certain chickens have a better flavour than others, but most chickens these days are tender, with a mass of white flesh whether they have flavour or not.

As it is still possible to buy poultry that has been neither plucked nor drawn, it is therefore useful to know some of the old methods of recognizing whether a feathered bird is all it is said to be.

In young chickens the legs are smooth, the scales not coarse and only slightly over-lapping, and in the male bird the spurs are scarcely more than scaley knobs. There is a flexibility at the end of the breast and the beak is pliable. The bird should be heavy in proportion to its size and with unwrinkled flesh. The quills in the wings will not be difficult to remove; also there is an absence of pin-feathers and of long hair.

If the chicken is fresh there will be no unpleasant odour coming from between the wings and the body. The flesh will be firm without a trace of bluish or green tinge. The eyes of freshly killed poultry are clear and sunken, the feet still soft and the feathers full. All poultry should be kept without food for several hours before being slaughtered. The result is a clean, empty stomach and intestines.

Living in India as I have done for many years, I found many of these instructions very useful. We chose our birds alive, prodding the poor creatures as they lay warm and trembling in our hands. With most of them it was obvious that they had not been fed for a long time before they came to the poultry market; one knew as well that they had had to scratch for every grain they ate. Being most definitely free-range birds, they were full of muscle and sinew and were usually very tough. However, chicken hatcheries have now arrived in India.

As with meat, poultry must be hung until the period of *rigor mortis* has passed and it becomes tender. Those of us who have sampled chickens killed 'on demand', de-feathered, cleaned and put into the pot within exactly the time it takes to kill and pluck them, will realize how important hanging is. A newly killed bird should be hung by the feet in a cool, dry larder or in a corner of the kitchen. The time of hanging depends on the kind of bird and its size. A fowl or chicken hangs for 24 hours; geese and duck for about the same time, perhaps a few hours longer; while the turkey is best left for 3–5 days. However, much of this instruction has become obsolete since most poultry is bought oven-ready: plucked, drawn, cleaned and even trussed. Also, if we prefer, it can be purchased cut into portions, the legs, breast and the wings. All of this one must admit is very convenient.

A bird is a chicken until it is nine months old, after that it becomes a fowl. The skin of a chicken may be white or yellow, depending on the breed of the bird. When buying chickens for roasting, frying or grilling, select birds which are plump and fresh with well-rounded breasts. For braising, stewing and boiling, where cooking is long and often slow, a fowl or elderly bird answers the purpose. If for some reason an elderly bird is to be roasted, steam it first until it is half-cooked, then roast it in the normal fashion, basting frequently.

In dealing with duck, the following instructions do not apply to the choosing of deep-frozen duck.

When ducks are young they have yellow, pliable feet and light bills which become darker as they mature. The webbing of the feet should be soft and easily torn, and the underside of the bill soft and pliable. The breast of the bird should be plump but not over-fat, and its skin white and smooth. One of the surest ways to determine the age of a duck is to open the wing fully. Near the beam feather are two small, pointed, hard feathers. At the extreme end of the longest one a triangular groove will be found if the bird is no more than a year old. If more than a year old, the bird has as many grooves as the years it has lived.

For table purposes, ducks are best when they are one year old. Ducklings seldom reach more than three months. Nowadays, especially in the United States, most ducks are ducklings, since commercial raisers do not find it economical to keep the birds longer.

A voracious eater, the duck is his own worst enemy, for the duckling can be nursed and fed to reach a weight of 5–6 lb. in the first ten or twelve weeks of its life.

The goose is a valuable bird which makes good eating but is extravagant in use. Its bone structure is bulky and it loses a good deal of its weight in cooking. If possible, choose a bird that has seen but one summer. The breast should be plump, the legs smooth and the feet yellow with smooth and easily torn webbing. There should not be too much fat, and this must be pale yellow or white, while the flesh, if the goose is young, is light red or rosy.

Geese vary in size, from goslings weighing as little as 8 lb. to fully-grown geese averaging 12–14 lb., with some even reaching 16 lb.

The turkey is a bird that used to be eaten only at Christmas time in Britain and on Thanksgiving Day and Christmas in America, but they are now eaten all the year round. Poultry breeders in Britain recognize two quite distinct breeds of domesticated turkey, the black-plumed Norfolk and the variegated Cambridge. The former, it is believed, is descended from the North American bird and the latter from breeds found further south.

The turkey cock is larger than the hen and usually less economical to use as its bones are heavier. As a rule, the hen is more tender than her mate. The best eating turkey is a hen from 7–8 months old and has been reared in semi-liberty, given plenty to eat but made to scratch for some of it. Its legs should be black, the neck short, the breast plump, and the flesh snow-white. Avoid birds with bluish colouring around the tail and the rear portions.

The drawing and trussing of turkey is done in much the same way as for chickens but, being larger birds, the operation is more cumbersome. However, nowadays, even when buying a farm turkey (as against a frozen bird) the bird comes to us ready for stuffing and cooking.

PLUCKING

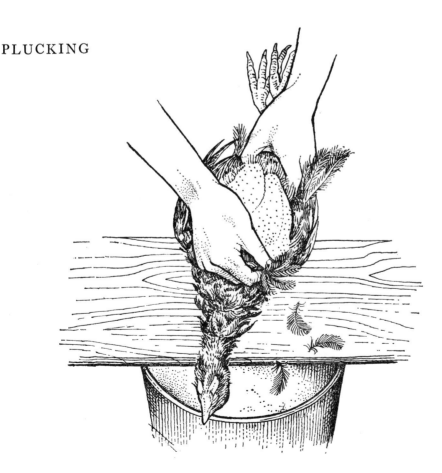

This means pulling off the feathers. Although today most of our poultry birds are purchased ready plucked, it does no harm to know how to pluck them. There are still many areas in the world where this is useful knowledge, and those who keep poultry in the back-yard should master this art.

First it is important to pluck the bird away from any draught, otherwise the feathers will fly all over the place. Plucking should be done over a large bowl, bucket or huge paper bag in which to catch and stuff the feathers. The bird should be laid on a cloth or paper or, better still, on a board. The feathers will come out more easily if the bird is still warm when being plucked. First remove the thin wing and tail feathers; then pluck from the tail towards the head, taking care not to break the skin, pulling the feathers out with a backward pull and against the direction in which they are set. If the bird is very young and the flesh tender, pluck from the head towards the tail to avoid tearing the flesh. For the wing feathers it is necessary to use a small knife and be sure to remove all stumps of feathers. If these feathers prove difficult to remove, the wings can be dipped into boiling water which will ease the process.

SINGEING

After the bird has been plucked it must be singed to remove all the small feathers and down. Rotate the bird over a gas flame or a torch of paper; take care not to blacken or

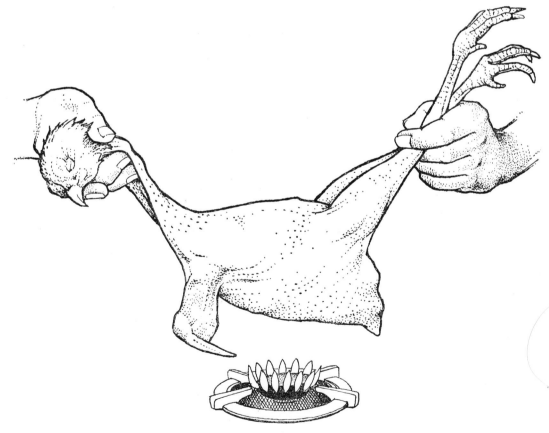

scorch the bird. Rub it with a cloth to remove any stubble and pluck out the quills which emerge with the heat. Cut the feet just below the drumsticks but do not cut through the tendons. Place the leg at the cut over the edge of the table, bend it downwards to break the bone and then pull off the feet. The tendons should come off with the feet.

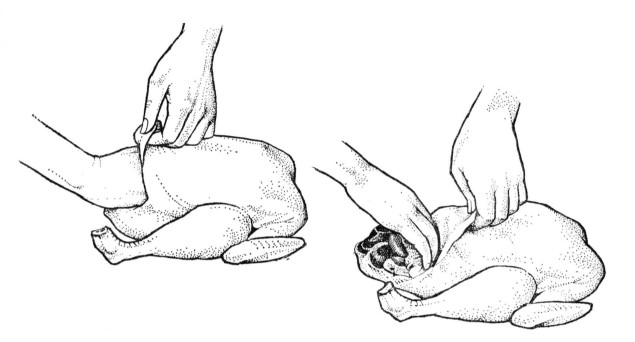

DRAWING

This always looks a messy job but it could be worse. Place the bird on a large sheet of paper. With scissors or a sharp knife slit it open from the vent towards the breast, making the slit as short as possible so that the bird keeps its shape. Carefully insert the hand into the cavity and loosen the entrails from the back and sides and pull then out towards the opening. With care it is possible to bring them out with one motion, but make certain that the lungs and kidneys, which lie close to the backbone, are removed. With a sharp knife cut out the oil sac which is found on the upper surface of the tail under a small white lump. Wipe the bird clean inside and separate the edible offal, i.e., the heart, liver and gizzard from the entrails or inedible offal. Attached to the liver is the gall bladder, a small greenish-tinged sac. Cut this away with great care for if it is broken it spills its bitter liquid and will spoil any meat it touches. Score along the curve of the thick outer skin of the gizzard down to the inner skin. Pry the inner skin apart and peel it away from the inner sac; discard this. Put the giblets into hot water. Pull off but reserve the soft layers of rich yellow fat which cling to the skin near the neck and the vent. The wishbone is often extracted to make carving easier but to do this is also to remove the pleasure of wishing on the breaking of the wish-bone. A pity.

TRUSSING

Trussing a chicken or turkey is not difficult and both are trussed in the same way. All that is needed is a trussing needle and a strong twine. The illustration shows how it is done. Before trussing the bird should be stuffed (it should be stuffed, otherwise trussing becomes difficult). Then the neck flap is sewn down. To fix the 'parson's nose' the butcher

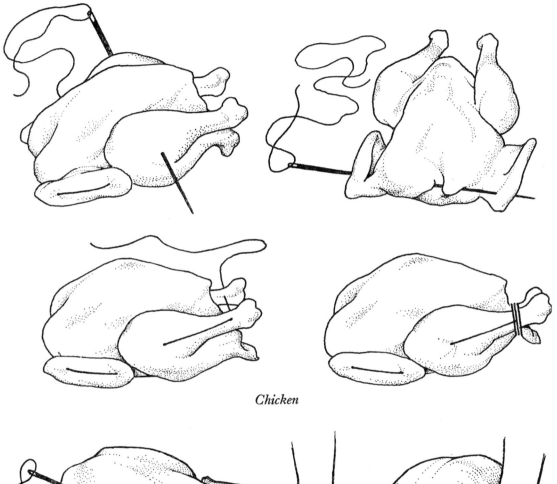

Chicken

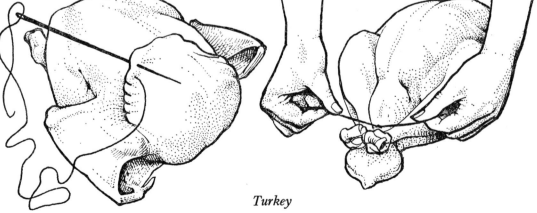

Turkey

makes a slit above the cavity which acts as a sort of button hole through which it is pushed.

Place the chicken (or turkey) on its back. Thread the needle with twine. Push the needle through the left thigh of the bird being trussed, through the breast and out the other side. Turn the chicken and push the needle through the wings. Break off the thread and tie the two ends together. Now pass the needle through the lower part of the drumsticks and under the breast from left to right. Pull the ends of the twine together and tie. Remove the trussing string before bringing the bird to the table.

FREEZING

Frozen poultry has come to stay, and the scope of its use is gradually increasing because of both the high quality of the products introduced by commercial methods, and the increasing numbers of freezing plants throughout the world. Another, and by no means the least reason, is the convenience of deep frozen poultry to the cook and the housewife who would find cooking just that much more difficult without such products.

All poultry freezes in both its uncooked and cooked states. However, freezing a fowl will not turn it into a chicken. If the bird starts out as ancient and tough, it will stay that way. Many people complain that frozen poultry has no flavour. It is not the freezing that produces a flavourless bird but the method of producing them. Birds kept in a battery in individual cages are more tender than those kept in a barnyard or free range where they can exercise and develop muscle. However, the latter has more flavour. So it is often a choice between a full-flavoured but less tender bird or one with less flavour but with meat that cuts like butter. Both can be frozen but will remain as they were.

When choosing poultry for putting into a deep freezer do so with discrimination. Poultry is not cheap, neither for that matter, is one's deep freeze space, so buy the best for deep freezing.

The method for preparing all poultry for deep freezing is the same. The bird must be plucked, drawn and trussed. The legs must be tied down so that there are no sharp bones to break through the polythene bag. Wipe the bird with a damp cloth both inside and out. Place the birds in the bag, press out as much air as possible and then tie the opening securely.

To thaw the bird, take it out of the bag and let it thaw at room temperature for at least 8 hours, even overnight. Chickens must be defrosted at least 8 hours before using, as they may contain salmonella, a toxic substance which is rendered harmless after this amount of time. A capon must most certainly be left overnight and, incidentally, these deep freeze splendidly. A large turkey will take up to 48 hours to thaw, a smaller one 36 hours. Smaller birds obviously take less time. By treating poultry kindly and thawing the birds slowly they gain a lot. Chickens may be stuffed before they are frozen, but it is better to stuff them after they have thawed.

Cooked poultry may be frozen on the carcass. If the bird is stuffed, scoop out the stuffing and freeze this separately. To serve cooked poultry, let it thaw for several hours before using. Sliced poultry is best covered in a gravy or sauce for freezing.

Chicken & Capon

'A chicken is a barnyard fowl', says André Simon, for him rather prosaically. But he continues more kindly, 'the chicken may rightly be called the best of the birds covered by the name of poultry'.

Brillat-Savarin pondered deeply on the chicken, as he pondered on most things culinary, and he came up with the provocative query, 'If Adam and Eve sold themselves for an apple, what would they have done for a truffled fowl?'

The common domestic or barnyard fowl or chicken (if there are still barnyards in this age of battery-fed hens) is descended from the wild jungle fowl of Eastern Asia. The earliest mention of the domestic fowl occurs in a passage by a Greek author, *circa* 570 B.C. It was at the same time that Aesop was admonishing the foolish milkmaid: 'Don't count your chickens before they are hatched'.

The Romans were scientific chicken breeders with a preference for red and black plumaged hens which they thought to be the best egg layers. They considered white ones delicate and these were unpopular.

Fowls were kept in poultry yards with the floors or ground strewn with sand and ashes. There were roosting poles and nest boxes which projected from the walls. Eggs were hatched by an incubation method. In fact, incubation was practised not only by the Romans, but earlier by the ancient Egyptians, who hatched eggs in especially adapted ovens.

And for those who deplore modern methods of force feeding, it must be said this is nothing new. The Romans fattened hens rather as the Strasbourg goose is fattened today, with balls of wheat moistened in water. Much later, in a book published in 1671, *The Closet of the Eminently Learned Sir Kenelm Digby, KT., Opened*, we are told how 'to fatten young chickens in a wonderfull degree'. The instructions run thus: 'Their drink must be onely Milk, in another little trough by a meat trough. Let a candle (fitley disposed) stand by them all night; for, seeing their meat, they will eat it all night long'. Yet another old poultry recipe advises: 'Let them have water or strong Ale to drink. They will be very drunk and sleep; and then eat again'.

Poultry culture has developed to a fine art today, and the average chicken, before it reaches the market or the freezer of the supermarket, passes through what can only be described as a metamorphosis. But whether barnyard bird or battery-fed, the chicken is, like potato, bread and rice, one of those items of diet which most of us can eat almost every day without nausea.

There is a story, told with variations, of King Henry IV of France who supposedly coined a slogan: 'I want each of my peasants to have a chicken in his pot on Sunday'. Well, if this story is true, and probably he said something very like this, surely the king, if he came back to earth today, would be pleased to see that not only can every peasant but every townsman too have his chicken not only on Sunday but every day of the week as well. The chicken, cooked and served in hundreds of different ways, has become the most popular table bird in the world.

Chicken is the general culinary term for the barnyard fowl, bred for egg production and for the table, and covering a range of birds from the 4–6 week-old poussin to the elderly laying hen. Between these are spring chickens (sometimes called broilers) which may weigh up to 3 lb., then the 3–5 lb. roasting chicken, and finally the capon, a young cock which has been castrated and fattened up so that it may be stuffed, roasted and eaten in place of turkey or goose.

In Britain the free range chicken is still most popular, either roasted or fried, and the same applies in many parts of the United States. In both countries there is now a large industry producing battery-fed, frozen birds which, though cheaper to buy and consistently tender, are so often tasteless and flabby that only a well-flavoured sauce and other embellishments will make them at all appetizing.

In France, however, the chicken still remains an important part of the menu at all tables, and free range, fresh chickens of every size are cooked and served in a wide range of ways, varying from province to province. Young birds are roasted, braised or fried and served in one of a huge range of rich and subtle sauces, often accompanied by a dish of rice; the older birds are stuffed with rich ingredients such as pork or truffles and then slowly simmered for several hours. In nearly all French recipes, however, there is an unmistakable blending of herbs, vegetables and wine to complement the delicate flavour of chicken; fresh tarragon is considered to be the perfect herb in many of these dishes.

In country districts of Britain, where free range chickens are still available, roasting birds are stuffed with a variety of forcemeats based on breadcrumbs and flavoured with garden herbs, parsley and lemon. In Italy the whole bird may be stuffed with ham or truffles, or the white meat cooked with ham and cheese.

But in all countries the good cook chooses a bird with an eye to the particular dish to be prepared, bearing in mind that the youngest birds are tender but inclined to lack flavour, while the oldest need the most care to produce an agreeable dish.

SERVINGS

The number of servings given in the following recipes are purely as a guide to assist the cook and are not to be taken as inflexible. Appetites vary and so does the weight of birds. For example, two people can buy an 8-lb. bird each; one may be heavy with bone, the other more happily with flesh. All weights given are dressed, i.e., after the bird has been cleaned, plucked, trussed, etc.

The following is a general guide to the number of servings dressed poultry will give.

Chicken		*Goose*	
poussin	1–2 servings	8-lb goose	5–6 servings
spring chicken	1–2 servings	9-lb. goose	6–7 servings
2-lb. chicken	2–3 servings	10–12-lb. goose	8–10 servings
3–3½-lb. chicken	3–4 servings	12½ lb. goose	10–12 servings
4½–5-lb. chicken	4 servings		
5½–6-lb. chicken	6–8 servings		

Duck		*Capon and Turkey*
3½–4-lb. duck	3–4 servings	Allow approximately ¾ lb. of dressed weight
4½-lb. duck	4 servings	per person.
5½–6-lb. duck	5–6 servings	

TO BONE CHICKEN BREASTS

It is possible nowadays, I know, to buy chicken breasts, as well as other portions of a chicken, already boned. Even so, it is not all that difficult to strip off the breasts.

First split the chicken into two halves and place these on a flat surface. Using the fingers, pull off the skin; it comes off with the minimum of effort. Then make an incision with a small knife between the meat and the breast bones at a point away from the wing bone. Again using the fingers and the knife carefully, pull and strip the flesh away from the bone, taking care not to tear the flesh.

If breasts, boned French style, are required, leave the main wing bones attached. See illustration below for alternative method of boning a chicken.

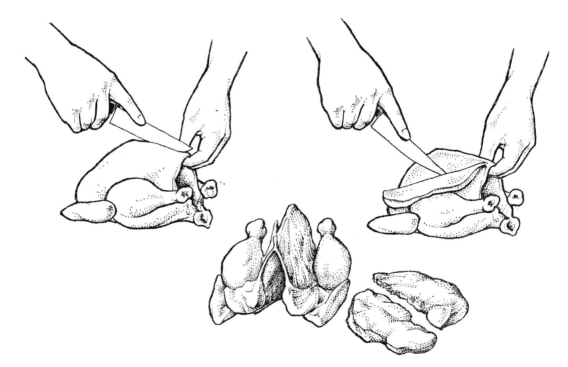

CARVING

Only large birds are carved, smaller birds can be simply jointed or cut into half.

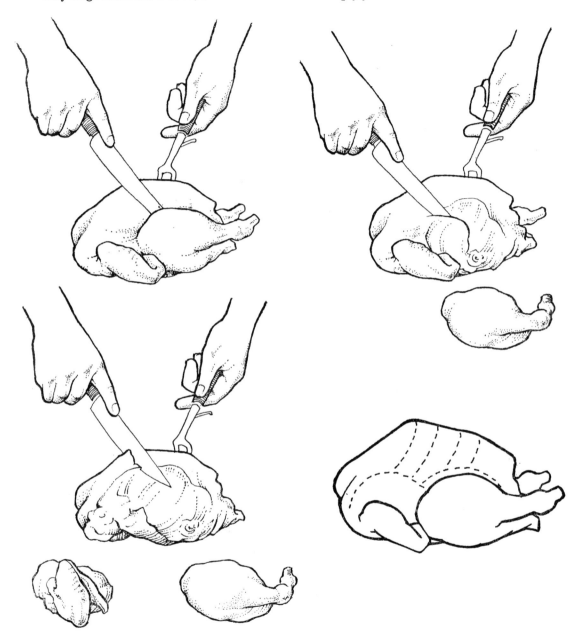

POT ROASTED CHICKEN

This is a popular method of cooking on the Continent but less so in Britain and the United States.

Pot roasting is a simple method of cooking, particularly for chicken which is past its pristine youth. To pot roast is to cook meat, poultry and game in a pot on top of the stove and is very similar to braising. The difference between pot roasting and oven roasting is that with the first the heat is direct from the top of the stove, and with the second, radiated from the oven. To pot roast meat and poultry, first sear or brown it in fat and then add a little liquid, always at the side of the pot, not touching the ingredient being roasted. Cover the pan and cook slowly and long. Vegetables may be added to the pot; it may be plain or spicy cooking.

Heat some fat in a pot (all quantities in this recipe depend on the size of the chicken being cooked and even on the size of the pot). Add the chicken, trussed and ready for roasting, breast downwards. Brown the skin evenly by turning the bird round and round. This is done simply with the help of two wooden spoons or forks. Do not prick the bird or its precious meat juices will seep out and the flesh will become dry. When the bird is evenly and nicely browned, add salt and pepper to taste. Add enough liquid at the side of the pot to cover the bottom of the pan to ensure there will be no burning. Cover the pan and continue cooking over a low heat so that cooking is long and slow. Turn the bird from time to time and baste frequently. If the liquid should evaporate, add a little more, always at the side of the pan so that the bird is not moistened.

It is not possible to tell how long it will take to cook the chicken until it is tender, as this depends on the size, age and quality of the bird. Test with a skewer; if this easily penetrates the breast and leg, the bird is ready for serving, tender and plumped-up.

ROASTING A CHICKEN

To give exact directions for the roasting of a chicken is a little perplexing. When being tested for 'doneness' and the juices run clear, it is done. If they are still streaked with blood, it is usual to continue roasting the chicken until clear juices are obtained.

However, there is a school of thinking which prefers to take the chicken from the oven while there is still a streak of pinkness in the juices. This results in a juicier and more succulent flesh and at the same time a certain touch of pink in the dark flesh of the joints, desirable by some, disastrous for others. For my own taste, I stop cooking the chicken when the juices still have a trace of blood running through them, as I do not like dry meat.

Generally speaking a roasting chicken of 4–5 lb. is ample for 4 people; but much depends on how it is carved. I have seen men carving a chicken with deliberate and splendid care, producing slices as thin as paper and managing to place untold amounts of thin white breast on plate after plate. This is economical but I prefer myself to divide my chicken into good-sized portions – with the aid of game shears.

ROAST CHICKEN

6 servings:

1 large roasting chicken	**2–3 slices fat bacon (optional)**
fat for basting	**1 cup (1¼) stock**
salt, pepper	**watercress as garnish**

Truss the chicken for roasting, spread it generously with fat and lightly sprinkle with salt and pepper. Place it on its side on a rack in a roasting pan and place in a moderate oven (the bacon may be placed on it if liked but it is not necessary). After 20 minutes turn the bird and roast on the other side, then for the last 20 minutes or so or until the chicken is tender, roast with the breast uppermost, basting frequently. To test whether the chicken is tender insert a fork between the thigh and the body without puncturing the skin. Hold up the chicken over the roasting pan and let the juices run. If these are clear, the chicken is cooked; if still streaked with blood let the chicken continue roasting. When the chicken is tender, take it from the pan, remove the trussing strings and place the bird on a hot platter. Keep hot until the gravy is made.

For the gravy pour off most of the fat from the pan leaving only the sediment. Add the stock, scrape round the sides of the pan, add salt and pepper and bring this to the boil. Cook for 2 minutes. Strain into a sauceboat. Serve the chicken garnished with watercress, the gravy, rolls of fried bacon, game chips (see page 206) and a bread sauce (see page 206).

ROAST CHICKEN (Spanish)

4–6 servings:

1 large chicken or capon	1 tablespoon (1¼) brandy
½ lb. button mushrooms	2 small truffles
1 oz. (2 tablespoons) butter	2 oz. (¼ cup) cooking fat
1 tablespoon (1¼) oil	4–6 slices bacon
1 medium onion, finely chopped	1 cup (1¼) white wine
½ lb. chicken livers	a sprig parsley
salt, pepper	1 teaspoon (1¼) cornflour (cornstarch)
½ cup (⅔) sherry	watercress as garnish

Finely chop two-thirds of the mushrooms putting aside the rest to be used whole as a garnish. Heat half the butter with the oil in a shallow pan, add the chopped mushrooms and the onion, chicken livers, salt and pepper. Cook over a moderate heat; add half the sherry and all the brandy, stir well, reheat, take from the pan and leave to cool. Chop the truffles and mix with the remaining butter. Gently lift the skin of the chicken and spread the butter and truffle mixture over the breast underneath the skin. Smooth the skin back into place. Stuff the cavity of the chicken with the mushroom and liver mixture.

Heat the fat in the same shallow pan and when it is hot add the chicken and fry it very slowly, basting it often and carefully until it becomes golden brown. Put aside but keep hot. In the same fat fry the bacon and the remaining mushrooms. Transfer the fat with the bacon and mushrooms to a baking pan, add the white wine, the remaining sherry and the chicken, parsley, salt and pepper. Roast the chicken in a hot oven for 40 minutes or until tender, basting from time to time with the juices in the pan. When the chicken is tender place it on a hot plate and garnish it with the bacon and mushrooms. Strain the gravy into a small pan and bring this to the boil. Mix the cornflour with enough cold water to make a thin paste. Pour this into the pan, bring it again to the boil, stirring all the while, and cook for 3 minutes. Serve this sauce in a sauceboat. Garnish the chicken with watercress and serve a bowl of watercress separately.

ROASTING AN ELDERLY CHICKEN

6 servings:

a 4-lb. chicken
salt, pepper

some fresh marjoram, finely chopped
4 oz. (½ cup) butter or other fat

Put the chicken into boiling water to cover, add salt and pepper (an onion and carrot as well if liked) and cook gently for 1 hour. Take the chicken from the stock, rub it inside with salt and marjoram and place it on a rack in a roasting pan. Heat the fat until it is boiling and pour this over the chicken. Put the pan into a hot oven and roast the chicken for 30 minutes or until quite tender, basting often.

If fresh marjoram is not available, dried may be used instead.

PEPPERED ROAST CHICKEN (Thai)

2–4 servings:

1 roasting chicken
1 tablespoon (1¼) pepper, coarsely ground
salt to taste

6 cloves garlic, crushed
parsley or fresh coriander, finely chopped to taste

Blend all the flavouring ingredients thoroughly and rub these well into the chicken. Leave for an hour, rub back any of the seasonings which might have fallen off the chicken, then roast in the usual manner. Serve with watercress and sautéed potatoes.

SAUTÉED CHICKEN

4 servings:

2 frying chickens
2–3 oz. (4–6 tablespoons) butter
2 large onions, sliced
½ cup (⅔) brandy

½ cup (⅔) cream
juice 1 lemon
slices truffle (optional)

Cut each chicken into halves or quarters. Heat the butter and fry the onions until they begin to change colour. Add the chicken pieces and fry these until brown and tender. Take them from the pan. Add to the pan the brandy and cream, bring to the boil and add the lemon juice; stir the sauce well but do not boil it. Pour this sauce over the chicken pieces and garnish with truffle.

Serve with watercress, a green salad or other vegetables to choice, i.e. beans, peas, artichokes or broccoli.

SAUTÉED CHICKEN WITH CUCUMBER

4 servings:

2 frying chickens
butter for frying
1 cucumber, peeled and cut into 'marbles'

juice 1 lemon
½ cup (⅔) white stock

Cut the chickens into halves. Heat the butter in a sauté pan. Add the chickens. As they cook add the cucumber. Cover the pan and continue cooking until the chickens are tender. Add the lemon juice and stock, bring to the boil and serve hot.

VIENNESE FRIED CHICKEN (*Wiener Backhendl*)

This method of cooking chicken is as Viennese as Vienna itself.

2–4 servings:

1 young chicken, cut into 2 or 4 pieces	**1–2 eggs, well beaten**
salt, pepper	**fine breadcrumbs**
flour	**pork fat or lard, for deep frying**

Preferably this should be a whole chicken neatly cut into four by an obliging butcher. In Vienna the butcher will chop the chicken for his customers and for some curiously macabre reason leave the skinned head on one of the pieces. Most of us will be able to dispense with this touching proof that the chicken is indeed chicken.

Rub the chicken pieces lightly with salt and pepper, then coat in flour, beaten egg and finally in breadcrumbs. Heat plenty of fat; there must be at least 1 in. of boiling fat in the pan. Carefully place the chicken pieces in the boiling fat, fry them to a golden brown, then lower the heat so that the chicken will continue to cook through without further browning. The chicken takes between 10 and 15 minutes to cook. Drain off the pieces of chicken on crumpled, absorbent paper. Serve on a heated platter with a green salad and wedges of lemon. Fried parsley is also served with *Wiener Backhendl*.

The liver and the stomach are usually cleaned, also coated in flour, egg and breadcrumbs and fried in deep fat. As both take only a moment or so to fry, throw them into the boiling fat just before the chicken pieces are ready.

CHICKEN FRIED IN DEEP FAT

2–4 servings:

2 spring chickens (broilers)	**½ cup (⅔) brandy**
oil, lard or butter	

In a deep pan put sufficient oil to completely cover the chickens. Heat until it is bubbling hot then carefully drop the chickens into it. Turn them to brown on both sides. They will take up to 10 minutes to fry but probably less, depending on the chickens. Take the birds from the fat and put them in a hot oven to dry and keep hot. In the meantime heat the brandy and warm a serving plate. Place the fried and dried chickens on the plate, pour over them the hot brandy, set this alight and serve at once with a green salad.

CASSEROLE OF CHICKEN WITH GREEN OLIVES

4 servings:

a 3-lb. chicken	**3 oz. (6 tablespoons) butter**
4 cups (5) water	**1 tablespoon (1¼) flour**
salt, pepper	**24 green olives, pitted**
1 onion, coarsely chopped	**1 tablespoon (1¼) capers**

Cut the chicken into 4 pieces. Put these into a casserole with the water, salt, pepper and onion. Cook slowly on top of the stove until tender. Lift out the chicken pieces; drain, dry, then fry them in butter until brown. Mix the flour with enough cold water to make a thin paste. Bring the liquid in the casserole to the boil. Add the flour and water paste and stir this until the sauce is medium-thick and smooth. Add the olives, capers and the chicken pieces. Reheat and serve with rice or puréed potatoes.

CHICKEN CASSEROLE (Hungarian)

6 servings:

a 4-lb. boiled chicken
4 oz. ($\frac{1}{2}$ cup) butter
4 tablespoons (5) flour
4 cups (5) chicken stock
salt, pepper
4 egg yolks, beaten

6 tablespoons ($7\frac{1}{2}$) grated cheese
  (Cheddar type)
1 oz. (2 tablespoons) butter
$\frac{1}{2}$ lb. mushrooms, peeled and sliced
1 tablespoon ($1\frac{1}{4}$) finely chopped chives
1 tablespoon ($1\frac{1}{4}$) capers

Skin the chicken and strip off all the meat from the bones. Heat the first quantity of butter, stir in the flour and cook this until it is smooth and even begins to appear somewhat frothy. Gradually add chicken stock until a smooth and fairly thick sauce is achieved. Put the pan aside, add the salt and pepper, then the egg yolks, beating these in gradually and stirring all the while to avoid curdling. Beat the sauce thoroughly, add the cheese and continue stirring until smooth; put aside. Heat the remaining butter in a pan, fry the mushrooms until they soften, then add them to the sauce. Add the chives and capers. Pour half of this mixture into a casserole, cover with the chicken then add the remaining sauce. Cook in a moderate oven for 30 minutes. Serve with any vegetables in season, but in particular peas, carrots, green beans and boiled potatoes.

COQ AU VIN

French classical recipes for this dish often add a cup of chicken's blood to the sauce to thicken it.

4 servings:

a 3-lb. chicken, cut into pieces
1 tablespoon ($1\frac{1}{4}$) olive oil
2 oz. ($\frac{1}{4}$ cup) butter
1 large onion, chopped
2 tablespoons ($2\frac{1}{2}$) flour
4 tablespoons (5) brandy or marc

2 cups ($2\frac{1}{2}$) red burgundy wine
salt, pepper
2 cloves garlic, finely chopped
$\frac{1}{4}$ lb. fat smoked bacon, sliced
12 button onions, peeled
$\frac{1}{4}$ lb. button mushrooms, sliced

Heat the oil and butter in a pan and add the chopped onion and the chicken pieces. Sprinkle with flour and stir well, then add the brandy and set this alight. When the flame dies down, add the wine, salt, pepper and garlic. Let this cook gently for 1 hour or until the chicken is tender. Remove from the heat, leave until the following day. Reheat over a low heat in a fireproof casserole and in the meantime deal with the remaining ingredients. Cut the bacon into small pieces and very lightly fry this with the button onions and the sliced mushrooms. (If the bacon is not sufficiently fatty, add a little butter or oil to the pan.)

Shortly before serving, add these ingredients to the casserole. Blend well and serve in the casserole. When button onions are not available, use the equivalent in mild onion, coarsely chopped. Serve with straw potatoes (see page 206).

CHICKEN CASSEROLE WITH TOMATOES

4 servings:

a 2½–3 lb. chicken
2 lb. ripe tomatoes, peeled
2 medium-sized onions

salt, pepper
1 teaspoon (1¼) powdered ginger

Cut the tomatoes into halves; peel and slice the onions. Put the chicken in a deep casserole, surround with tomatoes and onions. Season, add ginger, cover and bake in a moderate oven for about 2 hours or until the chicken is tender. The juice of the tomatoes provides sufficient liquid.

CHICKEN WITH CHEESE

4–6 servings:

6–8 chicken pieces
¼ lb. Gruyère cheese, thinly sliced
½ lb. mushrooms, thinly sliced

2 cups (2½) cream
salt, pepper

Cook the chicken pieces either in a chicken stock or in water to cover until tender. Take the chicken pieces from the pan and strip the flesh from the bones. Cut this into neat strips. Put the chicken meat, cheese and mushrooms into a shallow, fireproof dish, cover with the cream and leave covered in a cool place for 12 hours. Add the salt and pepper and bake the chicken in a moderate oven until the top is a golden brown. Serve with spinach soufflé or creamed spinach and plainly boiled potatoes. Buttermilk may be used instead of cream.

CHICKEN COOKED WITH PEACHES

4–6 servings:

a 4-lb. chicken
salt, pepper
flour
4 oz. (½ cup) unsalted butter
1 tablespoon (1¼) sugar
1 tablespoon (1¼) mild vinegar
good pinch grated nutmeg

½ teaspoon (⅔) paprika
1 medium-sized can peaches
½ lb. carrots, sliced into rounds
a little fresh rosemary
½ cucumber, peeled and thinly sliced
parsley, finely chopped

Cut the chicken into serving portions, 4 or 6, rub with salt and pepper and roll in flour. Heat the butter in a large pan, add the chicken pieces and brown these all over. Mix the sugar with the vinegar in a cup, add the nutmeg and the paprika and enough peach juice to fill the cup. Arrange the carrots in a casserole and add the chicken pieces. Pour the contents of the cup into the pan in which the chicken was fried, let it come to the boil, stir well and scrape away at the sides of the pan. Pour this sauce over the chicken. Add the rosemary, cover the casserole and cook in a moderate oven for about 1 hour. Ten minutes or so before the end of cooking time add the peaches and the cucumber. Sprinkle with parsley before serving. Serve with a green salad and creamed potatoes.

CHICKEN KIEV

4 servings:

4 chicken breasts	**salt, pepper**
1 oz. (2 tablespoons) butter, melted	**1 cup (1¼) soft white breadcrumbs**
4 walnut-sized knobs butter, frozen hard	**2 eggs, beaten**
	oil for frying

Blanch the chicken breasts in boiling water for 5 minutes then carefully strip off the flesh from both sides of the breastbone with a sharp pointed knife. Divide each breast into two, skin them carefully and then gently pound the flesh until pliable, but not broken. Brush each breast with the melted butter and put in the centre of each piece a knob of frozen butter. Sprinkle with salt and pepper, wrap the pieces (each separately) round the butter and form them into hollow cutlets the size and shape of a carrot. Seal firmly by overlapping the sides to keep the knob of butter intact and put the cutlets into a refrigerator for 2 hours. Spread out the breadcrumbs or have them in a shallow bowl. Dip the cutlets first into beaten egg then into breadcrumbs. Repeat this process. Return them to the refrigerator for about 30 minutes or long enough to allow the coating to set.

Have ready a pan of deep, smoking oil and fry the cutlets for 5 minutes. Make slits in each portion before serving and warn the family or guests of the danger of the butter squelching out, as it does sometimes with some force when a fork is dug into them. Serve the Kiev cutlets very hot with straw potatoes (see page 206) and peas and garnish with sprigs of fresh parsley or watercress and wedges of lemon. Instead of putting plain frozen butter into each cutlet, a smaller amount of butter may be mixed with salt, pepper, chopped parsley and chopped yolk of hard-cooked eggs or, if feeling extravagant, with *pâté de foie gras* and truffle.

CHICKEN BAKED IN ALUMINIUM FOIL (German)

4 servings:

a 3-lb. chicken	**juice 1 small lemon**
salt, pepper	**2 oz. (¼ cup) softened butter**
1 tablespoon (1¼) French mustard	**1 small onion, finely chopped**
2 teaspoons (2½) sugar	

Rub the chicken inside and out with salt and pepper and place it on a large piece of aluminium foil. Mix the remaining ingredients together to make a spread. Rub the chicken with the mustard spread and wrap it carefully in the foil making sure the ends are well tucked in. Put the package in a hot, dry baking pan and bake in a moderate oven for between 1 and $1\frac{1}{2}$ hours. Serve the chicken in a deep dish in its foil.

The advantages of foil are that the oven and the pan do not require cleaning after cooking and the chicken retains all its flavour. Serve with any of the usual chicken accompaniments. The juices in the foil can be served as a gravy.

CHICKEN HOPPITY (American)

4–6 servings:

1 large roasting chicken	**salt, pepper**
2 cups (2½) cream, stiffly whipped	**1 teaspoon (1¼) each mushroom ketch-**
1 teaspoon (1¼) prepared mustard	**up and Worcestershire Sauce**

Roast the chicken in the usual manner. Cut it into serving pieces and arrange these in a fireproof shallow dish. Blend the cream with the remaining ingredients and pour this mixture over the chicken pieces. Return the chicken to the oven and continue cooking until the sauce has browned. Serve with a potato soufflé to which has been added a little sweet chutney.

Instead of roasting a whole chicken, chicken pieces fried until tender in butter may be used.

The origin of the curious name of this dish is obscure, but early American cooks had a penchant for giving unusual names to their dishes for no other reason, it would seem, than the fun of saying them.

CIRCASSIAN CHICKEN (Turkish)

Serve Circassian chicken as a first course, without accompaniment.

4–6 servings:

1 cold, boiled chicken	**salt, pepper**
1 lb. blanched walnuts	**2 cups (2½) chicken stock**
2 thick slices crustless white bread, soaked in chicken stock, milk or water	**walnut oil if available or olive oil** **paprika**

Put the walnuts twice through a grinding machine. Squeeze the bread dry, mix it with the walnuts and put this mixture through the grinder. Add salt and pepper and put it all once more through the grinder. A liquidizer (blender) shortens this process. Add enough stock to turn the paste into a thick sauce.

Strip the flesh off the chicken, cut this into strips and arrange on a serving plate. Pour about half of the sauce over the chicken pieces and see they are well coated. Put aside until required. Just before serving add the remainder of the sauce, making sure that the whole of the chicken meat is blanketed in the sauce. Mix 1 tablespoonful (1¼) of oil with enough paprika to make it a vivid red. Pour this over the walnut sauce in a thin trickle as a garnish. Serve cold but not chilled.

For a richer sauce dispense with the bread and use only the walnuts plus a little cream. The walnut sauce is a pale beige colour when finished. It can be prepared a day ahead of time.

CHICKEN À LA KING (American)

4 servings:

the white meat of 1 boiled chicken, cut in chunks	**¼ cup (⅓) sherry**
2 oz. (¼ cup) butter	**1 cup (1¼) cream**
¼ lb. mushrooms, peeled and thinly sliced	**2 egg yolks, beaten**
1 sweet pepper, thinly sliced	**salt, white pepper and cayenne pepper**
	hot buttered toast

Heat the butter in a pan, add the mushrooms and sweet pepper, cover the pan and cook gently for 5 minutes. Add the chicken meat and, still cooking gently, reheat. Add the sherry and the cream (retain just 2 tablespoonfuls (2½) of the latter) and cook carefully for 5 minutes. Mix the egg yolks with the reserved cream and add this at the last moment. Add the salt, white pepper and cayenne. Should the mixture be a little thick, add a little more sherry. Serve on hot buttered toast or in puff pastry patty cases or *vol-au-vent* shells or with rice. Truffles are sometimes added as a garnish.

CHICKEN PEASANT STYLE (Rumanian)

4 servings:

a 4-lb. chicken	**large sprig parsley, coarsely chopped**
2 oz. (¼ cup) cooking fat	**salt**
6 large onions, finely chopped	**¼ cup (⅓) sour cream or yoghourt**
pepper	**hot water**

Cut the chicken into 4 neat pieces. Heat the fat in a large pan or casserole, add the onions and cook these gently until soft and a golden brown; add the pepper and parsley. Stir well, add the chicken pieces and salt. Cover the pan tightly and cook over a gentle heat until most of the liquid has been absorbed. Add the sour cream, stir and cook covered for another 5 minutes. Add just enough hot water to cover the chicken, let this come to the boil and continue cooking over a low heat until the chicken is tender. Serve hot with tiny dumplings, noodles, rice or potatoes.

CHICKEN BREASTS WITH TRUFFLES

A splendid if somewhat expensive dish. The second main ingredient, mozzarella cheese, is usually available in Italian delicatessen stores. It is a pressed white curd cheese.

2–4 servings:

4 chicken breasts	**thin slivers white or black truffles to**
flour	**taste**
2 oz. (¼ cup) butter	**8 slices mozzarella cheese**
salt, coarsely ground black pepper	

Carefully pound the chicken breasts until thin (if making 4 servings, cut each breast into two). Dredge with flour. Heat the butter in a frying pan (skillet), add the chicken breasts and fry them until tender, browning on both sides. Take the chicken pieces from the pan, put into a shallow casserole and sprinkle with salt and pepper. On top of each chicken breast arrange as many slivers of truffles as desired and cover with 2 slices of mozzarella cheese. Put the pan under a hot grill (broiler) and leave until the cheese melts. Serve at once.

Small artichokes, green-tipped asparagus, peas, French beans and sautéed potatoes go well with this dish.

FRIED BREASTS OF CHICKEN IN PARMESAN CHEESE

3 servings:

6 chicken breasts	**fine breadcrumbs**
flour seasoned with salt and pepper	**Parmesan cheese, grated**
1 egg, well beaten	**4 oz. (½ cup) butter**
½ cup (⅔) milk	

Coat the chicken breasts with seasoned flour. Mix the egg with the milk. Drop the chicken breasts into this, then roll them in breadcrumbs and cheese. Heat the butter in a large frying pan (skillet) and fry the chicken breasts on both sides until brown and tender. The breasts are now ready to be served. For variation, at this point place them in a casserole, pour tomato sauce over them, sprinkle them lightly with fresh or powdered oregano, cover with thin slices of mozzarella cheese and bake for about 15 minutes in a moderate oven.

Serve with a green salad, sliced tomatoes or green peas.

CHICKEN COOKED WITH SHERRY

4 servings:

a 3-lb. chicken	**2 large onions, thickly sliced**
salt, pepper	**1 red sweet pepper, cored, seeded and**
3 oz. (6 tablespoons) unsalted butter	**sliced**
4 slices bacon	**6 tomatoes, peeled**
½ cup (⅔) dry sherry	

Cut the chicken into 4 serving pieces and rub each piece with salt and pepper. Heat the butter, add the bacon, let this cook until it begins to brown, then add the chicken pieces. When these are brown, add the sherry, onions, sweet pepper and tomatoes. Cover the pan and cook very slowly until the chicken is tender. Serve with rice, straw potatoes (see page 206) or potato purée and courgettes cooked in butter.

CHICKEN WITH RICE – 1

4–6 servings:

a 4-lb. boiling chicken	sauce:
salt, pepper	1 oz. (2 tablespoons) butter
2 carrots, peeled and chopped	1 tablespoon ($1\frac{1}{4}$) flour
1 large onion, peeled and chopped	2 cups ($2\frac{1}{2}$) strained chicken stock
bouquet garni	1 egg yolk, beaten
8 oz. ($1\frac{1}{3}$ cups) rice	a little cream
1 oz. (2 tablespoons) butter	

Put the chicken into a pan with plenty of hot water, add salt and pepper to taste and bring it to the boil. Skim off any surplus fat, then add the carrots, onion and bouquet garni. Lower the heat and cook the chicken gently until the flesh is really tender. Take the chicken from the pan, cut into pieces, with or without the bones, and keep hot. Strain the stock.

About 30 minutes before the chicken is ready bring, in another pan, enough water to the boil to cook the rice, add salt, then the rice and boil this for 15–20 minutes. Strain off the water. Keep the rice in the strainer for a few minutes. Melt the first quantity of butter in the same pan, return the rice, stir, cover and put the pan at the side of the stove to let the rice dry but remain warm. Leave until required.

Prepare the sauce. Melt the butter, add the flour and stir until blended. Gradually add enough chicken stock to make a medium-thick sauce, stirring all the time. Let this slightly cool, then beat in the egg yolk. Add the cream and reheat the sauce without boiling. Turn out the rice on to a hot platter, arrange the chicken pieces on top and cover with the sauce. Serve with stewed dried apricots.

CHICKEN WITH RICE – 2 (French)

6 servings:

a 4-lb. chicken	salt, pepper
5 cups ($6\frac{1}{4}$) water	bouquet garni
3 carrots, sliced	8 oz. ($1\frac{1}{3}$ cups) rice
2 onions, sliced	

Pour the water into a large pan, add the chicken, carrots, onions, salt, pepper and bouquet garni. Cook over a low heat until tender. Skim off the fat, raise the heat and bring the liquid to a gentle boil. Add the rice and continue cooking for 30 minutes. Take out the chicken, cut it into serving pieces, arrange them on a hot serving plate and keep hot. Strain off any liquid: there will not be much after the long slow cooking and the rice will also have absorbed most of it. Pile the rice round the chicken pieces and serve immediately.

CHICKEN COOKED WITH ONIONS

4 servings:

a 3½–4 lb. chicken	¼ cup (⅓) olive oil
12 large onions	1 bay leaf
small bunch parsley, coarsely chopped	salt, pepper
	1 cup (1¼) brown sauce (see page 208)

Cut the chicken into 4 serving pieces. Coarsely chop or slice the onions. Place half of these with half of the parsley at the bottom of a casserole. Add the chicken pieces and then the remainder of the onions and parsley, completely covering the chicken. Add the olive oil, bay leaf, salt and pepper, and cook the chicken over a slow heat until it is tender. Turn the pieces of chicken from time to time. Serve on a hot serving plate with the onions piled in the centre of the plate and the chicken pieces surrounding them; over the top pour a brown or *sauce espagñole*.

The chicken can equally well be cooked in a very slow oven.

CHICKEN WITH NOODLES

4–6 servings:

a 3½–4 lb. boiling fowl	peppercorns
onion, celeriac, celery root or parsnip, peeled and chopped	½ lb. wide noodles
salt	parsley or chives

All the above ingredients are to taste; a carrot may be added and turnips instead of parsnip.

Put the chicken with the vegetables, salt and peppercorns with plenty of water into a large pan. Bring it all slowly to the boil, reduce the heat and cook until the chicken is tender. Take out the chicken and cut it into pieces. Put aside but keep hot. Strain the stock, return it to the pan, bring to the boil, add the noodles and cook these at a boil until soft, 5–15 minutes according to size and type. (Fresh noodles cook in a matter of 5 or 7 minutes; dry or commercial noodles take longer.) Return the chicken pieces to the pan and cook for a few minutes. Serve the chicken with the noodles in deep plates garnished with finely chopped parsley or chives.

'A WAY WITH AN ANCIENT FOWL' (country recipe)

4 servings:

1 large elderly fowl	dust of powdered mace
1 cup (1¼) washed brown rice	salt, pepper
4 cups (5) milk	4 small whole onions, peeled

'First thing in the morning, say as early as 8 o'clock, put the fowl into a deep casserole. Surround it with the rice. Add the milk, mace, salt, pepper and one onion in each corner of the casserole. Cover tightly and put the casserole in a very slow oven and leave it all day to take care of itself. Around midday look to see if any more liquid is required to keep the rice soft, if so add either more hot milk or water and continue the slow cooking until the fowl is tender, around dinner time. If the oven has not been too hot the fowl will not be dried up but will be, despite its age, exceedingly tender. Serve the fowl cut into joints and surrounded with the rice.'

White rice may be used in place of the brown.

BAKED CHICKEN WITH NOODLES

6 servings:

a 3½–4 lb. chicken	**1 lb. noodles**
salt, pepper	**butter**
1 each onion and carrot, coarsely chopped	**mixed grated Gruyère and Parmesan cheese**
4 egg yolks, well beaten	
1 cup (1¼) each hot strained chicken broth and cream	

Boil the chicken in water with the salt, pepper, onion and carrot. When it is quite tender, take it from the pan and cut the flesh into medium-sized strips.

While the chicken is cooking, make a sauce by pouring the eggs into the top of a double boiler over hot water. When hot gradually add the cream and broth, stirring all the time. Cook gently until the sauce thickens and put it aside.

Cook the noodles in plenty of boiling water for 15 minutes. Drain and season well with salt and pepper. Generously butter a round earthenware casserole and fill to three-quarters of its depth with noodles. Add the chicken pieces and cover with the sauce. Sprinkle the top generously with grated cheese and brown in a hot oven.

BAKED CHICKEN AND BACON

4–6 servings:

a 4-lb. chicken	**6 slices bacon**
2 tablespoons (2½) flour	**small sprig thyme**
salt, pepper	**2 small leaves sage**
2 tablespoons (2½) finely chopped onion	**stock or water**
	butter

Cut the chicken into the required portions. Mix the flour, salt, pepper and half of the chopped onion. Toss the chicken pieces in this. Roll up each slice of bacon. Place the chicken pieces in a greased baking dish and push the bacon rolls into the spaces. Add the herbs. Over this sprinkle the remains of the flour and onion mixture. Add liquid to cover, dot with small pieces of butter and cover with a lid, aluminium foil or greaseproof paper. Cook in a very slow oven for 2½–3 hours, turning the chicken pieces occasionally and adding more liquid if necessary. Serve in the baking dish.

CHICKEN COOKED IN BUTTER

4 servings:

2 young chickens
4 oz. (½ cup) unsalted butter
salt, pepper
⅓ cup (scant ½) brandy or marc

1 cup (1¼) cream
2 egg yolks
1 tablespoon (1¼) strained lemon juice

Cut each chicken into halves. Heat the butter and fry the chicken halves on both sides until a light brown and almost cooked. Add salt and pepper and, if liked, a little thyme. Warm the brandy and pour this over the chicken pieces. Ignite and when the flame dies down add the cream. Cover and cook gently until the chickens are very tender. Arrange the chickens on a hot plate. Beat the egg yolks with the lemon juice until smooth. Take the pan from the heat and whisk the egg and lemon mixture into the cream. Blend thoroughly, then pour the sauce over the chicken. Surround the chicken with the small strips of toast, steamed asparagus tips or parsley-sprinkled, boiled new potatoes.

DIJON CHICKEN

4 servings:

a 3½–4 lb. chicken
2 oz. (¼ cup) butter
1 cup (1¼) dry white wine
bouquet garni
salt, pepper

2 egg yolks
2 tablespoons (2½) sour cream
2 tablespoons (2½) Dijon mustard
pinch cayenne pepper

Cut the chicken into 4 pieces. Heat the butter in a large pan and fry the chicken pieces until browned all over. Add the wine, bouquet garni, salt and pepper. Bring slowly to the boil and simmer until the chicken is tender. Take out the chicken and keep hot. Discard the bouquet garni, beat the egg yolks and stir these carefully into the gravy. Add the sour cream, mustard and cayenne pepper. Pour this sauce over the chicken immediately before serving.

Dijon mustard is considered by many the best of the French mustards.

CHICKEN COOKED IN MILK

3–4 servings:

a 2½–3 lb. chicken
salt, pepper to taste
about 2 pints (2½) milk
2 oz. (¼ cup) butter
3 tablespoons (3¾) flour

1 tablespoon (1¼) capers
lemon juice to taste
cream to taste
lemon slices
sprigs parsley

Cut the chicken into 4 serving pieces. Put these into a pan with the salt, pepper and milk to cover. Cook over a low heat, preferably with asbestos between the fire and the pan, until the chicken is tender. Take the chicken pieces carefully from the pan. Drain, put on to a hot plate and keep hot. Knead the butter and the flour together and stir into the milk. Continue stirring until the mixture is smooth. Still stirring add the capers, salt, pepper, a little lemon juice and, finally, enough cream to loosen the sauce (if necessary) and to add richness. Pour this sauce over the chicken pieces and garnish with slices of lemon and sprigs of parsley. Serve with rice or puréed potatoes and braised courgettes.

CHICKEN ITALIAN STYLE

4 servings:

a 3-lb. chicken
1 tablespoon (1¼) each butter and
  olive oil
6–8 tomatoes, peeled
1 chilli pepper, finely chopped

1–2 green sweet peppers, cored,
  seeded and quartered
salt, pepper
garlic
1 cup (1¼) strained meat stock

Cut the chicken into 4 pieces. Heat the butter and the oil in a large pan, add the chicken pieces and brown these all over. Add the remaining ingredients, bring to a slow boil, lower the heat and cook gently for 1½ hours, keeping the pan tightly closed.

Serve with rice, noodles or puréed potatoes.

SPATCHCOCK

1 serving:

Take a plump young frying chicken and slit it straight through the backbone but not through the breast. Season it well inside and outside with salt, pepper, chopped parsley, finely chopped onion and a few finely mixed fresh herbs. (When fresh herbs are not available, use dried.) Open out the chicken quite flat and thread it on to a skewer. Brush it well with warm butter and grill (broil) until half-cooked. Take it from the grill, sprinkle generously with browned breadcrumbs and return it to the stove to finish grilling it. Take it off the skewer and serve with any preferred sharp sauce and surrounded with crisply fried streaky bacon. Grated horse-radish mixed with a vinegar dressing from a beetroot salad makes a good sauce for spatchcock chicken.

GRILLED (BROILED) CHICKEN (for the home rotisserie)

2 servings:

2 grilling (broilers) chickens or
  poussins
salt, pepper
lemon juice
oil for rubbing the chicken
4 tablespoons (5) olive oil
2 tablespoons (2½) mild vinegar

1 teaspoon (1¼) Worcestershire Sauce
1 tablespoon (1¼) tomato sauce
1 shallot or small onion, finely
  chopped
sugar, salt, paprika and garlic salt to
  taste
parsley, finely chopped

Rub the inside of the chickens with salt, pepper and lemon juice. Spear them on to the rotisserie skewers. Rub well with oil and securely fix the skewers into the rotisserie (the grill should be preheated). Prepare a sauce with the olive oil, vinegar, Worcestershire Sauce, tomato sauce, shallot, sugar, salt, paprika and garlic salt. As the chickens grill, baste them with the sauce. The chickens can be served with watercress or with grilled bananas, peaches or apricots, stuffed apples, plain boiled rice, boiled new potatoes, a green salad, or sprinkled with parsley.

GRILLED (BROILED) CHICKEN

2–4 servings:

2 poussins
marinade:
3 tablespoons (3¾) soy sauce
2 tablespoons (2½) dry sherry

2 tablespoons (2½) oil
good pinch each aniseed, ground cinnamon, pepper
¾ tablespoon (1) brown sugar

Cut each chicken into halves and lightly flatten. Mix the remaining ingredients in a bowl and marinate the chicken pieces in this for at least 30 minutes but preferably for 1 hour. Turn the pieces as often as possible. Grill (broil) them on both sides until brown and crisp, basting frequently with the marinade. Serve with watercress, a green salad, rice or cooked spinach.

WHOLE CHICKEN KEBAB (Pakistani)

2–3 servings:

1 grilling chicken (broiler)
4–6 onions
4 cloves garlic
3 cardamom seeds

salt
chilli powder to taste
3 oz. (6 tablespoons) butter, melted

Mince the onions and crush the garlic and the cardamoms. Mix with the salt and chilli powder and pound to a paste, adding a little water. Rub this mixture well into the chicken and leave for 30 minutes. If any paste slips off, rub it back into the chicken. Brush the chicken with some of the melted butter. Insert a long skewer through the centre of the chicken and grill (broil) it over a hot charcoal fire or in a rotisserie. Occasionally brush the chicken with the remaining butter and cook steadily, but not too quickly, until the chicken is tender; turn the skewer from time to time to ensure even cooking. Cut into halves, serve with a raw onion salad garnished with chilli peppers.

BUTTERED POUSSIN

A bird 4–6 weeks old is a poussin and it can be prepared in several ways: roasted, boned and stuffed, pot roasted or split and grilled (broiled). They weigh between 1–1¼ lb. each. There is also a double poussin, some 8–10 weeks old and weighing between 1¾–2 lb.

and these serve two people. Such young chickens should be cooked as quickly as possible to preserve their delicate flavour.

2–4 servings, according to size:

1–2 poussins	1 cup (1¼) fresh green peas
6 young carrots	1 teaspoon (1¼) sugar
12 spring (green) onions	salt
stock	4 oz. (½ cup) butter

Prepare and trim the carrots and spring onions, keeping them whole and simply taking off the green part of the latter; cook gently in stock to cover for 10 minutes. Add the peas, sugar and salt and cook gently uncovered until a coating glaze forms. Heat the butter and fry the poussins in this until tender, between 15 and 20 minutes. Serve garnished with the glazed vegetables.

CHICKEN AND TOMATO STEW (Greek)

4–6 servings:

a 4-lb. boiling chicken	¼ cup (⅓) olive oil
juice 1 lemon	6 tomatoes, peeled and chopped
¼ teaspoon (⅓) ground cloves	2 tablespoons (2½) tomato purée
½ teaspoon (⅔) ground cinnamon	2 cups (2½) hot water
salt, pepper	

Joint the chicken. Mix the lemon juice, cloves, cinnamon, salt and pepper together and with it rub each piece of chicken. Heat the oil in a large pan and fry the chicken pieces. Take them from the pan, put aside but keep hot. Add the tomatoes and the purée to the pan, stir both well into the hot oil and gradually pour in the hot water, stirring all the time. Cook over a gentle heat until the tomatoes are soft and the sauce is thick. Return the chicken pieces to the pan. Turn each piece over and over again until coated with the sauce. Cover the pan and continue to cook over a moderate heat until the chicken is so tender that the meat literally falls off the bones. Serve with noodles.

CHICKEN COOKED WITH VEGETABLES

3–4 servings:

a 3½-lb. chicken	½ lb. small onions or coarsely chopped
salt, pepper	large ones
2 slices very fat bacon	1 cup (1¼) green peas, fresh or frozen
2 oz. (¼ cup) butter	artichoke bottoms or small artichokes
½ lb. small young carrots	to taste
½ lb. small young turnips	½ oz. (1 tablespoon) melted butter
½ lb. small new potatoes	2 teaspoons (2½) flour

All the vegetables should be peeled and cleaned as required but left whole. Where fresh artichoke bottoms or small fresh artichokes are not easily obtainable, canned ones may be substituted, but put these into the pan towards the end of cooking as they require a minimum of cooking. This instruction also applies to frozen peas.

Rub the chicken inside and out with salt and pepper. Cut the bacon into small pieces and put into a large pan with the butter; fry until the bacon fat runs. Add the chicken and fry it until lightly brown, then add about 1 pint (2½ cups) of boiling water or stock and the vegetables. Cover the pan and cook for about 1 hour or until the chicken is tender. Take the chicken and the vegetables from the pan, put aside to keep hot. Mix the melted butter and flour together and stir into the liquid remaining in the pan. Cook for a further 5 minutes. Serve the chicken with the vegetables as a garnish and the sauce poured over the top.

If preparing this dish in winter, use canned new potatoes but add these a few minutes before the chicken is ready as they are pre-cooked.

CHICKEN MARENGO (Italian)

4 servings:

a 3-lb. chicken	**¾ tablespoon (1) flour**
¼ cup (⅓) olive oil	**1 cup (1¼) dry white wine**
4 tablespoons (5) butter	**juice 1 large lemon**
salt, pepper	**about ½ cup (⅔) chopped parsley**
freshly grated nutmeg	

Clean and dry the chicken and cut it into 4 pieces. Heat the oil and butter in a large pan, add the chicken pieces, fry until brown, then add salt, pepper and nutmeg. Cover the pan and cook gently for 20 minutes. Take the chicken pieces from the pan; add the flour, wine and half the lemon juice to the pan, stirring all the while. Return the chicken to the pan and continue cooking slowly for 10 minutes, stirring constantly. Arrange the chicken pieces on a hot plate, sprinkle with the remaining lemon juice and garnish with parsley. Serve the gravy separately.

This recipe demands a really tender bird. Serve with rice, a green salad, spinach, broccoli etc.

CHICKEN COOKED IN APPLE JUICE (German)

4–6 servings:

a 4-lb. chicken	**¼ lb. mushrooms, peeled**
2 large carrots, thickly sliced	**2 firm green apples, peeled and**
3 tablespoons (3¾) oil	**quartered**
1 large onion, thickly sliced	**1 cup (1¼) apple juice**

The typical German apple juice, *Apfelsaft*, is not cider and the flavour of this dish is quite different from that of chicken cooked in cider.

Cut the chicken into serving portions. Cook the carrots until almost tender in boiling salted water. Heat the oil in a large pan, add the onion and fry until a golden brown.

Add the mushrooms, fry these for 3 minutes, then take the onion and mushrooms from the pan. Add the chicken pieces and let these brown. Return the onion and mushrooms to the pan, add the apples and apple juice. Drain and add the carrots; cover the pan and cook gently until the chicken is tender. Serve with rice or puréed potatoes.

PAPRIKA CHICKEN (Hungarian)

There are several versions of this dish from Hungary but the following is probably the most used.

6 servings:

a 4-lb. boiling chicken
2–3 oz. (4–6 tablespoons) butter
2–3 onions, thickly sliced
2–3 red sweet peppers, cored and
 quartered
1 tablespoon ($1\frac{1}{4}$) Hungarian paprika

2 tablespoons ($2\frac{1}{2}$) mild vinegar
salt, pepper
strained stock or water
3 tablespoons ($3\frac{3}{4}$) sour cream
small boiled potatoes

Heat a large pan, add the butter and lightly fry the onions without browning them. Add the peppers and simmer them gently, then add the paprika and the vinegar. Add the chicken, salt and pepper and cook for 15 minutes. Add enough stock to cover, cover the pan and cook the chicken over a moderate heat until tender. Just before serving add the sour cream and the potatoes, which should be hot. Continue cooking for a few minutes longer. Take the chicken from the pan and cut into serving pieces. Put these into a deep serving dish, add some of the sauce (put the rest in a sauceboat) plus the onion, peppers and potatoes. Serve very hot with noodles or tiny dumplings.

BUTTERED CHICKEN WITH WINE AND GRAPES

2–4 servings:

2 spring chickens
4 oz. ($\frac{1}{2}$ cup) unsalted butter
salt, pepper

$\frac{1}{2}$ cup ($\frac{2}{3}$) strained chicken stock
1 cup ($1\frac{1}{4}$) white wine
1 cup ($1\frac{1}{4}$) seedless white grapes

Cut each chicken in half, lengthwise. Heat the butter in a large deep frying pan (skillet) and fry the chicken pieces on both sides until half-cooked. Add the salt, pepper, chicken stock and wine. Cover the pan and cook the chickens gently until tender. Five minutes before serving add the grapes.

Serve with a green salad and creamed potatoes, rice or new potatoes, boiled and sprinkled with parsley.

CHICKEN COOKED IN CREAM AND WHITE WINE (French)

4–6 servings:

a 4-lb. chicken
4 oz. ($\frac{1}{2}$ cup) butter
salt, pepper

1 cup ($1\frac{1}{4}$) white wine
$\frac{1}{2}$ lb. button mushrooms
2 cups ($2\frac{1}{2}$) cream

Cut the chicken into 4 or 6 pieces. Heat the butter in a large, heavy pan but do not let it brown. Add the chicken pieces, turn them until they are well-coated with butter, cover the pan and cook gently for 30 minutes. Add the salt and pepper to taste, wine and mushrooms; stir, cover the pan again and continue cooking gently for another 20 minutes or until tender. Take the chicken pieces from the pan, put aside but keep hot. Stir the cream gradually into the mushrooms. When hot pour the sauce with the mushrooms over the chicken. Serve with a lettuce salad and paper-thin sliced cucumber sprinkled with chopped chives, chervil and French dressing.

SPANISH CHICKEN

6 servings:

6 fat chicken legs, skinned
$\frac{1}{2}$ cup ($\frac{2}{3}$) olive oil
6 cloves garlic or to taste
1 onion, thinly sliced
6 small red chilli peppers

salt, pepper
$\frac{1}{2}$ cup ($\frac{2}{3}$) long grain rice
1$\frac{1}{2}$ cups (scant 2) clear stock
6 tomatoes, quartered

Heat the oil in a large pan, add the garlic, onion and the chicken legs. Fry the legs until they begin to brown, turning them from time to time. Add the chilli peppers, salt, pepper, rice and stock, cover and cook gently until the chicken legs are very tender. After 20 minutes add the tomatoes and continue cooking until these are soft but still retaining some of their shape.

As chilli peppers vary in strength, six might well be rather too many for some people.

CHICKEN FRICASSEE

4–6 servings:

a 4-lb. chicken
4 cups (5) boiling water
bouquet garni
6 very small onions
1–2 carrots, chopped

2 oz. ($\frac{1}{4}$ cup) butter
salt, freshly ground white pepper
white wine
2 egg yolks
juice 1 lemon

Cut the chicken into 4–6 pieces and soak in a bowl of warm water for 30 minutes. Drain, put the pieces into a pan with the boiling water, bouquet garni, onions and carrots and cook for 20 minutes. Take out the chicken pieces and pat them dry. Strain the stock and reserve it. Heat the butter in a pan and fry the chicken pieces without browning them. Add salt and pepper and enough wine and stock to cover. Bring to a quick boil and boil for 2 minutes. Take the chicken pieces from the pan and keep hot. Beat the egg yolks into the lemon juice and add a little of the hot liquid. Take the pan from the fire, stir in the egg and lemon mixture and pour this at once over the chicken. Serve hot with boiled rice and triangles of fried bread.

The fricassee can be garnished with mushrooms simmered in butter.

CHICKEN COCOTTE (French)

4–6 servings:

a 4-lb. chicken
1 pint (2½ cups) water
¼–½ lb. salt pork
12 small onions
2 oz. (¼ cup) butter

1 lb. large old potatoes, peeled and
    cubed
4 artichoke bottoms (optional)
salt, pepper

The *cocotte*, which is a heavy iron or copper pan with handles on both sides, must be large enough to hold a chicken. It is usually oval in shape with a close fitting lid and is an indispensable item in a French kitchen. *Cocotte* also is the French nursery word for chicken.

Bring the water to the boil and add the salt pork and onions. Cook for 5 minutes. Drain thoroughly and reserve the liquid. Heat the butter in a *cocotte* and fry the pork and onions to a light brown. Take from the pan but keep hot. In the same pan fry the chicken until brown all over. Return the pork and onions to the pan, add the potatoes, artichokes, salt, pepper and the pork and onion liquid. Cover and cook over a moderate heat for 1½ hours or until the chicken is tender. Serve the chicken in the *cocotte* and carve at table.

Artichoke bottoms in tins are obtainable these days in delicatessen stores but whole small artichokes may be used instead.

BLANQUETTE OF CHICKEN

3 servings:

1 lb. boiled white chicken meat,
    neatly chopped
1 cup (1¼) white sauce (see page 215)
½ cup (⅔) milk or white stock

1 egg yolk
¼ cup (⅓) cream
salt, pepper
juice ½ lemon

Put the sauce into a pan, reheat it gently, stirring in the milk at the same time. Bring it slowly to the boil. Add the cooked chicken, lower the heat and let it slowly reheat. Beat the egg yolk into the cream and mix this into the sauce. Add salt, pepper and lemon juice, stir and serve at once. If the sauce boils at this stage it will curdle.

To the above may be added a little cooked ham, tongue or oysters. Serve the *blanquette* sprinkled lightly with chopped parsley and garnished with fingers of toasted or fried bread.

CHICKEN POTPIE (American)

6 servings:

a 4-lb. chicken
2 cloves
1 each onion, carrot and stick
    celery
salt

1¼ cups (1¾) plain (all-purpose) flour
2 eggs
3–4 medium-sized potatoes, thickly
    sliced
parsley, chopped

Cut the chicken into pieces. Push the cloves into the onion. Put the chicken, carrot, onion and celery into a pan and cover with cold water. Add salt. Bring to the boil, reduce the heat and cook until the chicken is tender. Take out the vegetables and discard them. In the meantime sift the flour into a bowl, add salt to taste and make a well in the centre. Break and drop in the eggs and blend the mixture to make a firm dough; add a little cold water if necessary. Roll this out as thinly as possible on a floured board and cut into 1-in. squares. Bring the chicken to the boil, add the sliced potatoes and pastry squares (potpies) and cook over a moderate heat for 20 minutes. Serve very hot and immediately, in soup plates, sprinkled with parsley.

CHICKEN WINGS WITH RICE

4 servings:

2 lb. chicken wings
6 tablespoons (7½) olive oil
2 large onions, finely chopped
2 cloves garlic, finely chopped
1 cup (1¼) rice
salt, pepper to taste

1 small can tomatoes (preferably Spanish or Italian)
1 cup (1¼) chicken stock
a few strands saffron, dissolved in water for 20 minutes
1 cup (1¼) green peas, cooked
3–4 canned pimientos, chopped

Heat the oil in a large pan until hot but not smoking. Add the onions and garlic; cook until soft and golden, stirring all the time. Take both from the pan and put aside. Add the chicken wings and fry them in the same oil until lightly browned, turning frequently to ensure even browning. Return the onions and garlic to the pan and add the rice. Stir this until it is transparent, then add salt, pepper, tomatoes and the stock. Add the saffron (and its liquid) and bring this all to the boil. Cover tightly and cook gently until the rice and chicken are tender and all the liquid has been absorbed. Add the peas and the pimientos, continue cooking for a moment or so and serve hot.

Pimientos are sweet peppers. The canned varieties have plenty of flavour and add colour to this dish which is a type of risotto.

CHICKEN MARYLAND (American)

2 servings:

1 small chicken
salt, pepper
1 egg, beaten
fine breadcrumbs or flour

4 oz. (½ cup) butter
¼ cup (⅓) cream
juice ½ lemon

Cut the chicken into quarters and carefully remove the breast bone and the thigh bones and make an incision down the legs so that the pieces will lie flat in the pan. Sprinkle each piece with salt and pepper, dip in egg and roll in breadcrumbs. Heat the butter and gently brown the chicken pieces. The white breast will cook first and should be removed and kept hot on a hot platter in a warm oven. Cook the legs for a further

10 minutes and transfer them to the hot dish. Add the cream and the juice to the pan and stir well, scraping at the sides of the pan to collect all the sediment and brown bits that cling to the bottom and sides of the pan. Pour this sauce over the chicken.

The usual garnishings for this dish are corn fritters, crisply fried bacon and floured and fried bananas.

STUFFED CHICKEN COOKED IN CHAMPAGNE (French)

6 servings:

a 4-lb. chicken	stuffing:
¼ lb. larding	**1 medium-sized onion**
4 slices fat bacon, diced	**1 clove garlic**
1 small onion, sliced	**2 shallots**
2 each shallots and carrots, sliced	**1½ oz. (3 tablespoons) unsalted butter**
½ calves' foot	**1 cup (1¼) brut champagne**
1 stick celery	**chicken liver**
½ bottle brut champagne	**1 lb. pork sausage meat**
	1 tablespoon (1¼) chopped parsley
	salt, pepper

First prepare the stuffing. Chop the onion, garlic and shallots and combine. Melt the butter in a pan, add the chopped vegetables and brown lightly. Drain off the butter. Add the champagne and cook until this is reduced by half. Chop the liver and mix with the sausage meat. Rub through a sieve and stir into the champagne sauce. Mix thoroughly then add the parsley, salt and pepper.

Fill the chicken with the stuffing, close the opening and wrap the breasts in the slices of larding. Fry the bacon in a heavy pan until the fat runs, add the sliced vegetables and the stuffed chicken, the calves' foot and celery. Over a moderate heat cook the chicken until it is brown all over, then add the champagne, and cook over a good heat until it boils. Cover the pan, reduce the heat and continue cooking until the chicken is tender. Place the chicken on a platter, remove the larding and keep the bird hot. Skim off the surplus fat, strain the sauce and serve this separately in a sauceboat. Serve the chicken either with new potatoes or a green salad or any of the finest vegetables in season. Instead of brut champagne, a *champagne nature blanc de blanc* may be used.

TANDURI CHICKEN (Pakistani)

This now internationally known and popular dish hardly needs a translation, although certainly an explanation. It is chicken roasted in an extremely hot primitive oven (a *tandur* from which it gets its name) which looks like one of the jars used by the forty thieves of Ali Baba. It is heated by a fierce fire of wood at the bottom. The chicken, which is marinated for 24 hours, is spiced and threaded on to a long skewer and thrust into the oven. It roasts quickly, so only tender chickens are suitable for this treatment. The chicken comes out of the oven looking rather fearsome. Tanduri chicken is attacked with the fingers and served with an onion salad prepared from very strong onions.

The following recipe is for 1 chicken. It is, or was, usual to offer a whole chicken per person. Nowadays one often sees tanduri chicken cut into serving portions. Tanduri chicken must be served piping hot, otherwise it falls exceedingly flat.

1–2 servings:

1 spring (broiler) chicken

marinade:

1 small onion, finely chopped
garlic, to taste (but be liberal)
½ teaspoon (⅔) chilli powder
juice 1 lemon

1 heaped teaspoon (1¼) mixed ground
black pepper and green cardamom
seeds
1 cup (1¼) curds or plain yoghourt

Clean and skin the chicken and with a sharp knife make cuts in the flesh on the breast and legs but without separating the joints.

Grind the onion with the garlic to a paste. Mix this with the remaining ingredients into the curds and pour it all into a bowl. Rub this mixture into the chicken and leave it for several hours (it is usual to leave it overnight) in the bowl.

Now the chicken can be either roasted in a very hot oven without any fat or grilled (broiled) in a modern rotisserie, in which case it may be brushed with a little oil from time to time.

Serve the chicken garnished with coriander or parsley and a dish of sliced red-peppered onions.

In the Indian subcontinent, with tanduri chicken is served hot *nan roti*, which is a type of unleavened bread.

COUNTRY CAPTAIN

This is a type of chicken curry. The chicken is cut into serving portions, fried with onions in butter, and flavoured with curry spices. When the chicken pieces are brown, stock is added and the chicken is cooked until tender, then served with rice.

It is an everyday manner of cooking in India although the original recipe is often credited to the southern United States (Georgia). There is a little mystery attached to the name country captain, but it would seem that since so many captains in the days of the British in India travelled Up Country, as it was called, and were always served chicken curry in this fashion, it became jocularly known as country captain.

'CRYSTAL CHICKEN' (Cantonese)

4 servings:

a 3–4 lb. chicken
a slice or so of fresh ginger

1–2 spring (green) onions or thickly
sliced mild onion

In a heavy pan bring plenty of water to a fast boil. Insert into the chicken 2 or 3 metal spoons to act as heat conductors. Put the chicken with its spoons into the boiling water, add the ginger and onion and bring the water once again to the boil. Let it bubble for 30 seconds, turn off the heat and leave the chicken in the boiling water until it is quite cold. The chicken will be cooked. Remove the spoons.

At this stage the chicken is ready for slicing and eating but instead it can be put into a large jar, covered completely with a Chinese wine or dry sherry, tightly sealed and left in a refrigerator for 1 week.

The chicken is now 'drunken chicken' for it has become thoroughly impregnated with the wine and has developed a splendid flavour. Cut the chicken into small pieces to serve. It is used by the Chinese as a party dish, with wine, and 'should be eaten slowly to relish all its flavour'. The sherry can be drained and used to flavour soups, sauces, etc.

MAYONNAISE OF CHICKEN

4 servings:

a 2½–3 lb. cooked chicken	1 truffle (optional)
1 cup (1¼) aspic jelly (see page 243) partially set	1–2 lettuces, depending on size
	2–3 hard-cooked eggs, quartered
1 cup (1¼) mayonnaise	2 tomatoes, peeled and quartered

Cut the chicken neatly into 4 portions, removing the skin. Put the chicken pieces aside. Mix ¼ cupful (⅓) of aspic jelly with the mayonnaise and let this begin to set. Brush the chicken pieces with this, giving them several layers until the pieces are completely covered. Decorate each piece with a little chopped truffle. (Instead of truffles, sliced olives may be used.) When the mayonnaise is firmly set, glaze each chicken piece with the remaining half-set aspic jelly, taking care not to disturb the mayonnaise coating. Let this set. In the meantime wash, dry and break the lettuce(s) into small pieces. Put some of the lettuce in the centre of a shallow bowl and place the chicken pieces on top. Tear the remaining lettuce leaves into yet smaller pieces and surround the chicken with this, garnishing the whole with the eggs and tomatoes.

COLD TIMBALE OF CHICKEN AND HAM

6–8 servings:

½ lb. cooked white chicken meat	1 truffle (optional)
¼ lb. lean ham	1 red sweet pepper
2 cups (2½) aspic jelly, partially set (see page 243)	1 cup (1¼) cream

Rinse a timbale mould in cold water and then mask it with a thin layer of aspic jelly. Cut the truffle and the pepper (removing the core and seeds) into fancy shapes. Arrange these at the bottom of the mould in the aspic. Gauge the remaining aspic and take enough of it to lightly cover the pepper and truffle shapes and mix it with the same quantity of cream. Leave this to set. Cut the chicken and ham into small pieces and then either pound in a mortar or grind in a mincer, aiming at a paste-like mixture. Put this into a bowl, whip and add the remaining cream and then pour all this into the mould. Add a layer of aspic jelly over the top to completely cover the paste and leave in a cold place until set. Turn out to serve on a round dish and garnish with coarsely chopped aspic jelly and small sprigs of parsley.

Bottled peppers are the easiest to use in this recipe.

CHICKEN IN JELLIED WHITE SAUCE (*Chaudfroid de Volaille*) (French)

6 servings:

a 4–5 lb. chicken
1 onion stuck with a clove
salt, peppercorns
bouquet garni

chaudfroid sauce (see page 65)
garnish:
truffle, pimiento or tarragon

Put the chicken into a pan, add the onion, salt, peppercorns, bouquet garni and enough water to cover. Bring to a gentle boil and cook until the chicken is tender. Let the chicken become cold in its own liquid. Skin and trim the chicken; it may be left whole or jointed or the flesh taken off in large solid pieces. Strain the stock. Make the chaudfroid sauce (using the strained stock), cool it and when it is on the point of setting coat the chicken. Let this set, then apply another coat of sauce. Garnish with truffles, pimiento or tarragon leaves, cut into shapes, as imagination dictates. The chicken can be served as soon as the sauce is set or covered with a thin layer of aspic and garnished with small clumps of aspic, tomatoes and sprigs of parsley.

POTTED CHICKEN

1 cooked chicken
salt, pepper
grated nutmeg

stock and cream
melted butter

Strip all the flesh from the chicken and pound it to a pulp in a mortar or finely grind 2 or 3 times. Add salt, pepper and nutmeg to taste and enough stock and cream to make a soft pulp. Put into a china mould and pour a thin layer of melted butter over the top. Chill and serve like pâté very cold with hot thin toast and butter.

CHICKEN SALAD

6 servings:

1 boiled chicken
1–2 lettuces
12 green olives or black and green
  mixed, stoned
1 tablespoon (1¼) capers

6–8 anchovy fillets
salt, pepper
a little vinegar and oil dressing
4 hard-cooked eggs, sliced

Strip all the meat carefully from the chicken and cut this into neat strips. Put aside. Thoroughly wash the lettuce(s), pull off the leaves, dry and tear into strips larger than the chicken pieces. Just before serving mix the olives, capers and anchovies with the chicken. Arrange the lettuce pieces in a shallow salad bowl, add the chicken, olives, capers and anchovies and pile these high in the centre of the bowl. Sprinkle with salt and pepper, add the dressing (not too much) and garnish with the eggs.

THE CAPON

Not as large as the turkey nor as small as the fowl, the capon is a happy compromise between the two and owes its existence to a curious law called the Fannius Law or *Lex Fannius*. This law was passed in Rome when the city was at its height of glory and extravagance. The senators viewed with dismay the gluttony of the wealthy, and the Consul, G. Fannius, feared that the enormous consumption of hens would lead to their extinction. Therefore came his edict, that the Romans should dispense with the fattening and eating of hens; but he said nothing about the cock. This omission is possibly explained because the cock was honoured among the Romans as a warlike bird but enjoyed no great reputation in culinary circles.

Amidst considerable grumbling at what was reckoned as an infringement of their personal freedom, the Romans gave serious thought to their culinary problem and it was a skilled surgeon who, remembering how eunuchs were created, performed a neat operation of 'snipping' on some doubtless protesting cocks and transformed these warlike birds into cackling eunuchs of the barnyard. They waxed fat, their flesh became more tender and succulent than that of the forbidden hen, and furthermore they increased in size. The fate of the cock was sealed, the extinction of the hen prevented and when Fannius himself was served some roast capon he pronounced his praises. From then on nearly all male chickens underwent the ingenious transformation which made them so welcome at the epicure's table.

So our capon is a rooster which has been gelded. There is more flesh on him after caponizing than on any other bird, his fat is marbled and worked through the lean tissue, rather than pocketed as with other fowl. He can be cooked and served in all the ways of chicken as well as of turkey. His minimum weight is about 6 lb., and the maximum 10 lb., and his age for eating is between 7 and 10 months.

Capons continued in high favour throughout the centuries. Shakespeare wrote: 'And then the Justice, in fair round belly, with good capon lined'. At the beginning of this century capons went out of fashion, possibly because their gelding became too expensive or too troublesome. Again great minds set to work and came up with the pill. Today's capon is injected in the neck with a hormone tablet, a quick and easy gelding. So capons have regained favour. In France, as so much poultry is sold undressed this method of caponizing is forbidden as occasionally the tablet does not dissolve and there is a risk of it being eaten by humans. In England the necks of the capons are removed before they are sold, thus there is no danger.

There is plenty of fine white and tender flesh on the capon. When buying a capon, unfrozen that is, feel the breast; the bone should be straight and free from blisters. The pelvic bones will be supple, or they should be, and the flesh on the breast and legs should be plump, with no spurs on the legs. Capons retain their tenderness and delicacy of flavour even when somewhat elderly.

Boned, rolled, stuffed turkey, with chipolatas,
chestnut purée and potato salad.

Hens are also caponized to increase their size and these are called *poulardes* or simply fat hens.

A Norfolk capon is not a fowl but a red herring. Capon was used in old English as a jocular form to describe a certain fish.

ROAST CAPON – 1

6–8 servings:

a 6-lb. capon
salt
chestnut stuffing (see page 219)
2 oz. ($\frac{1}{4}$ cup) unsalted butter or
    other fat

1 small onion, very finely chopped
a few celery leaves, chopped
$\frac{1}{2}$ cup ($\frac{2}{3}$) cream

Rub the inside of the capon generously with salt then stuff it lightly with chestnut stuffing. Close the opening, and rub the capon with half the butter. Melt the remaining butter in a roasting pan, add the onion and the celery leaves and fry these until the onion browns. Place the capon, breast side up, in the pan and cover it with foil smeared with butter. Put the pan into a slow oven and roast the capon until tender, allowing 30 minutes per pound. Baste it frequently with the drippings. Half an hour before the capon is ready remove the foil and continue roasting until the breast is brown and the capon is completely cooked. Take it from the pan, put aside but keep hot. Strain the gravy, pour it back into the pan, then return the capon to the pan, sprinkle lightly with salt and brush the breast with the cream. Continue to cook the capon for a further 10 minutes. Serve the capon with any of the usual chicken accompaniments and the sauce separately in a sauceboat.

ROAST CAPON – 2

6–8 servings:

a 6-lb. capon
$\frac{1}{2}$ cup ($\frac{2}{3}$) cream
1 cup ($1\frac{1}{4}$) breadcrumbs
4 oz. ($\frac{1}{2}$ cup) suet
butter

6 button mushrooms, peeled and
    chopped
1 teaspoon ($1\frac{1}{4}$) finely chopped parsley
salt, pepper
2 egg yolks

Boil the capon liver, then chop it as finely as possible. Pour the cream over the breadcrumbs and leave for 30 minutes. Finely shred the suet. Heat a little butter and lightly fry the mushrooms. Mix all these ingredients together; add the parsley, salt, pepper and egg yolks. Stuff this mixture into the capon and close the opening. Rub the capon generously with butter and put on the rack in a roasting pan. Add a little water to cover the bottom of the pan and roast in a moderate oven until the capon is tender, allowing 25–30 minutes to the pound. If the breast begins to get too brown, cover it with oiled greaseproof paper or aluminium foil.

Roast pheasant with grapes, game chips and watercress.

ROAST CAPON WITH TRUFFLES (French)

8 servings:

1 capon	**salt, pepper**
1 lb. fat pork	**2 medium-sized black truffles**

Prepare the capon 24 hours before it is to be roasted. Loosen the skin at the breast and legs. Slice off 2 thin pieces of pork and 12 thin slices of truffle. Put aside. Put the rest of the pork and truffle trimmings through the finest blade of a grinder. Add salt and pepper and spread this mixture smoothly under the skin of the capon. Top the stuffing with the slices of truffle so that they are immediately under the skin. Cover the breast of the bird with the slices of pork. Truss the legs and wings close to the body. Wrap loosely in foil and leave it overnight in a cold place or the refrigerator. The aroma and the flavour of the truffles thus permeate the capon.

Next day remove the foil and place the capon on the rack of a large roasting pan. Put this into a slow oven and roast until the capon is very tender allowing 25–30 minutes to the pound. In the same way as with roast chicken, pierce it with a fork between the leg and the body to test whether it is tender. If the juice runs clear it is ready. Place the capon on a hot platter and strain the gravy. Pour this over the capon and serve with potato croquettes Duchesse (see page 206).

HUNGARIAN STUFFED CAPON

6–8 servings:

a 5-lb. capon	**2 eggs, well beaten**
salt, freshly ground pepper to taste	**½ lb. mushrooms, peeled and chopped**
¼ lb. calves' liver	**1 heaped tablespoon (1¼) finely**
1 bread roll, soaked in milk and	** chopped parsley**
** squeezed dry**	**4 oz. (½ cup) butter or goose fat**
1–2 slices bacon, diced	**1 cup (1¼) red wine**
fresh or dried marjoram to taste	**¼ cup (⅓) sour cream**

Rub the capon with salt and leave for 1 hour. In the meantime trim the capon liver and gizzard and put through the fine blade of a mincer (grinder) with the calves' liver and the roll. Add the bacon, salt, pepper, marjoram and eggs and knead the mixture thoroughly. Chill for 30 minutes. Mix the mushrooms and the parsley. Lift up the skin of the capon carefully (it can be done with the handle of a wooden spoon) and loosen it from the breast. Push the liver stuffing inside this and ease it down to spread evenly all over the breast. Smooth the skin back into place. Fill the mushroom and parsley mixture into the cavity. Place the capon on the rack in a roasting pan. Heat the butter and pour it over the capon. Add half the wine. Roast the capon in a moderate oven until tender, allowing 25 minutes to the pound, basting frequently and each time adding a little more of the wine, but retaining some for the gravy. If the capon is browning too quickly, cover it with foil. When the capon is tender, take it from the pan and then add the sour cream and the remaining wine to the gravy in the pan. Stir well, scraping the sides and bottom of the pan to collect the sediment. Strain and serve the sauce in a sauceboat. Serve the capon with potato croquettes and any vegetable in season.

WALNUT STUFFED CAPON

8–10 servings:

a 6-lb. capon
½ lb. calves' liver
1 cup (1¼) milk
½ lb. (1¾ cups) shelled walnuts
butter

3 tablespoons (3¾) soft breadcrumbs, soaked in milk
salt, pepper
2 egg yolks, beaten
⅓ cup (scant ½) madeira

Soak the calves' liver in the milk for several hours or overnight. Blanch the walnuts, chop finely or better still put through a nut grinder. Drain the liver and chop it finely. Take the capon liver, chop this, mix it with the calves' liver and lightly fry in a little butter. Pound the cooked liver and mix with the walnuts, breadcrumbs, salt and pepper, 1 tablespoonful (1¼) of butter and the egg yolks. Knead well. Stuff this mixture into the capon, through the neck and rear end, and sew up the openings or fix with skewers. Rub the bird with butter (using any surplus from cooking the liver) and put on the rack in a roasting pan. Add enough butter to baste the capon from time to time, cover and bake in a moderate oven, allowing 25 minutes to the pound, until the capon is tender. Just before serving add the madeira.

Serve with sautéed potatoes, broccoli, Brussels sprouts or spinach.

Duck

'Prisoner, God has given you good abilities, instead of which you go about the country stealing ducks.'

WILLIAM ARABIN 1773–1841

Perhaps the unknown prisoner felt it was a challenge to go a-duck stealing, for 'the duck is one of the most intelligent of our domestic creatures, it seems at times to possess a sense of right and wrong, and in many ways it resembles a little child, except it is more easily taught', wrote Mr Bernard Reddaway some time in the nineteen-twenties in *The Feathered World*. Ducks also, it appears, have good hearing, are cheerful and can be called from a mile away.

Many people regard the duck as an extravagant bird and it has not quite achieved the popularity of the chicken either in Britain or the United States of America, although in Long Island there is probably the largest duck breeding industry in the world. The jibe, 'too much for one not enough for two' seems to have stuck. France, or rather French cuisine, has a great regard for the delicacy of the flavoursome, succulent duck and almost all of the French duck recipes are internationally acclaimed.

In English the culinary term for duck is used both for the male and the female bird, as in France *canard* and *caneton* (duck and duckling) in culinary parlance covers all. In North America most duck is duckling, for the breeder, taking advantage of the voracious eating habits of the duck, feed them up and in a matter of weeks get a duckling to the required weight for a duck.

The ancester of the domesticated duck was the mallard, but history does not recall when the first mallard gave up his freedom for the certainty of a daily meal. This may have seemed intelligent but it was not far-sighted, for the daily meal for the duck meant the pot for them in the end.

The duck has an ancient history. It was offered as a sacrifice to Neptune, and one historian wrote: 'The god of the seas never found fault with this offering'. And why indeed should he? Cato is said to have given his family a diet of duck whenever he felt they were run down in health.

The Greeks sprinkled roast duck with wine from Chios, while the Romans, eating only the breast and curiously the brains of the duck, liked to garnish them with white truffles, doubtless from Piedmont.

In China the duck has never been despised, and has long been connected with Chinese superstitions and thought. To the Chinese it means felicity, and when ducks are found in pairs it indicates to the Chinese conjugal fidelity, or it did to the Chinese of earlier regimes. Mandarin duck, with their exquisite colouring, develop a strong attachment to their mates and often pine and die when separated.

Fidelity, conjugal bliss or not, this has not prevented the Chinese cooks from developing a hundred and one different, often exciting ways of cooking and serving duck, from the whole duck to the tiniest morsels of the bird, which might well be discarded in the average Western kitchen. The Chinese were raising duck for the table long before the Romans were sacrificing them to Neptune. The finest of them all, the White Peking Duck, came from the aviaries of the Imperial Palace and were intended for the Imperial chopsticks.

The duck, it is true, is not the most economical item in the poultry group but it is usually lower in price, which makes up for some of the waste. Its bones make excellent soup. A 5-lb. duck should serve 4 to 5 people.

In French classical cooking there are three distinct types of duck, the Nantais, a small duck from 3 to 4 lb., which is killed by having its head chopped off and is then left to bleed before it is cooked. The second is the Rouennaise, a larger duck from 5 to 6 lb., which is smothered so that it has lost none of its blood before it is cooked. And thirdly is the *canard sauvage*, wild duck, which is generally a sort of mallard but may be any wild sort, sometimes reared in the barnyard from wild duck eggs.

In Britain the flavour of the Aylesbury duck or duckling, which are large and rather similar to the Rouen duck, is highly thought of.

In the United States it is the Long Island duck which is favoured, descended from the Imperial aviaries of China. The first nine of these ducks were imported into North America in March 1873, a date still honoured by Long Island duck raisers.

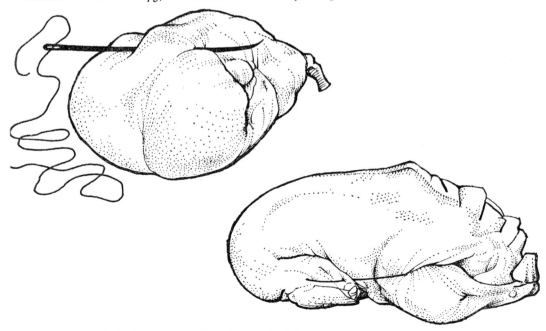

To truss a duck first remove the wings and pinions.

ROAST DUCK (English)

3–4 servings:

a 4–5 lb. duck
sage and onion stuffing (see page 224)
fat for basting

½ oz. (2 tablespoons) flour
1 cup (1¼) stock
salt, pepper

Fill the duck with the stuffing and truss it for roasting (see page 55). Place it on a rack in a roasting pan and roast in a moderate oven for 1–1½ hours, or until tender, basting frequently. Take the duck from the pan and keep hot. Pour off most of the fat, leaving about 1 tablespoon (1¼). Stir the flour into this remaining fat and let it brown. Gradually add the stock, salt and pepper. When the sauce is smooth, strain it and pour into a hot sauceboat. Remove the trussing strings from the duck. Serve the duck with apple purée, watercress as a garnish, and the gravy separately.

ROAST DUCK (Normandy)

4 servings:

a 5½-lb. duck
1 oz. (2 tablespoons) butter
1 cup (1¼) diced white bread
1 lb. tart apples
ground cinnamon

salt, pepper
½ cup (⅔) each white wine or cider and
  stock
2 tablespoons (2½) calvados
½ cup (⅔) cream

Heat the butter in a pan, add the bread and fry this until it is lightly browned. Peel, core and chop the apples, add them to the pan with the bread, sprinkle with cinnamon, salt and pepper and just moisten with some of the wine. Cook until the apples are soft, then stuff this mixture into the duck. Sew up the opening and sprinkle the duck lightly with salt and pepper. Place it breastside up on a rack in a roasting pan and roast uncovered in a moderate oven 25 minutes for each pound. Prick the skin several times to release the fat. At this stage the fat can be poured off from the pan. Heat the remaining white wine and stock, pour this over the duck and continue to baste frequently. When the duck is tender take it from the pan and arrange on a hot platter. Keep hot. Skim off as much fat as possible from the pan, add the calvados, stir briskly and then add the cream. Gently reheat the sauce, then strain it over the duck. Serve with red cabbage or peas, celery or spinach and potatoes.

ROAST DUCK (French)

2–3 servings:

a 3½–4 lb. duck
4 tablespoons (5) white wine or dry
  cider
1 small onion, sliced
a little carrot and tomato, sliced
celery leaves, parsley and thyme

olive oil
salt, pepper
flour
grated orange peel and stoned black
  cherries

First make a stock. Put the duck giblets into a pan, add the wine, vegetables and herbs and bring to a bubbling boil. Boil for 2 minutes, then add 2 cupfuls (2½) of water. Lower the heat and simmer for 1 hour. Strain.

Place the duck on its side on a rack in a roasting pan, rub it with olive oil, salt, pepper and flour. Let it cook uncovered for 30 minutes in a moderate oven. Take the pan from the oven, pour off all the fat and prick the skin of the duck over the breast and thighs, between the legs and the body (pricking the skin lets the fat run out so that when the duck is cooked the flesh will not be too greasy and the skin crisp and thin). Return the duck to the pan, place it on its other side and over it pour the strained hot stock. Let it cook for a further 30 minutes. Now turn again, this time breast upwards to allow the skin of the breast to brown and cook for a further 10–15 minutes. Baste frequently with the liquid in the pan. If necessary skim off any surplus fat.

Put the duck on to a hot platter, remove the trussing strings, and keep hot. Strain off the liquid from the pan, flavour it with grated orange peel, stoned black cherries, or any of the orange-flavoured liqueurs, i.e. curaçao, and serve this separately as a sauce.

Serve with an onion or apple purée and garnish with oranges.

DUCK, FARMER'S STYLE

4 servings:

Stuff an Aylesbury duck weighing about 5½ lb. with a mixture of seedless raisins, peeled and quartered apples and oranges. Close the opening and roast in a moderate oven, basting very frequently with hot water and the drippings from the pan until tender.

Serve with a purée of green peas, giblet sauce and cubes of crisply fried salt pork.

ROAST DUCK WITH STUFFED VINE LEAVES

3–4 servings:

a 4–5 lb. duck
salt, pepper
1 can stuffed vine leaves
butter
12 small onions, peeled
2 oranges

maraschino cherries
4 slices lean bacon, diced
a sprig summer savory, rosemary or
sage
1 cup (1¼) clear stock or bouillon
watercress

Wipe the duck inside and out with a damp cloth and sprinkle with salt. Fill the cavity with the stuffed vine leaves and truss the bird for roasting. Smear it lightly with butter and place it breast down on a rack in a roasting pan. Preheat the oven to hot and roast the duck for 30 minutes. Take from the oven and pierce the breast and thigh skin with a sharp pronged fork. Return the duck to the oven, breast upwards, add the onions, reduce the heat to moderate and cook for another hour or until the duck is tender. In the meantime cut the oranges into halves and scoop out the flesh. Pull off the thin skin, discard the pips and return the flesh to two of the orange shells. Top each with 2 or 3 maraschino cherries. Thinly slice the remaining half (keep the peel on) and crimp the edges of each slice.

Heat ½ oz. (1 tablespoon) of butter and fry the bacon. Put aside but keep hot. Take the pan from the oven and put it on top of the stove, put the duck aside but keep hot, drain off almost all of the fat, add the herbs, gradually stir in the stock and bring this to the boil. Add the seasoning, lower the heat and simmer for 5 minutes or so.

Place the duck on a hot serving dish and remove the trussing strings. Arrange the bacon and a few cherries along the breast. Put an orange 'basket' at either end of the bird and surround it with orange slices and watercress.

Cooked peas and small new potatoes may be added as a garnish if liked.

Vine leaves, usually stuffed with rice, are available in delicatessen shops.

ROAST DUCK WITH ORANGE SAUCE

3–4 servings:

a 4–5 lb. duck	a little curaçao
salt, pepper	1 oz. (2 tablespoons) butter
2 large oranges	1 tablespoon (1¼) flour
white wine	

Put the duck liver aside. Wipe the bird with a damp cloth and rub inside and out with salt and pepper. Peel 1 orange, cut the flesh into pieces and push this into the duck. Reserve the peel. Put the duck on a rack in a roasting pan and add enough water to cover the bottom of the pan. Roast in a hot oven for 15 minutes. Pour off the fat, reduce the heat and continue roasting in a moderate oven until the duck is tender, allowing 20 minutes to each pound. Prick the breast and thigh skin with a sharp pronged fork every 30 minutes or so. Baste from time to time with white wine and gravy from the pan.

Chop the reserved orange peel into thin strips and boil these in water for 15 minutes. Finely chop the liver. Drain the peel and mash this into the liver. Moisten with a little curaçao. Take ¼ cup (⅔) of the duck gravy (scrape the bottom of the pan well) and put this into a small pan. Add the butter and mashed liver, sprinkle with flour, stir and bring to the boil, stirring all the while. Let it boil for 2 minutes, then rub through a sieve. Take the bird from the pan, remove the trussing and carve. Discard the stuffing. Garnish with the remaining orange (thinly sliced) and serve the sauce separately.

ROAST DUCK (American)

3–4 servings:

a 4–5 lb. duck	1 cup (1¼) each strained stock and
bacon fat	water
flour	¾ cup (1) sherry or madeira
1 each apple, onion and stick celery	

Rub the duck with bacon fat and coat with flour (this is to prevent the duck from browning too soon). Peel and thickly slice the apple, onion and celery and put as much as possible into the duck. Put the duck into a roasting pan, preferably one with a lid. Add any remaining apple, onion, celery and the stock and water. Cover tightly, put the pan into a slow oven and cook for 1 hour, basting frequently. Uncover, add the sherry and cook uncovered for a further 20 minutes. When the breast is brown, take the duck from the pan, remove the trussing strings and serve with baked apples.

SAVOURY ROAST DUCK (Hungarian)

3–4 servings:

a 4–5 lb. duck
salt
4 anchovy fillets, mashed
2 oz. ($\frac{1}{4}$ cup) butter
rind $\frac{1}{2}$ lemon, grated

1 tablespoon ($1\frac{1}{4}$) capers
4 tablespoons (5) fine breadcrumbs
2 eggs, beaten
$\frac{1}{2}$ cup ($\frac{2}{3}$) each stock and red wine

Rub the outside of the duck with salt. Mix the anchovy fillets, butter, lemon rind, capers and breadcrumbs with the eggs. Trim the liver. Spread the anchovy mixture inside the duckling, then return its liver. Place the duckling breastside down in a deep casserole, add the stock and wine, cover and bake in a moderate oven for 1 hour; then turn the bird over and cook, without the cover, another 30 minutes. If the duck appears to be browning too quickly, cover with waxed paper or foil. Take the duck from the casserole, remove the trussing strings. Carve the duck and arrange it on a hot platter. Keep hot. Drain off the liquid in the casserole, strain it and either make a thick gravy, or simply leave as it is after straining. The Hungarians take the duck liver, slice it thinly and use this as a garnish. Roast potatoes and sliced green beans are recommended as accompaniments.

CASSEROLE OF DUCK

2–4 servings:

1–2 ducks
$\frac{1}{2}$ cup ($\frac{2}{3}$) oil
1 oz. (2 tablespoons) butter
1 lb. small onions
garlic to taste (plenty)
2 oz. ($\frac{1}{2}$ cup) flour

1 bottle dry white wine or cider
3–4 sweet peppers
6–8 tomatoes, peeled and halved
bouquet garni
salt, pepper

Heat the oil and butter in a deep casserole (preferably an iron one). Cut the duck into serving pieces. Add the duck pieces and cook these gently until they are a light brown. Take them from the pan, put aside but keep hot. Peel the onions and garlic and drop these into the pan, cooking them gently until brown. Sprinkle with flour and stir this into the fat, then gradually pour in the wine to make a smooth sauce. Cut each sweet pepper into 4 pieces; discard the core and seeds. Add to the pan and gently bring everything to the boil, stirring often and particularly at the bottom of the pan to prevent sticking. Add the tomatoes, bouquet garni, salt and pepper. Stir all these ingredients gently together, add the duck pieces, cover the pan and continue gently cooking for $1\frac{1}{4}$ hours. Serve in the sauce with boiled long grain rice.

BRAISED DUCKLING WITH GREEN PEAS AND LETTUCE

2–3 servings:

a 3½–4 lb. duckling	juice 1 lemon
2 oz. (¼ cup) butter	1 lb. peas, shelled
2 cups (2½) clear stock or water	6 lettuce leaves
salt, pepper	1 tablespoon (1¼) flour

Heat the butter in a large pan and brown the duckling all over. Add stock, salt, pepper and lemon juice and cook for 30 minutes over a low heat. Take the duckling from the pan and pierce the skin thoroughly over the breasts and thighs. Pour off surplus fat from the pan. Continue cooking another 30 minutes. Add the peas and lettuce leaves and cook for a further 15 minutes. Take out the duckling and the peas, put aside but keep hot. Discard the lettuce leaves. Mix the flour with enough water to make a thin paste, add to the pan, bring this to the boil and cook for 5 minutes, stirring all the time. Carve the duckling, coat it with the sauce and serve surrounded with peas.

DUCK WITH SAUERKRAUT

3 servings:

a 4-lb. duck	1½ lb. sauerkraut
3 oz. (6 tablespoons) fat	½ cup (⅔) red wine
salt	½ cup (⅔) sour cream

Cut the duck into serving pieces and carefully remove the breast bone, keeping the pieces of meat as large as possible. Rub the duck pieces with a little fat, sprinkle lightly with salt and leave for 1 hour. Heat the remaining fat in a pan and quickly fry the duck pieces to a golden brown. Put a layer of sauerkraut on the bottom of a casserole, arrange the duck pieces on top, add the duck liver, thinly sliced and cover with the rest of the sauerkraut. Mix the wine and the sour cream together and spoon this mixture over the top. Cover and cook in a fairly hot oven for 1–1½ hours. Do not overcook or the sauerkraut will become a rather sad brown. Serve with dumplings or potatoes. Partially cooked red cabbage may be used instead of sauerkraut.

DUCK WITH CABBAGE (Rumanian)

A recipe for farm-yard and wild duck.

3 servings:

1 duck, about 4 lb.	1 large white cabbage
salt	8 peppercorns
1 tablespoon (1¼) paprika pepper	1 tablespoon (1¼) tomato purée
6 oz. (¾ cup) butter or other fat	

Rub the duck generously inside and out with salt and paprika pepper and half the butter. Put the duck on a rack in a roasting pan and roast in the usual manner (see page 56) for 30 minutes. While the duck is cooking, wash and shred the cabbage, discarding any old leaves and thick stalks. Heat the remaining butter in a pan, add the cabbage, turning it from time to time until it changes colour. Add salt and peppercorns. Dilute the tomato purée with a little water or stock, add this to the pan and continue to cook the cabbage until it is soft. By this time the duck will be half-cooked; take it from the oven and out of the pan. Remove the rack. Spread the cabbage on the bottom of the pan in which the duck was roasting, place the duck on top of this, return it to the oven and continue cooking until the duck is quite tender.

Serve with straw potatoes or game chips (see page 206).

PORT SIMMERED DUCK

4 servings:

a 5-lb. duck
1½ oz. (3 tablespoons) butter
1 cup (1¼) port
1 tablespoon (1¼) cornflour (cornstarch)
½ cup (⅔) orange juice, preferably
  fresh

2 teaspoons (2½) lemon juice
2 tablespoons (2½) brandy
bouquet garni
salt, black pepper
pinch allspice
2 tablespoons (2½) pâté de foie gras

Cut the duck into 4 serving pieces. Heat the butter in a shallow saucepan, add the duck pieces and brown these all over. Add the port, cover the pan, bring to a gentle boil, lower the heat and cook until the duck is tender. Remove the duck, place on a hot plate and keep hot. Mix the cornflour with enough water to make a thin paste. Blend this with the remaining ingredients and pour the mixture into the pan in which the duck was cooked. Stir it well, until it is all blended (duck fat and scrapings as well), and continue stirring and gently cooking until the sauce is thick. Remove the bouquet garni. Return the duck pieces to the sauce, cook for another 5 minutes. Serve the duck hot, garnished with sliced oranges or tangerines and a watercress salad.

Instead of using *pâté de foie gras* (which is expensive) try using the duck liver. Cook it until tender in water, mash and mix it with a little liver paste. This makes quite a good substitute.

BRAISED DUCKLING WITH GREEN GRAPES

4 servings:

a 5-lb. duckling
mixed dried herbs
salt, pepper
a little ground nutmeg
1 oz. (2 tablespoons) butter or
  other fat

1 cup (1¼) muscatel wine
2 tablespoons (2½) redcurrant jelly
2 teaspoons (2½) cornflour
  (cornstarch)
1 cup (1¼) seedless green grapes

Mix a little of the mixed dried herbs with salt, pepper and nutmeg and rub the mixture well into the duck. Heat the butter in a pan, add the duckling and brown it all over.

Add the wine and the jelly, cover tightly and bring to a gentle boil. Lower the heat and cook gently until the duckling is tender, about 1½ hours. Take out the duckling, place it on a hot plate, remove trussing strings and keep hot. Mix the cornflour with enough water to make a thin paste. Stir this into the duck gravy and continue stirring until the mixture boils and thickens. If the sauce should be too thick, thin it down with either water, strained stock or more wine. Add the grapes, gently stir and heat them thoroughly. Serve the duckling with the grape sauce poured over it.

Serve with rice or puréed potatoes and other seasonal vegetables.

DUCK WITH OLIVES (Italian)

4–5 servings:

a 5–6 lb. duck	1 small onion, diced
salt, pepper	1 small carrot, diced
sage to taste	1 teaspoon (1¼) minced parsley
1 bay leaf	1 cup (1¼) red wine
2 tablespoons (2½) olive oil	½ lb. green or black olives, pitted

Wipe the duck with a damp cloth inside and out. Rub inside with salt and pepper; add the sage and bay leaf. Heat the oil in a deep casserole and brown the duck on all sides very quickly. Take it from the casserole and pierce the skin with a sharp pronged fork over the breast and the thighs. In the same fat brown the onion, carrot and parsley. Return the duck to the casserole. Add the wine, bring to the boil and cover tightly. Lower the heat and cook for about 1¼ hours or until the duck is tender. Remove the duck. Strain the sauce and return it to the pan, add the olives and simmer for 3–4 minutes. Cut the duck into serving pieces and cover with its sauce.

Serve with rice or riced potatoes.

DUCKLING COOKED IN WINE WITH GREEN OLIVES (French)

3 servings:

a 4-lb. duckling	½–1 lb. green olives, pitted
1 tablespoon (1¼) flour	1 onion, chopped
salt, pepper	parsley
2 tablespoons (2½) butter	bouquet garni
1 bottle saumur (a rather sweet sparkling wine)	1 clove garlic

Cut the duckling into 3 serving pieces. Lightly sprinkle with flour, salt and pepper. Heat the butter in a pan, brown the duck pieces, add the saumur, olives, onion, parsley, bouquet garni and garlic. Bring to the boil, cover, lower the heat and cook the duckling gently until tender. Take out the bouquet garni before serving. Serve with boiled rice.

If preferred, the duckling may be cooked whole. A sparkling cider can take the place of the wine.

SALMI OF DUCK

2 servings:

1 lb. cooked duck meat, without
   bones
1 oz. (2 tablespoons) butter
salt, pepper

½ cup (⅔) red burgundy
1 tablespoon (1¼) water
2 egg yolks
½ cup (⅔) fresh or sour cream

Heat the butter in a pan, add the duck meat, salt, pepper, burgundy and water. Bring to the boil, lower the heat, cover the pan and simmer for 10 minutes. Beat the egg yolks, add the cream and thoroughly blend. Pour this mixture over the duck, stirring all the while to prevent curdling. When the sauce is thick, the salmi is ready.

Serve with red cabbage and puréed potatoes.

RAGOÛT OF DUCK

4 servings:

a 4-lb. duck
1½ oz. (3 tablespoons) butter
1 tablespoon (1¼) flour
2 cups (2½) strained stock
1–2 sprigs parsley

salt, pepper
1 teaspoon (1¼) lemon juice
bouquet garni
1 tablespoon (1¼) redcurrant or
   cranberry jelly

Cut the duck into 4 neat serving pieces. Heat the butter in an earthenware casserole and brown the duck pieces. Add the flour, sprinkling it in carefully and fry this until brown. Add the stock, stirring until the gravy is smooth. Add the parsley, salt, pepper, lemon juice, bouquet garni and jelly. Cover and cook gently for 45 minutes. Serve the duck in the casserole. Small new potatoes may also be cooked with the duck.

Serve with peas and redcurrant or cranberry jelly.

SPOON DUCK (Duck cooked in white wine)

3–4 servings:

a 4–5 lb. duck
4 oz. (½ cup) butter
3 each onions and carrots, sliced
1 cup (1¼) white wine

very clear stock, strained
bouquet garni
salt, pepper
1 tablespoon (1¼) arrowroot

Heat the butter in an iron casserole and brown the duck. Take it from the pan and put aside; then add the onions and carrots to the casserole. Gently cook these until soft. Pour off any remaining butter and add the wine. Stir round the sides and the bottom of the casserole to loosen the sediment attached to the pan. Add enough stock to cover the duck, then the bouquet garni, salt and pepper; finally, return the duck to the pan. Cook gently for 3 or 4 hours. This dish can be cooked on top of the stove or in the oven. The flesh of the duck should be so tender that it can be 'spooned', thus the long cooking. Take the duck from the casserole and put it on a hot platter. Strain the gravy, return it to the casserole and bring it to the boil. Mix the arrowroot with sufficient warm water or stock to make a thin paste, pour this into the boiling liquid, stir, bring to the boil and cook for 5 minutes, stirring all the time. Pour this sauce over the duck which should be served whole.

Accompany with an orange salad (see page 206).

BRAISED DUCK WITH VEGETABLES

4 servings:

a 5-lb. duck
2 large onions
6 sticks celery or the equivalent
　tinned
1 teaspoon (1¼) ground ginger
1 bay leaf
peppercorns to taste

4 oz. (½ cup) unsalted butter
6 each medium-sized carrots, onions,
　potatoes
salt to taste
1 cup (1¼) peas, fresh or frozen
1 cup (1¼) cream

Chop the 2 large onions, the celery and the duck liver, combine and stuff into the duck. Cook the duck giblets, ginger, bay leaf and peppercorns in 2 cups (2½) of water. Heat the butter in a large heavy pan and brown the duck evenly. Strain the giblet stock. Add the carrots, onions, potatoes and the stock. Cover the pan and cook the duck for about 1½ hours or until it is tender, adding salt to taste. Add the green peas and continue cooking until these are soft. Add the cream, bring the whole gently almost to the boil and serve at once.

BRAISED DUCK WITH AN ORANGE AND CURAÇAO SAUCE

3 servings:

a 4-lb. duck
salt, pepper
sprig sage and 1 bay leaf
3-4 cloves
a little onion, chopped
peel 1 orange
2 oz. (¼ cup) butter

½ cup (⅔) curaçao
½ cup (⅔) clear stock
1 tablespoon (1¼) white wine
1 tablespoon (1¼) soft brown sugar
juice 1 orange
3 sweet oranges, peeled, skinned and
　cut into thick slices

Wipe the duck with a damp cloth both inside and out and sprinkle the inside with salt and pepper; then add the sage, bay leaf, cloves and onion. Close the opening. Insert between the skin and the flesh of the duck thin parings of orange peel. Heat the butter in a deep casserole and cook the duck until brown all over. Cover the dish, lower the heat to simmering and cook the duck gently for 30 minutes, turning it from time to time and pricking its skin. Pour off most of the fat and then add two-thirds of the curaçao; continue cooking for another 5 minutes. Add the stock, wine, sugar and orange juice, bring to a gentle boil, again reduce the heat and continue cooking until the duck is very tender, about another hour.

Transfer the duck on to a platter and keep hot. Bring the sauce to the boil, stirring all the time and scraping the sides of the casserole. Lower the heat and simmer for 10 minutes, skimming off any surplus fat. Pass the sauce through a fine sieve and return it to the pan. Add salt and pepper to taste, the rest of the curaçao and half the orange slices; again bring gently to the boil. Strain a little of this sauce over the duck and serve the rest in a sauceboat. Garnish the duck with the remaining orange slices and watercress.

Instead of curaçao, marsala or vermouth may be used in this recipe. Serve with potatoes Anna and watercress.

GALANTINE OF DUCK

6 servings:

a 5-lb. duck	2 large slices cooked smoked tongue
3 tablespoons ($3\frac{3}{4}$) brandy	2–3 hard-cooked eggs
salt, pepper	4–6 chicken livers
3 tablespoons ($3\frac{3}{4}$) sour cream	3 tablespoons ($3\frac{3}{4}$) blanched pistachio
1 lb. pork sausage meat	nuts
dash grated nutmeg	chaudfroid sauce (see below)
2 large thin slices cooked ham	aspic (see page 66)

Ask the butcher to bone the duck. Spread the boned duck on a board, skin side down. Brush the inside with 1 tablespoonful ($1\frac{1}{4}$) of brandy and sprinkle with salt and pepper. Blend the sour cream into the sausage meat, add the remaining brandy, salt, pepper and nutmeg. Spread three-quarters of this stuffing over the duck and cover it with the ham and the tongue. Spread with the remaining stuffing. On top of this put the eggs, chicken livers, the duck liver and pistachio nuts. Cautiously fold the skin over the stuffing, pushing it into shape, then sew up the overlapping skin with thread. Roll first in wax paper, then in foil and finally in a white cloth. Fasten each end with string and suspend the duck in a deep (preferably cast iron) pot by tying the string to the handles on either side. Pour in enough water to cover. Bring to a gentle boil, reduce the heat and cook gently for $1\frac{1}{2}$ hours. Take from the pan, place in an oblong bread baking tin and cover with a heavy weight. Chill overnight. Next morning unwrap and wipe off all surplus fat. Stand the duck roll on a rack over a flat baking pan or tray and coat with chaudfroid sauce.

chaudfroid sauce:

8 tablespoons (10) water	salt, cayenne pepper
3 tablespoons ($3\frac{3}{4}$) oil	2 cups ($2\frac{1}{2}$) milk
$6\frac{1}{2}$ tablespoons (8) flour	$\frac{1}{3}$ cup ($\frac{1}{2}$) cream
2 tablespoons ($2\frac{1}{2}$) gelatine	

Slowly heat the water and oil together. Mix the flour, gelatine, salt and cayenne in a bowl. Take the water and oil off the heat, add to the flour mixture and stir until smooth. Gradually pour in the milk and stir over a moderate heat until the sauce comes to the boil. Take from the heat and stir over cracked ice until the sauce begins to cool. Add the cream and continue stirring over the ice until the mixture thickens to just coat the spoon. Cover the duck with this sauce as evenly and smoothly as possible. Put into a refrigerator to set (still on its back and in the baking pan). Take out, coat again with the sauce and again let it chill and set in the refrigerator.

aspic:

6 cups (7½) stock	**sherry-glass dry sherry**
3 tablespoons (3¾) gelatine	**3 egg whites, beaten**

Put the stock, gelatine, sherry and the egg whites into a pan and beat with a whisk over a moderate heat until it comes to a rolling boil. Put aside and leave for 15 minutes without touching. Strain through fine cloth wrung out in cold water and stir over ice to the point of setting.

garnish:

1 hard-cooked egg	**3–4 strips of truffle or 3–4 black or green olives**

Garnish the top of the duck with rings of hard-cooked egg whites, strips of truffle or black and green olives, dipping each piece of garnish into aspic just before being added. When the garnish is firmly affixed, brush the duck with a thin coating of aspic and then put into the refrigerator. Put the left-over aspic in the refrigerator to set.

Serve the duck on a platter garnished with the remaining aspic, chopped, a few olives, if liked, and watercress.

DUCK WITH CHESTNUTS (Chinese)

2–3 servings:

a 3–4 lb. duck	**1 teaspoon (1¼) cornflour (cornstarch)**
2–3 Chinese dried mushrooms	**1 teaspoon (1¼) salt**
1 lb. chestnuts	**peanut or vegetable oil for deep**
1-in. piece fresh ginger	**frying**
1 teaspoon (1¼) soy sauce	**a few spring (green) onions, finely**
1 teaspoon (1¼) sugar	**chopped**

Soak the mushrooms for 30 minutes, then slice. Cut a gash on the flat side of the chestnuts, drop them into a pan of hot water and cook for 15–20 minutes or until their skins show signs of bursting for easy peeling (or fry them in a little butter over a low fire, shaking them from time to time). When the chestnuts are cool they can be easily peeled. Finely chop the ginger.

Chop or have chopped the duck, bones and all, into bite-sized pieces. (This is meant for easy eating with chopsticks; if not eating with chopsticks, cut the duck into larger portions.) Mix together the soy sauce, sugar, cornflour and salt and rub this mixture into the duck pieces. Heat the oil and fry the duck pieces for 3 minutes. Take these from the pan, add the onions, ginger, mushrooms and chestnuts and fry these for a few minutes. Drain off any excess fat, return the duck pieces to the pan, add hot water to cover and continue cooking until the duck is tender (about 30 minutes but depending on the tenderness of the duck). Serve with rice.

Roast haunch of venison with red cabbage, mashed potatoes and watercress.

PRESSED DUCKLING (*Caneton à la Rouennaise*)

3 servings:

a 4½-lb. duckling

1 oz. (2 tablespoons) butter

2 tablespoons (2½) finely chopped shallots or onions

mixed herbs, finely chopped

coarse salt, pepper

3 tablespoons (3¾) brandy, marc or calvados

1 extra duck liver

¼ cup (⅓) red burgundy

The duckling should not bleed when killed as its blood must be preserved. Therefore it must be killed by strangulation. Clean the carcass, still taking care not to bleed the bird. Remove the breast bone, take the spleen from the liver, discard it, and put the liver inside the duck. Place the duck in a roasting pan and roast, breast side upwards, for 20 minutes in a hot oven. Take the duck from the oven, remove the wings and legs and put these aside. Rub an oblong platter with butter and spread with the shallots and herbs, and sprinkle with salt and pepper. Slice the breast flesh into long narrow strips and arrange these on the platter. Warm the brandy and pour it over the pieces of duck, set alight and put aside but keep warm.

Pulverize the breast bone and the extra liver in a duck press. Rinse the bones with the burgundy and press them again to collect all the blood. Strain. Pour the mixture of wine and blood over the pieces of duck in the platter and put the platter in a moderate oven. Leave until the blood coagulates but do not let it come to the boil or it will curdle and the result be disastrous.

In the meantime grill (broil) the legs and wings of the duck and arrange them as a garnish on the platter. Serve with fried chips (French fried potatoes) or with croûtons.

Roast goose with pickled beetroot, fried potatoes and spinach.

Goose

The goose is the favourite of our nursery rhymes. When we call someone a 'silly goose' it may not be a compliment, but it is no insult either. 'He can't say boo to a goose' suggests that geese are cowards. When we have 'cooked our goose' it means all is finished; and we all know what happens when we 'kill the goose that lays the golden egg'.

According to Egyptian mythology, it was a goose that laid the golden egg of all eggs, the sun. Even so, goose was a favourite dish with the Egyptians. And an Egyptian still-life in the British Museum depicts a shoulder of veal and a goose, plucked and trussed for the table, ready for the spit.

Some defenders of the goose maintain it is a wise bird and the true harbinger of spring. Only when spring is truly with us do we hear the bold cackling of the geese in the yard. 'The spring is near when the green geese are breeding', wrote Shakespeare, always a man of the country, in *Love's Labour's Lost*.

There is a story of a traveller in France a century or so ago who saw a goose turning a spit on which a turkey roasted – the silly goose oblivious of the tragic-comedy of the situation. A famous goose story is the one of the grey geese on the Capitoline hill whose disturbed cackling warned the Romans of the approaching attack by the Gauls. And there is the story of the geese whose cackling gave away the hiding place of the modest St Martin, Bishop of Tours, who was seeking sanctuary in the barnyard away from those who would make him a bishop. Goose is eaten on this day, St Martin's Day or Martinmas, to perpetuate the anger of the good saint against the geese.

The goose, silly or astute, has been with man thousands of years and some are reputed to have reached great ages. One goose is claimed to have been 102 years old before he died. Pliny wrote at some length about the goose. 'Our people esteem the goose on account of the excellence of the liver which attains a very large size when the bird is crammed. When the liver is thoroughly soaked in honey and milk, it becomes especially large. It is a moot question who made such an excellent discovery – whether it was Scipio Metellus, a man of consular rank, or Marcus Sestius, a Roman knight. However, there is no doubt that it was Messalinus Cotia who first cooked the webbed feet of geese and served them with cocks' combs, for I must award the palm of the kitchen to the man who is deserving of it. This bird, wonderful to relate, comes all the way from Morini to Rome on its own feet: the weary geese are placed in front and those following by a natural pressure urge them on.'

The Roman geese were not the only ones who travelled on their own feet. Those in Britain had their walking marathons too. Journeys to the famous goose fairs often took a week or so, and the gooseherd used to 'shoe' his flock. First he dipped the feet in tar and then in sand, and thus shod the geese could travel for miles at the rate of one mile an hour. Not bad going for a goose.

Goose in Scandinavia and on the Continent is the Christmas treat, as it once was in Britain, but in the form of a pie. In England during the nineteenth century it was the poor man's Christmas dinner and goose clubs were formed to make sure poor families got their Christmas goose. A typical Cockney song of the period, of the tear-jerking type, has a verse which runs:

'Twas hungry time, last Christmas Day,
Old lady, you remember,
This year might bring the same ill-luck,
so to ensure some spruce grub
I'll tell you what I'll do, my duck,
I'll take and join the goose club.'

Formerly more honour was done to the goose at Martinmas and Michaelmas, when the young stubble-fed bird appeared on the table, tender and juicy and quite distinct in flavour from the super-fatted Christmas goose.

In Central Europe the goose takes precedence over the turkey and probably even more so in Germany, where they say: '*Eine gute gebratene Gans ist eine Gabe Gottes*' (a fine roast is a gift from God).

France probably has the most by-products from the goose, *foie gras* is one of them, the geese being reared for the inflated liver, half the size of a football, and they produce masses of fat. In goose-eating countries, goose fat is a favourite item of diet. Smeared on soft fresh brown bread, sprinkled with salt and freshly milled pepper, it is diet for the gourmet. Goose fat takes the place of butter or other cooking fats, even in baking. What is left of the flesh is usually cooked and preserved in crockery jars as *confit d'oie*. Goose necks are stuffed and eaten, not only in France, but in Hungary, a great goose-rearing country.

The goose and the gander look alike and at a quick glance it is not easy to tell which is which. They are of similar size and marked alike. When trussed and ready for the oven, both are goose, since the culinary world knows no distinction as male and female goose, any more than it concerns itself with the sex of the duck.

ROAST GOOSE

There are several ways to roast a goose, often erroneously considered a rather fat bird.

Nowadays our butchers all but cook our goose as they sell it dressed ready for the oven and the pot. However, even in these days the following general instructions will not go amiss.

Select a goose with a clean white skin, plump breast, a clear yellow beak and feet. If it is over a year old it is not fit for the table. Hang it, if possible, for a few days as this will improve its flavour. Pluck and singe the outside, rub with a cloth and wash in warm water containing flour or bran. Remove the excess fat, but keep this as it can be used for cooking. Cut off the goose's neck close to the back leaving the skin long enough to fold over; cut off the wings and the feet at the first joint. Flatten the breast bone with a mallet and put a skewer through the under part of each wing. Draw up the legs close to the body and the skewer through each. The legs of the goose are too short to allow trussing in the same manner as with turkey or chicken. If the skewer does not work, tie a trussing string around one leg and then around the other, leaving about 2 inches of string between the legs. Bring the ends of the twine under the back and then tie securely.

Rub the goose all over with salt. Cut off the end of the vent and make a hole in the skin large enough to slip the rump through. Fill the inside with stuffing (see page 216) – or if preferred simply rub it with a cut lemon and put a peeled lemon inside – and sew up the opening. Put the goose on the rack in a large roasting pan. Put boiling water and 1 onion into the roasting pan and cook in a moderate oven for 1 or $1\frac{1}{4}$ hours. Baste frequently with the liquid in the pan and from time to time prick the goose under the wings and legs to let the fat escape. This fat falls into the pan and helps in the basting. During the last 20 minutes pour 1 tablespoon ($1\frac{1}{4}$) of cold water over the breast to make the skin brown and crusty.

The usual timing for roasting a goose is 20–25 minutes to each pound, although it varies slightly according to the age of the bird. Test the bird by wriggling its legs; if they move easily, the goose is done. When the goose is tender, take it from the pan and place on a hot dish. Pour off most of the fat, simply leaving enough to make a gravy. Scrape around the sides and bottom of the pan, add 1 cupful ($1\frac{1}{4}$) of hot stock (made from the giblets etc.), salt and pepper. Bring this to a slow boil, stirring all the time. Strain, pour a little of the gravy over the goose and the remainder into a sauceboat.

Serve the goose with such sauces as apple, apricot or prune; with red cabbage, Brussels sprouts, sauerkraut or shredded cooked white cabbage; chestnuts or floury plain cooked potatoes sprinkled with melted butter and chopped parsley.

The typical stuffing for goose in Britain is sage and onion but there are many other stuffing (see pages 216). In the United States I have also been served halved, tinned white peaches as a garnish. Sautéed in butter they appeared flaming, surrounding the goose. Brandy and orange liqueur had been mixed and warmed, poured over the peach halves and ignited.

In Greece a mixture of chopped apples and chestnuts is used as a stuffing. In Germany whole apples peeled and cored and stuffed with chestnuts, walnuts or raisins, make a popular stuffing.

ROAST GOOSE (Hungarian)

One of my memories of Hungary in the late thirties was my first sight of a 'living' goose girl. Until then these pretty creatures with their plaits, bare legs and short full skirts, using willow sticks to drive their geese through the fields and along the lanes, had been to me only pictures in a story book.

8–10 servings:

1 plump goose about 10–12 lb.
salt, pepper
4 hard-cooked eggs, coarsely chopped
1 lb. mushrooms, peeled and
   coarsely chopped
¼ cup (⅓) sour cream

1 teaspoon (1¼) finely chopped chives
good pinch marjoram
2 eggs, beaten
2 tablespoons (2½) red wine
2 oz. (¼ cup) goose or pork fat

Rub the goose all over with salt and leave for 2 hours. In the meantime prepare the stuffing. Put into a deep bowl the hard-cooked eggs, mushrooms, sour cream, chives, the goose liver cut into small pieces, salt, pepper, marjoram, beaten eggs and wine. Mix well and stuff the mixture into the cavity of the goose; pin the skin flaps together with small skewers. Spread the fat on a piece of foil, cover the goose with this and put it into a baking pan, preferably on the rack. Pour in just enough water to cover the bottom of the pan and roast it in a hot oven for 30 minutes. Reduce the heat and continue cooking until the goose is tender, basting frequently. After the first hour discard the foil and let the goose brown. Test with a skewer to see if it is tender.

Roast goose is rich; the Hungarians prefer to serve it simply with a green salad, letting the gravy and the stuffing be sufficient garnish. Red cabbage or any of the early greens are also served with goose in Hungary.

If the goose is very young, no water is required.

To make the gravy, drain off all but 2 tablespoons (2½) of the fat in the pan, add 1 tablespoon (1¼) of flour to the pan, mix together and add enough clear stock or water to make a thin gravy. Cook for 5 minutes. If the giblets have been cooked to make a stock, these should be finely chopped and added to the gravy.

ROAST GOOSE (Danish)

According to time-honoured tradition, roast goose in Denmark is served on Christmas Eve, after the rice porridge, another favourite Scandinavian Christmas dish.

8 servings:

1 goose weighing 10–12 lb. when
   dressed
½ lemon
prunes and green apples
salt, pepper

1 cup (1¼) stock or water
1 teaspoon (1¼) redcurrant jelly
1 teaspoon (1¼) arrowroot

The quantity of prunes and apples depends on the size of the goose. Allow 1 cupful (1¼) of stuffing for each pound of bird, ready-to-bake or dressed weight. The apples and prunes are used in equal proportions. Some prunes require soaking, some not. In any case, they must be cooked until tender and then pitted. Pare, core and chop the apples. Mix the fruit and lightly sweeten to taste.

Rub the inside of the goose with lemon, salt and pepper and stuff it with the apple and prune mixture. Sew up the opening and turn the skin of the neck backwards. Secure it with a small skewer or sew it on its back. Truss the bird and tie its legs loosely to the tail. Prick well with a fork, preferably two-pronged. Heat the oven to moderate. Place the goose breast side up on a rack in an open roasting pan. Baste frequently while roasting. It is difficult to state the roasting time exactly but allow 20 minutes roasting time per pound for a young goose and 25 minutes per pound for an older bird. Test with a skewer. Baste frequently with a sprinkling of water. The goose is tender when the flesh is soft and the leg joints move easily. Pour off the gravy when the goose is almost cooked. Baste with a few tablespoonfuls of cold water to crisp the skin. Half an hour before serving, open the oven door and leave it ajar; this is to help to crisp the skin. Tap the skin with a spoon to test its crispness. Take out the goose and transfer it to a hot serving dish. Skim off the excess fat. Put the pan over a low heat on top of the stove, add the stock and redcurrant jelly to the pan and swirl the gravy around to collect all sediment. Mix the arrowroot with a little water to a thin paste, add this to the gravy, stir, raise the heat, bring to the boil and cook for 3 minutes. Strain and serve in a sauce-boat.

Serve the roast goose with red cabbage and fried potatoes sprinkled with sugar. Pickled beetroots are also served with goose in Denmark.

GOOSE FAT

Cut the goose fat into pieces, put into a pan and add water to cover. Add a peeled small green apple and shallot or a piece of onion. Cover and cook until the fat is dissolved. Uncover and continue cooking until the water has evaporated. Strain, pour into a bowl and let the fat set.

ROAST GREEN GOOSE

4 servings:

Green geese are from 2 to 3 months old. They are not usually stuffed as their own flavour is much appreciated. Empty and truss the goose and rub it with salt and pepper inside and out. Crush a few juniper berries and mix them with a small piece of butter and place this inside the bird. Green geese can be roasted on a spit or in an oven. A young goose requires no water in the pan. Baste frequently and 10 minutes before it is ready sprinkle lightly with flour, baste again and let the breast get brown and frothy.

Serve with stewed gooseberries, brown gravy and a watercress salad, or with baked apples stuffed with loganberries or mountain cranberries.

ROAST GOOSE STUFFED WITH SAUERKRAUT (Russian)

6–8 servings:

1 goose, 8–10 lb. dressed weight	**1 large onion, finely chopped**
salt, pepper	**caraway seeds**
2 lb. sauerkraut	**1 large tart apple, chopped**
goose fat	**2 cups (2½) stock or water**

Cut out the fat from the inside of the goose. Pierce the flesh of the goose all over to release its fat when it is cooking. Rub inside and out with salt and pepper. Wash the sauerkraut. Heat a little of the goose fat and slowly fry the onion until it begins to change colour, then add the sauerkraut, caraway seeds, pepper and apple. Stir these ingredients together until the sauerkraut begins to dry out, then add the stock. Cover and stew gently until the sauerkraut is soft. Stuff this mixture into the goose and sew up the opening. Brush the flesh with goose fat and put the goose on a rack in a large roasting pan. Put it into a very hot oven and let it roast at this heat for 15 minutes, then reduce the heat to slow and continue cooking until the bird is tender (a fork should pierce the flesh without too much pressure when the goose is done), between 2 and 3 hours roasting according to the size of the bird.

Since the stuffing is of sauerkraut, serve the goose with floury potatoes or a purée of lentils, and with the sauerkraut stuffing as a garnish.

BOILED GOOSE WITH APPLES (French – Normandy style)

6–8 servings:

an 8–10 lb. goose
1 tablespoon (1¼) butter
2 medium-sized onions, sliced
½ lb. each lean and fat belly pork
2 eggs, beaten
6 apples, peeled and chopped
salt, pepper
2 tablespoons (2½) calvados
strips fat salt pork

2 oz. (¼ cup) goose fat or other fat
3 each carrots and leeks, sliced in
  rounds
1 stick celery
¼ cup (⅓) dry cider
mixed herbs
garnish:
2 lb. stewed apples

Heat the butter and fry the onions. Grind or chop the lean pork, pork belly and goose liver. Mix with the fried onions, eggs, apples, salt and pepper, adding the calvados slowly, a teaspoonful at a time. Fill this into the goose, sew up the opening and brown in a very hot oven for 15 minutes. In the meantime fry the strips of fat salt pork in a very large pan with the goose fat, adding the goose giblets, carrots, leeks and celery. Moisten with cider and cook until the vegetables are soft. Add the goose, herbs, salt and pepper and cook over a moderate heat until the goose is tender. Take the goose from the pan, place on a hot platter and keep hot. Skim off surplus fat and strain the vegetables. Serve the strained vegetables as a garnish. Surround the goose with apples (stewed until very soft) and serve with any of the usual vegetables.

DEVILLED GOOSE (American)

8–10 servings:

a 10–12 lb. goose
salt
potato stuffing (see page 223)

4 tablespoons (5) vinegar
1 teaspoon (1¼) white pepper
2 tablespoons (2½) prepared mustard

Clean and truss the goose (see page 72) and wipe it thoroughly with a damp cloth. Plunge it into a large pan of boiling, salted water and boil it gently for 1 hour. Take it from the pan, drain well and wipe dry. Fill the body with potato stuffing, sew up the openings and lay it in an earthenware casserole. Mix the vinegar, pepper and mustard together and pour this mixture over the goose. Roast in a very hot oven until very tender, basting it frequently. Serve with boiled rice and red cabbage.

BOILED STUFFED GOOSE

This method of cooking is suitable for an old goose.

8–10 servings:

a 10–12 lb. goose
1 lb. cooked or canned whole chestnuts
¼ lb. (1 scant cup) currants
1 small carrot, chopped
1 medium-sized onion, chopped

salt, pepper
12 small onions
1 lb. small turnips
1 head celery
1 tablespoon (1¼) arrowroot or potato flour

The goose should be trussed in the usual manner (see page 72). Mix the next 4 ingredients together to make a stuffing and stuff the goose with this. Sew up the opening, fold the skin back over the neck opening and rub the outside with salt and pepper. Place the goose on a rack in a large pan adding 2 cups (2½) of warm water. Cover the pan and cook gently for 1 hour, basting frequently. In the meantime prepare the remaining ingredients. Peel the small onions (if small ones are not available, coarsely chop larger ones). Peel and cut the turnips into halves unless they are very small (in which case leave them whole). Cut the celery into thick slices. Add all these to the pan and continue cooking gently until the goose is tender, approximately another hour. Take the goose from the pan, place on a hot plate, surround with the vegetables, put aside and keep hot. Strain the liquid and return it to the pan. Mix the arrowroot with enough water to make a thin paste. Stir this into the goose gravy, bring to the boil and cook for 3–4 minutes, stirring all the while. Pour a little of the sauce over the goose and serve the rest in a sauceboat.

GOOSE IN ASPIC

8–10 servings:

a 10–12 lb. goose
meat stock made from a hambone
   and veal knuckle
2–4 onions, according to size
2–3 carrots
1 slice lemon
mixed herbs

salt, pepper
prepared mustard, preferably
   French or German
½ oz. (1 envelope) gelatine
garnish:
sliced hard-cooked eggs, capers,
   cooked green peas

Cook the goose gently in a large pan with plenty of stock, adding the onions, carrots, lemon, herbs, salt and pepper. When tender take the goose from the pan and let it cool. Strip off all the meat from the bone, return the bones to the pan and let it all continue to cook slowly for another hour. Strain the bone stock through a cloth, cool and remove the surplus fat. In the meantime cut the pieces of goose meat into neat strips. Add the salt, pepper and mustard. Dissolve the gelatine in water and then add to it 1 quart (5 cupfuls) of the strained stock. The gelatine assures that the liquid will jell, although it will probably do so of its own volition. Line the bottom of a mould with the aspic and garnish this with slices of egg, capers and peas. Let this set then cover with a layer of goose meat. Cover with aspic and leave to set. Continue in this manner until all the ingredients are finished and the mould is full. The top layer must be of aspic. Leave overnight to set. Turn out to serve on a bed of lettuce with apple sauce, potato salad, etc.

STUFFED GOOSE NECKS (French)

This is a speciality of the French town of Rocamadour, a place of pilgrimage. As few people are able to buy enough geese to collect goose necks, an obliging butcher or poulterer might get them if asked nicely. It is the neck portion from just under the beak to where the neck ends in the breast which is required.

12–18 servings:

6 goose necks	12 peppercorns
2 goose legs	1–2 cloves garlic
¾ cup (1) vinegar	salt, pepper
2 tablespoons (2½) brandy	¼ lb. ham
½ cup (⅔) white wine	1 lb. sausage meat
2 cloves	2 ducks' livers, chopped
1 bay leaf	1 small truffle, finely chopped
2 sprigs thyme	(optional)
1 each small onion and carrot,	½ cup (⅔) white wine
thinly sliced	lard or goose fat for frying

Strip the skin from the goose necks; do this carefully to avoid tearing by separating the skin from the neck at one end with a sharp knife. Peel back the skin and pull it off inside out. This leaves a tube of skin. Strip the meat from the legs and put it with the neck meat. Make a marinade from the vinegar, brandy, first measure of white wine, cloves, bay leaf, thyme, onion, carrot, peppercorns, garlic, salt and pepper. Put the goose meat into the marinade and leave overnight.

Thoroughly cleanse the skins and put them aside until required.

The next day, take the goose meat from the marinade. Put the meat aside and strain the marinade.

Prepare a stuffing by putting the goose meat and the ham together once through a grinder, then again with the sausage meat and livers. Add the truffle (if wanted), second amount of white wine and just enough of the marinade to moisten the stuffing. Sew up one end of each of the neck skins and push some of the stuffing into each, packing it as tightly as possible but allowing a little space for swelling. Sew up the other end. Fry the goose necks in hot lard or, better still, in goose fat until crisp and brown or poach gently in stock for 40–60 minutes. If poaching, let the necks cool in the stock before serving.

Serve the goose necks thinly sliced; if fried and hot, serve on a bed of creamed potatoes or purée of peas with a foamy wine sauce; if cold, with a green salad.

Truffles are not essential; either pistachio nuts or *foie gras* may be used instead. If there is not enough meat to stuff all the necks, add some bread soaked in water and squeezed dry to the mixture before pushing it into the skin.

The goose necks can be kept in earthenware jars as pieces of *confit d'oie*.

BOILED AND GRILLED (BROILED) GOOSE WITH SHERRY (American)

6–8 servings:

an 8–10 lb. goose	1½ cups (scant 2) cream or milk
salt	dash grated nutmeg
1 each onion, carrot and turnip	1 clove
2 eggs, well beaten	1 clove garlic
3 tablespoons (3¾) sherry	1 bay leaf
breadcrumbs	1 teaspoon (1¼) minced shallot or
sauce:	onion
1 oz. (2 tablespoons) unsalted	salt, pepper
butter	2 tablespoons (2½) sherry
1 tablespoon (1¼) flour	1 extra tablespoon (1¼) butter

Put the goose into a large pan, cover it with cold water, add salt and the vegetables and cook very slowly until the goose is tender. At this point make the sauce.

Heat the first quantity of butter, add the flour and stir to a roux. Add the cream, nutmeg, clove, garlic, bay leaf and shallot. Bring this to a gentle boil, stirring all the time; lower the heat and simmer for 15 minutes, still stirring. Strain through a fine sieve, return the mixture to the stove and continue cooking until the sauce is reduced to one-third of its volume. Add salt, pepper, sherry and the extra butter. Put to the side, but keep warm.

When the goose is tender, take it from the pan, cool it and carve into serving portions. Beat the eggs with the sherry. Dip the pieces of goose first into the sherry-egg mixture and then into breadcrumbs. Grill (broil) on both sides until golden brown. Serve on a hot platter with the sauce.

HASHED GOOSE LEGS À LA LYONNAISE

2 servings:

2 cooked goose legs	1–2 onions, sliced
goose fat	

Slice the flesh off the legs as neatly as possible. Heat enough fat to fry both the onions and the meat. First fry the pieces of meat until brown; place these on a hot plate. In the same fat fry the onions until a golden brown and soft. Spread these over the goose meat and serve with a *sauce poivrade* (see page 212).

CASSEROLE OF GOOSE AND BEANS

This is a *cassoulet* and a typical French dish. Being rather heavy, it is best served as a midday meal. It can be accompanied by a green salad and a young, full-bodied red wine or a strong dry rosé.

6 servings:

a 9-lb. goose	$\frac{1}{4}$ lb. lean salt pork, diced
1 lb. dried white beans	1 teaspoon ($1\frac{1}{4}$) flour
4 onions, coarsely chopped	4 cups (5) beef stock
salt, pepper	a good sprig thyme and parsley
1 garlic sausage	1 small bay leaf
2 oz. ($\frac{1}{4}$ cup) butter	2–3 tomatoes, peeled and chopped
2 cloves garlic	soft white breadcrumbs

Soak the beans in water overnight. Next day cover them with fresh water, add 2 of the onions, a little salt and pepper and cook slowly until the beans are barely tender, about 2 hours. Cut the goose into 12 neat pieces and the garlic sausage into 1-in. lengths. Heat the butter and brown the goose pieces and the garlic sausage. Transfer both to a shallow earthenware baking dish (variously known as a *cassole, turpin* or *cassoulet*) first rubbed with a cut clove of garlic. Drop the salt pork into boiling water for a few minutes then drain and brown it quickly in the hot butter. Add the remaining onions and garlic and cook until the onions are lightly browned. Sprinkle in the flour and continue cooking, stirring, until the flour is brown. Add the stock, still stirring, bring it to the boil, add the herbs and the tomatoes, cover the pan and cook over a low heat for 20 minutes. Drain the beans and spread them over the goose and sausage in the *cassoulet*, add the hot sauce and bake in a moderate oven for 1 hour. Take the *cassoulet* from the oven, sprinkle the top with breadcrumbs, then return it to the oven to brown the crumbs.

GOSLING PEASANT STYLE

4–6 servings:

an 8-lb. gosling	2 cups ($2\frac{1}{2}$) stock
salt, pepper	4 each carrots and turnips
4 oz. ($\frac{1}{2}$ cup) butter	12 very small onions
2 large onions, coarsely chopped	1 tablespoon ($1\frac{1}{4}$) flour
1 large carrot, coarsely chopped	$\frac{1}{2}$ cup ($\frac{2}{3}$) red wine
1 clove	$\frac{1}{2}$–1 lb. cooked peas
bouquet garni	

Cut the gosling into 4 portions or 6 serving portions; rub with salt and pepper. Heat half the butter in a pan, add the coarsely chopped vegetables, the clove and the pieces of gosling. Fry all this together until brown. Add the bouquet garni and stock. Cover and cook gently for 45 minutes or until the gosling is tender. In the meantime prepare the remaining vegetables. Cut the carrots and turnips into thick rounds and put with the onions into another pan with a little salted water. When they are tender drain off any remaining water and add the rest of the butter shaking the vegetables until they are well buttered. As soon as the gosling is tender, take the pieces from the pan, place them on a hot platter and keep hot. Strain the liquid from the pan into a smaller pan. Mix the flour with enough water to make a thin paste, stir this into the pan and simmer for 10 minutes. Add the wine, salt and pepper. Pour this sauce over the gosling. Garnish with the buttered vegetables and the peas.

GIBLET CASSEROLE STEW

4 servings:

1 set goose giblets, chopped	½ lb. mushrooms, sliced
1 oz. (2 tablespoons) butter	1 clove garlic
2 large onions, chopped	3 cloves and 1 blade mace
½ lb. green bacon, cubed	sprig marjoram, thyme and parsley
3 carrots, sliced	salt, cayenne pepper
3 tomatoes, peeled and sliced	2 cups (2½) stock

Melt the butter in a large pan, add the onions, fry these to a golden brown. Add the giblets (not the liver) and the bacon and fry until a light brown. Add the vegetables, garlic, cloves, mace, herbs, salt, pepper and stock. Bring to a gentle boil and then transfer to a casserole, cover and cook in a moderate oven for 3 hours. Twenty minutes before the stew is ready, dice and add the goose liver.

Alternatively, the stew can be cooked in a pan on top of the stove. If a thick sauce is preferred, thicken the gravy with a butter and flour paste (*beurre manié*, see page 208).

This stew can be served with apples cut into rather large slices and cooked until soft but not mushy. The Germans have a similar recipe, omitting the bacon but adding currants. They also cook giblets with pears. Turnips and potatoes make a conventional accompaniment.

PRESERVED GOOSE (French – *confit d'oie*)

This is a very fine preserve which will keep for several months if stored in a cool place. It can be used for impromptu lunches as the pieces of goose can be taken from the jar, heated and served with red cabbage, rice, noodles, sauerkraut or white cabbage, boiled potatoes, spinach etc. It is an important ingredient in a French *cassoulet*. As geese are not so rigorously fattened in Britain and the United States as they are in France, it will be necessary to add chicken fat or fine lard, since it is important the goose is covered with fat while it is cooking.

8 servings:

1 large goose	**a little fresh thyme**
coarse salt	**1 bay leaf, chopped**
a little ground allspice	**goose fat or lard**

Remove the fat from a thoroughly cleaned and drawn goose. Cut the goose into 4, 6 or 8 joints or even more, depending on the size of the bird. Put aside the pieces of fat, of which there should be plenty. Rub each piece of goose generously with salt mixed with a little allspice, thyme and bay leaf. Arrange in a deep earthenware bowl, cover with the lid and then with a board heavily weighted. Keep the goose in this for 6–10 days, preferable in a larder or other very cool place. After this period drain the goose and wipe carefully clean with a damp cloth.

Cover the bottom of a pan with the pieces of goose fat; if there is not sufficient add some pure lard. Arrange the goose pieces on this bed of fat and put the pan over a low heat. Gradually the fat will melt and the cooking should take between $1\frac{1}{2}$ to 2 hours. Prick the goose flesh; if no blood runs from it the meat is done. Take out the pieces of goose, drop them into an earthenware jar or crock. Strain the fat through several layers of cheesecloth, discarding every trace of the meat juices as these would spoil the *confit*. Cover the pieces of goose with the fat then cool. When thoroughly cold add yet more strained melted fat to make a cover at least 1 in. thick above the meat. Let this solidify. Cover the jar with greaseproof paper, tie it securely with string and put it in a cool place for future use.

To use, dig a long fork into the fat and dig out as much goose as required with its adhering fat. Fry it in its own fat with some thin slices of uncooked potatoes. Preserved goose can also be served cold, but must be wiped completely free of fat.

Turkey

The general and short form used for a turkey-cock, turkey-hen and turkey-poult (the young turkey). It is a large bird which has been domesticated for several centuries and is now one of our most valued table birds.

The name turkey was first given in England to the guinea fowl, which was originally introduced into the country from West Africa. Turkeys (in the present sense of the word) were discovered in Mexico, where they had been domesticated for some time by the Spaniards who are said to have brought them to Europe in 1530; but the matter seems not at all clear for there is a well-known jingle:

> Turkeys, carp, hops and beer,
> Came into England all in one year.

And that year was 1520. Then it is recorded that by 1555 the turkey (guinea fowl?) was a prized table bird in Europe. When Shakespeare talked of turkeys, he was talking of guinea fowl, and even as late as 1633, when we read Dr Hart's *Diet of the Diseased*, the mention of turkey obviously refers to the guinea fowl. It seems that not until the reign of Queen Anne was the turkey a turkey as we know it.

In the past when large flocks of turkeys were 'walked' to the London markets, the feet of the birds were wrapped in sacking and shod with leather boots to protect them from the cold.

The turkey-cock is larger than the hen and less economical, as its bones are heavier. A large specimen is better stuffed by the taxidermist than the cook. The best is the hen from 7 to 8 months old reared in semi-liberty, given plenty of food but made to scratch for at least some of it. Its legs should be black, the neck short, the breast broad and plump, and the flesh snow-white and firm, with thin layers of fat over the back.

Turkeys in the United States are by 'stern and inflexible tradition' eaten at Thanksgiving as well as at Christmas; while England still considers turkey as the Christmas bird. However, they are available now in both countries throughout the year, not only as whole birds but cut into portions to suit all pockets and sizes of families. A bird, as the turkey producers now say, not only can be served on festive occasions or at the week-ends, but also in the middle of the week.

ROAST TURKEY – 1

1 turkey	slices of fat bacon
stuffing or forcemeat	dripping or other fat
salt	pepper
lemon juice	stock and flour

There are no exact quantities given with this recipe since all depends on the size of the bird. A usual stuffing for a turkey in Britain is of chestnuts but it is preferable to have 2 or 3 kinds of stuffing in the same turkey (for other stuffings see pages 216–25).

Rub the turkey inside and out with salt and lemon juice and fill the bird with the chosen stuffing. Pack this into the turkey from the back in any preferred order; push well forward into the breast moulding it into a good shape. Sew up the loose crop skin neatly and firmly; this keeps the stuffing securely in place.

Place the turkey on the rack of a roasting pan, lay 2–3 slices of bacon over the breast and skewer them on firmly. Over the bacon and over the rest of the turkey thickly spread softened fat, sprinkle with salt and pepper and then cover with aluminium foil, pressing it well down over the bird. Roast in a pre-heated moderate oven allowing 18–20 minutes to each pound of weight.

Baste every 30 minutes (removing the foil, of course), the first time with boiling water, then with the drippings from the bird. Forty-five minutes before the turkey is ready remove the bacon and foil, baste the turkey again and continue roasting until the breast turns a rich brown but not too brown. When approaching the time when the turkey should be ready, test it with a skewer. When the turkey is quite tender, take it from the pan, place it on a large platter and keep hot. Pour off almost all the fat, add a little stock to the pan and stir well. Add enough flour to thicken the gravy. Cook for 5 minutes, stirring all the while. Strain and serve in a sauceboat (or prepare a giblet gravy as on page 84.)

Serve the turkey with small grilled sausages, bread sauce, Brussels sprouts and celery, if culinary tradition is being maintained.

In the United States, creamed onion is almost always served with it. Either roast or creamed potatoes may be served with roast turkey, and cranberry sauce (see page 209). Artichoke bottoms or small artichokes, cauliflower and boiled rice are other possible accompaniments.

ROAST TURKEY – 2 (Spanish)

8 servings:

an 8–10 lb. turkey	1 bay leaf and sprig thyme and
½ lb. each dried prunes and peaches	parsley tied together
1 lb. chestnuts	salt
butter or fat for frying	freshly ground white pepper
1 lb. pork sausages	cinnamon
½ lb. ham, chopped	4–5 slices fat bacon
	½ cup (⅔) red wine or sherry

Soak the prunes and peaches until soft, discard the stones. Boil the chestnuts for 20 minutes or until they peel easily, discard the outer and inner skins. Chop coarsely.

To make the stuffing, heat a little butter in a pan and fry the sausages until brown; take them from the pan and cut into small pieces. Return these to the pan, adding the turkey liver, ham, prunes, peaches, chestnuts and herbs. Mix well, add salt, pepper and cinnamon, and cook slowly for 10 minutes. Take from the fire, discard the herbs and fill the stuffing into the turkey cavity.

Cover the breast of the turkey with the bacon (leave this on for the first hour and a half of cooking, then remove it to let the breast brown). Put the turkey on a rack in a roasting pan and into a hot oven. Roast for about 2½ hours or until tender. Baste frequently, first with hot water and then with the turkey drippings and, after the turkey has been cooking for about 1 hour, baste it with all the wine. When the turkey is tender take it from the pan and place on a hot platter.

Make a gravy (see below) and serve this separately in a sauceboat. Serve the turkey with rice and Brussels sprouts.

GRAVY FOR ROAST TURKEY

While the turkey is roasting, it is important to cut the giblets into very small pieces and simmer in a little water until tender. After the turkey has been taken from the roasting pan, pour off all but 5 tablespoons (6¼) of the drippings. Scrape well round the sides of the pan to get all the sediment, which is full of flavour. Add 4 tablespoons (5) of flour, stir this well into the drippings and cook over a moderate heat until the mixture is smooth. Gradually add enough liquid, meat or vegetable stock for choice, to make a medium-thick gravy, stirring all the time. Let the gravy cook until it bubbles, then add the giblets and continue cooking for a further 5 minutes. Strain to serve.

For a darker colour, add approximately ½ cup (⅔) of strained black coffee.

ROAST TURKEY IN ALUMINIUM FOIL (German)

a turkey	**onions and mushrooms, peeled and**
salt	**chopped**
lemon juice	**butter**
	parsley and watercress

Rub the turkey inside and out with salt and lemon juice. Stuff it with onions, mushrooms and butter, all three ingredients well blended. Lightly rub a large piece of foil with butter, put the turkey in the middle and wrap it up, making sure that the ends are firmly sealed. Put the package into a hot oven and roast the turkey, allowing 20–25 minutes per pound. Twenty minutes before the turkey is ready, take it from the pan, discard the foil, scoop out the stuffing and return the bird to the oven. Increase the heat to very hot and continue to roast the turkey until the flesh is brown and crisp. Reheat the stuffing.

Serve the turkey garnished with the mushroom and onion stuffing, parsley and watercress. As an extra garnish, add cooked, mashed or chopped chestnuts. Serve with the usual turkey accompaniments, plus a gravy (see above).

ROAST AND TRUFFLED TURKEY (French)

8 servings:

1 young fat turkey	**1½ lb. pork sausage meat**
10 truffles	**2–4 chicken livers, chopped**
1 glass sherry	**salt, pepper**

Pare the truffles and cut them in quarters. Cook the truffle parings in the sherry for 2–3 minutes. Chop them finely and mix with the sausage meat, adding the sherry in which they cooked, the chicken livers and the quartered truffles. Rub the inside of the turkey generously with salt and pepper, push the stuffing into the cavity and leave for 2 days to let the stuffing flavour permeate the turkey. Roast in the usual manner (see previous recipe) and serve on a bed of watercress with game chips and a truffle sauce (see pages 206, 215).

TURKEY EN DAUBE (French)

Chicken can be cooked in the same fashion.

8 servings:

a small turkey	**sweet herbs (chervil, tarragon,**
onions and carrots, sliced	**parsley)**
slices fat bacon	**salt, pepper**
1–2 bay leaves	**dash freshly grated nutmeg**
	stock or water

For this recipe a large casserole with a tightly fitting lid which excludes all air is needed.

Arrange a 'bed' of onions, carrots and slices of fat bacon on the bottom of the pan. Add herbs, seasonings and nutmeg to taste and place the turkey on top. Cover the bird with another layer of onions and carrots, moisten with the stock and tightly cover. Cook the turkey on top of the stove for 3½–4 hours. Take it from the casserole but keep hot. Rub the vegetables through a fine sieve, reheat and pour as a sauce over the turkey.

A layer of stoned and soaked prunes may be added to the 'bed' of vegetables, and red wine to the stock. Almost any vegetables can be served with this dish.

BOILED TURKEY

'A turkey boiled is a turkey spoiled' is an old rhyme. It has more rhyme than sense, for a boiled turkey presents an agreeable change from the usual, rather rich roast turkey.

10 servings:

a plump hen turkey	**1 carrot**
oyster or celery stuffing (see pages 219,	**1 onion, stuck with 2 cloves**
222)	**2–3 sticks celery**
salt, pepper and lemon juice	**small bunch parsley**
flour	**10 peppercorns**

Hang the turkey in a cool place for 4 or 5 days before using. When ready to cook fill it with either oyster or celery stuffing or a mixture of both. Sew up the aperture, draw the legs into the body and bind the bird securely. Rub the outside with salt, pepper and lemon juice and dredge with flour. Put it into a large, preferably oval, pan adding just enough warm water to cover it. Add the carrot, salt, onion with the cloves, celery, parsley and peppercorns. Bring this all slowly to the boil, lower the heat and let the turkey cook until it is tender, approximately 15 minutes for each pound. (Cooking time starts from when the liquid reaches boiling point.) Take it from the pan and place on a hot platter. Serve with melted butter, an oyster or parsley sauce and celery or chestnut purée. It may be garnished with sliced ham and tongue, with sliced lemon or forcemeat balls.

BRAISED TURKEY

a turkey	2–3 cloves
slices fat bacon	parsley, chives and thyme to taste
1 knuckle veal	salt, pepper
1 calf's foot	stock
6 medium-sized onions, peeled	butter
3–4 carrots, scraped but left whole	1 egg

Cover the bottom of a large pan with bacon. Add the veal, calf's foot, onions, carrots, cloves and herbs. Add salt and pepper. Cover the turkey with plenty of bacon, fixing this with skewers, and put it into the pan, adding about 1 cup (1¼) of stock. Cover the turkey with buttered foil and the lid and cook gently for 5 or 6 hours. Take the pan from the stove and leave the turkey in it for a further 30 minutes. Take it from the pan, place on a hot serving plate and keep hot. Take out the calf's foot and veal knuckle. Strain the gravy through a fine sieve. Return this to the pan and cook until it is very hot. Beat the egg well and stir it into the gravy. Pour the gravy over the turkey and serve it with any vegetables in season, particularly celery.

This recipe is suitable for an elderly bird, which can also be stuffed with a savoury stuffing, i.e. veal or sausage meat. The knuckle of veal and the calf's foot can be omitted, their function is to give added flavour to the turkey.

SALMI OF TURKEY (French)

8 servings:

a young turkey	¾ pint (1½ cups) stock
4 oz. (½ cup) butter	salt, pepper
1 each carrot and onion, sliced	1–2 slices lean bacon, diced and
bouquet garni	blanched
1–2 cloves garlic	1 lb. small mushrooms
1 tablespoon (1¼) flour	1 tablespoon (1¼) armagnac or
2 cups (2½) red wine	brandy

Cut the turkey into 8 pieces, i.e., the breast into 2 pieces, the legs and wings into 2 pieces each. Heat half the butter and brown the turkey 'bits' (the neck, head, gizzard and feet), then add the carrot, onion, bouquet garni and garlic. Sprinkle in the flour and continue cooking, with some care, until this is a golden brown. Add half the wine and half the stock. Stir well, then simmer for 1 hour. In the meantime sprinkle the pieces of turkey with salt and pepper. Heat the remaining butter in a large pan and brown the pieces of turkey. Take from the pan and put into a hot dish.

In the same pan lightly fry the bacon and mushrooms. Take these also from the pan and put with the turkey. Add the remaining wine and stock to the pot with the turkey neck etc., and bring to a gentle boil. Return the turkey, bacon and mushrooms to the pan in which they were browned. Reheat, then strain the stock from the turkey neck etc. over it. Continue gentle cooking for 2 or 3 minutes. Warm the armagnac, pour it at once into the pan and ignite it. When the flame dies down, cover the pan and cook over a gentle heat for $1\frac{1}{2}$ hours.

Serve the turkey in the sauce, with sippets of fried bread and boiled rice.

CREAMED TURKEY WITH MUSHROOMS AND PIMIENTO

Chicken, duck and goose may be cooked in the above manner.

6 servings:

2 lb. cold cooked turkey
butter
1 lb. mushrooms, peeled and sliced
2 oz. ($\frac{1}{4}$ cup) butter
2 tablespoons ($2\frac{1}{2}$) flour

3 cups ($3\frac{3}{4}$) cream
salt, pepper
4 tablespoons (5) chopped canned
   pimiento

Heat enough butter to fry the mushrooms until soft. Put aside, keeping hot until required. Cut the turkey meat into thin strips. Heat the measured quantity of butter, add the flour and stir both to a *roux*. Gradually add the cream, stirring all the time over a low heat. When the sauce is thick and smooth add the turkey meat and cook this gently until thoroughly re-heated. Add the mushrooms, salt and pepper and finally the pimiento. Continue simmering for another 10 minutes. Serve the turkey in a ring of either hot cooked rice or creamed potatoes.

Instead of cream, buttermilk or a mixture of milk and cream may be used.

CREAMED TURKEY WITH GREEN OLIVES

2 servings:

1 lb. cooked turkey, chopped
1 oz. (2 tablespoons) butter
1 tablespoon ($1\frac{1}{4}$) flour
2 cups ($2\frac{1}{2}$) cream or milk

salt, pepper
$\frac{1}{2}$ lb. green olives, pitted
chopped parsley, to taste

Heat the butter, add the flour and stir to a *roux*. Gradually add the cream and stir to a smooth and creamy sauce. Add salt and pepper, then the turkey. Continue cooking until the turkey is hot. Add the olives and parsley, cook for a few minutes then serve in a ring of cooked rice or creamed potatoes, or on hot buttered toast. To make the sauce even richer, a well-beaten egg yolk may be added.

FRICANDEAU OF TURKEY LEGS

This recipe could be used with capon legs or very large chicken legs.

4 servings:

2 turkey legs	salt, pepper
butter	1 egg, well beaten
8 mushrooms, peeled and sliced	slices fat bacon
¼ lb. cooked ham, chopped	2 cups (2⅓) white stock
lemon peel, finely chopped	1 head celery
2 tablespoons (2½) breadcrumbs	1 cup (1¼) velouté sauce (see page 215)
sweet herbs (tarragon, chervil, parsley etc.)	

Carefully cut out and discard the bone from the turkey legs. Heat the butter and fry the mushrooms in it. Mix these with the ham and a little lemon peel. Add the bread-crumbs, herbs (if fresh, finely chopped), salt and pepper. Add the egg and mix all these ingredients into a paste. Stuff the legs with this mixture and flatten them back into their original shape, trimming the edges. Wrap in bacon. Put the stock into a shallow pan, add the turkey legs, cover the pan and cook the legs gently until tender. In the meantime wash the celery and cook until tender. Drain it and arrange on a serving platter. Place the turkey legs on top. Put aside but keep hot. Stir in a little of the turkey liquid into the velouté sauce, reheat until very hot and pour it over the turkey legs.

Serve with any vegetables in season and riced potatoes.

CASSEROLE OF LEFT-OVER TURKEY

3 servings:

1½ lb. cold turkey, thinly sliced	tomato sauce or purée
2 oz. (¼ cup) butter	butter
2 tablespoons (2½) flour	1 cup (1¼) cold cooked green peas
3 cups (3¾) stock, milk or water	breadcrumbs
salt, pepper	

Heat the butter, add the flour and stir this to a *roux*. Gradually stir in the stock and continue cooking gently until the sauce is thick and smooth. Add salt and pepper and enough tomato sauce to give taste and colour. Butter a small casserole, add a layer of turkey, then of peas. Continue until these ingredients are finished. Pour the hot sauce over the top, sprinkle with breadcrumbs, dot with butter and bake in a hot oven until the top is brown. If the breadcrumbs are first fried in butter their flavour is greatly improved. Grated Parmesan cheese may also be mixed with the breadcrumbs, and thinly-sliced, fried mushrooms, added at the same time as the peas.

HASHED TURKEY

4 servings:

1–1½ lb. cooked turkey
2 cups (2½) stock
onion, chopped
plenty of celery, chopped
1–2 carrots, diced

a little cucumber, chopped
salt, pepper
1–2 egg yolks
½ cup (⅔) cream or milk
creamed potatoes or boiled rice

Cut the meat into neat pieces. Put the stock into a pan, add the vegetables and cook these slowly until soft, adding salt and pepper to taste. Beat the egg yolks with the cream and add this to the pan, stirring all the time. Do not let the mixture boil. Add the turkey meat and cook over a very low heat for about 10 minutes or long enough to reheat. Arrange the potatoes or rice in a ring on a hot, round plate and pour the hashed turkey in the centre.

TURKEY PÂTÉ

10–12 servings:

1 lb. raw turkey meat, finely ground
12 slices streaky bacon
1 lb. pork sausage meat
1 turkey liver, cooked and finely chopped
salt, pepper

1 level teaspoon (scant 1¼) mixed spice
4 oz. (½ cup) butter
2 cloves garlic, crushed
2 medium-sized onions, peeled and minced

Grease a 2-lb. loaf pan and line it with bacon. Mix together the turkey meat, sausage meat, liver, seasoning and spice. Melt the butter in a pan, add the garlic and onion and fry gently to a golden brown. Add this, with the butter from the pan, to the turkey mixture. Work all this together to a smooth paste. Press the paste into the loaf tin and cover it with foil or greaseproof paper. Stand this in a baking pan of water so that the water comes half-way up the side of the loaf pan. Bake on the centre shelf of a moderate oven for 3 hours. Take from the oven and leave for 15 minutes. Turn out and cool. Chill before serving. Serve with hot crisp toast and butter or a green salad.

TURKEY CROQUETTES

3 servings:

½ lb. white turkey meat
¼ lb. ham and tongue, mixed
a little onion, minced
1 tablespoon (1¼) parsley, finely chopped
1 teaspoon (1¼) lemon juice

salt, pepper
½ cup (⅔) extra thick white sauce
1 egg yolk, well beaten
1 whole egg, well beaten
fine breadcrumbs
fat or oil for deep frying

Grind the turkey, ham and tongue and mix with the onion, parsley, lemon juice, salt and pepper. Stir this into the white sauce – the mixture must be thick and firm. Bind with the egg yolk. Shape the mixture into croquettes, dip into beaten egg and then into breadcrumbs. Leave in a refrigerator for 1 hour. Fry in deep fat or oil until a golden brown. Serve the croquettes with any sauce fancied but if using tomato sauce, let it be home-made (see page 214).

To the above recipe may be added ¼ lb. mashed potatoes and the same quantity of soft white breadcrumbs. This obviously increases the number of servings.

TO BONE A TURKEY

Cut through the skin down the centre of the back, lift the flesh carefully on each side with the point of a sharp knife until the sockets of the wings and thighs are reached. Bone these joints before proceeding further, for once these are detached nearly the whole of the bone may be separated from the flesh and taken out complete. Only the neck bones and merrythought (wishbone) remain to be removed and the empty body will then be ready to take the filling.

A chicken may be boned in the same manner.

It is my experience that a good-class butcher will always bone a turkey for a customer if asked to do so. Boning a turkey while not an impossible task does demand some experience or knack as well as time.

GALANTINE OF TURKEY

20 servings:

a 12–14 lb. turkey, dressed weight
1 lb. each lean veal and pork
1 lb. salt pork, cut into cubes
¼ cup (⅓) brandy or sherry
¾ cup (1) cream
2½ tablespoons (3) salt or to taste
coarsely ground black pepper, to taste
¾ teaspoon (1) nutmeg, freshly ground
½ lb. very fat bacon

½ lb. cooked tongue, cut into strips
2 truffles, sliced (optional)
½ cup (⅔) pistachio nuts, coarsely chopped
butter
2 carrots, scraped but left whole
1 stick celery, chopped into 3 pieces
1 good sprig parsley
¾ tablespoon (1) finely chopped tarragon

Bone the turkey and pull off the meat from the skin, keeping the skin intact. Put the meat aside and cook the bones to make a stock. Cut the best pieces of the flesh into small cubes, grind the rest once then grind again with the veal and the pork. Mix this with the cubes of salt pork and turkey, brandy, cream, salt, pepper and nutmeg. Lay the turkey skin as near flat as possible on the table, the inside uppermost. Spread it with the ground and seasoned mixture making sure that all the cavities left by the bones are filled. Cover the stuffing with alternate rows of the bacon, tongue and truffles. Sprinkle with pistachios. Carefully pull the edges of the skin together to make a sausage-like roll and then sew up the edges of the skin. Liberally spread a large piece of linen with butter and place the turkey roll on it. Roll it up tightly and tie at both ends and once or twice in the middle – it depends on the size of the roll. Pat it so that it becomes smooth and even in shape and size. Place the roll in a large, preferably oval, pan. Add the vegetables, parsley, tarragon and enough of the turkey stock to cover. Cover the pan, bring to a gentle boil, lower the heat and cook gently for 1–1½ hours. Let the turkey cool in its own liquid, then take it from the pan and carefully unwrap. Have ready another cloth; place the turkey roll in this and rewrap. Weight it down with a plate with a weight on it, and leave for 2 hours. Unwrap and take out the thread with which the turkey was sewn. At this point the turkey can be covered with a chaudfroid sauce, aspic jelly (see pages 65, 243) or glazed with aspic jelly made from the broth in which the bones were cooked. The galantine is served as a first course with buttered toast.

If garnishing with aspic, make sure the turkey is very cold before spreading it with the aspic, allowing it to set quickly. The aspic itself must be cold but still liquid before being used. Place the turkey with its layer of aspic on a wire rack over a shallow flat dish. Chill but do not freeze. When the aspic is quite set, spread the chaudfroid sauce over it and chill again. Repeat this until the glaze or coating is thick.

Truffles cut into shapes may be used as a decoration as may the green parts of spring (green) onions, hard-cooked egg whites and black olives. Having decorated the galantine, add more aspic, let this set and repeat this operation until all the aspic is used. Chill until required.

ROAST BONED AND STUFFED TURKEY

12 servings:

a turkey weighing 10 lb. dressed, 8 lb. when boned

forcemeat:

1½ cups (scant 2) soft breadcrumbs

3 oz. (¾ cup) grated suet

2 teaspoons (2½) lemon juice

2 teaspoons (2½) each finely chopped parsley and thyme

salt, cayenne pepper

1–2 eggs, beaten

2 lb. chestnuts, cooked and puréed

2 lb. sausage meat

salt, pepper

To bone the turkey, follow the instructions on page 90, or ask the butcher to do it. Mix the forcemeat ingredients together using sufficient beaten egg to bind them. This is a basic recipe which can be adapted according to the size of the bird to be stuffed.

Lay the turkey as near flat on the table as possible, the inner side uppermost. Spread it with the forcemeat, chestnut and sausage meat in layers making sure all the cavities left by the bones are filled. Season generously and carefully pull the skin together to make a neat roll. Sew up the edges with thread. Fasten it with skewers and string.

Place it on a rack in a roasting pan, add enough boiling water to prevent burning, and roast in a moderate oven until tender, about 2½–3 hours. Baste from time to time. Take the turkey from the oven, arrange on a dish and leave it until cold.

TURKEY FLORENTINE

A similar dish can be made with chicken, duck or goose.

6 servings:

2 lb. cooked turkey, neatly sliced
2 cups (2½) milk
½ cup (⅔) single (light) cream
2 tablespoons (2½) butter
2 tablespoons (2½) flour
salt, pepper

4 lb. spinach
good pinch ground mace or nutmeg
Parmesan cheese to taste, grated
fine breadcrumbs, fried in butter
butter

Combine the milk and cream and warm. Heat the measured quantity of butter in a saucepan, add the flour and stir it to a *roux*. Gradually stir the warmed milk into the *roux* to make a thick and smooth sauce. Add salt and pepper. Wash the spinach, drain and cook it until tender in the water adhering to its leaves; drain it and finely chop. Return it to the pan, add the mace and ½ cup (⅔) of the sauce. Blend thoroughly and spread the mixture in a shallow baking dish. Lay the sliced turkey on top. Stir the Parmesan cheese into the remaining sauce and pour this over the top, completely covering it. Sprinkle with breadcrumbs and dot with slivers of butter. Bake in a hot oven until the top is browned.

General Instructions
for Game

The designation game covers wild animals and birds which are hunted for sport and are protected by game laws. For the purposes of the British Game Laws, hares, pheasants, heath or moor game, black game and bustards are game. A licence is required to shoot woodcock, capercailzie, teal, snipe, quail, widgeon, landrail, conies (rabbits) and deer, although these are not classified as game, but come under the Wild Life Protection Act.

No one is quite sure what is meant by heath and moor game, and bustards are rare visitors to Britain. The game laws control the time of year when animals and birds may be hunted or shot, and it is an offence to shoot during the closed season, i.e. the nesting or mating season. It is, however, usual to include under the heading of game such animals as rabbits which, although not protected by game laws, are included in the Excise Licence to kill but have no closed season.

In Britain the game season is between August and March, starting on the day known as the 'Glorious Twelfth'. However, this does not mean that all birds are in season throughout these months. Birds, in particular, vary considerably. Wood pigeons, like rabbits, have no season; they are regarded as vermin and may be shot throughout the year. Many shooting men disagree with the official shooting dates for some birds, feeling they are legally shot but too early.

The chief British game birds are pheasant, grouse and partridge, favourite birds for shooting; usually considered as game birds also are snipe, teal and wild duck. The chief game animals are the hare, deer (venison) and rabbit.

In the United States there is no official beginning to the shooting season, which varies from state to state. Each state has independent game laws which are rigidly enforced. There is a tightly restricted bag limit on all types of game, and it is considered that all game is the property of the state and not the owner of the land where the game is found. This attitude to game exists also in Australia, Canada, New Zealand and in many other parts of the world. Broadly speaking, the shooting season in the United States starts on 1 November and ends on 14 February for upland game; that is birds and small game.

Big game shooting starts on 1 December and lasts about 30 to 90 days. Again each state determines its own period for shooting as well as for the limit of the bag.

American game may be broadly divided into four categories – water fowl, upland game, small game and big game. Water fowl are found and shot in all states to some degree. Generally, however, this category is limited to duck, geese, rail, gallinule and to any of the snipe family. This grouping is unique in one respect in that it is the one where shooting is controlled by an overall Federal Law and whose welfare is the concern of both state and federal agencies. Clearly defined laws outline the methods which may be employed by sportsmen, and bag limits are strenuously enforced.

Upland game is generally recognized as including the various members of the partridge and quail and pheasant families, the woodcock, and one member of the migratory bird family, the dove. America is particularly rich in upland game as many of the various birds introduced from other parts of the world have flourished with great success, two good examples being the Hungarian partridge and the chukkar partridge from the Himalayas. Another is the Chinese pheasant, which is found throughout the north-western central states. These game birds have not only flourished but have fulfilled a highly needed want in the ecology of those regions.

Small game consists of the rabbit, the squirrel, opossum, racoon and, though not all sportsmen agree on this, wild turkey. The last is possibly one of the finest game birds.

All would agree, however, that the foregoing list includes nothing which is hunted simply as a trophy but is edible and, when properly prepared, provides a most tasty addition to the housewife's menu.

America abounds in big game, both native and imported. The commonest of these is the bear, generally of the black bear family, and the deer in its various species. The population of the white-tailed deer has been estimated at 10 to 15 million head and is distributed throughout all states east of the Mississippi river. Specimens vary in weight from 160 to 250 lb. The meat is eaten in all the usual ways of venison.

In the western plains are found the antelope, the javelina (a wild pig of the peccary family), and the big western deer nicknamed the mule deer. This name supposedly originated from a story about an old Mountain Man who, on shooting his first large deer and seeing its size, said, 'this here animule is as big as a skinned mule'.

In the Rocky Mountains is found the bighorn sheep, the only wild sheep native to North America. Difficult to stalk, hard to kill, this splendid animal is a trophy highly prized by any sportsman. The elk and the moose are the largest of the ruminants classed as game in North America. Hunting of these fine animals was at one time drastically limited for some time as they were in danger of becoming extinct through over-shooting, but efficient conservation methods have reduced this threat.

The Russian boar is found in the mountains of Tennessee. Originally imported into the United States in the early part of this century, it has acclimatized well to the area and is ranked as one of the finest sporting trophies of the Eastern seaboard. This animal is the true wild boar of Europe and is not to be confused with the feralhog which abounds throughout the wild lands of the South. These hogs are domesticated swine which have gone wild and have reverted through many generations to their natural size.

Game in the kitchen is a luxury and not necessarily an expensive one, but it demands care when cooking. Its chief merit is its gamey aroma and flavour, and for most game lovers, it should be hung for at least a week before being cooked. The main difficulty in cooking game is to counteract the often extreme dryness of the flesh.

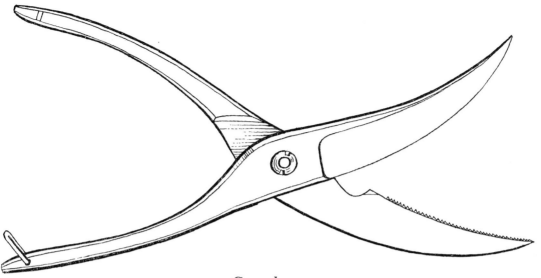

Game shears.

HANGING

The special flavour of game is lost if it is not hung for a length of time after being killed, but care must be taken that the game is not too high. Game birds are hung uncleaned and with the feathers left on.

Maximum and minimum time for hanging game birds and animals is variable. For example, pheasant will take 3–4 days to develop its flavour in hot weather, but 10 days in hard weather under perfect conditions. Capercailzie need an astonishing amount of hanging before they are tender and be really high before cooking. Older wild geese require hanging until obvious signs of ripeness are seen and it begins to smell high. Woodcock and snipe hang for 3 to 4 days, while venison and hare hang at least a week before they are cooked.

Game should be hung on hooks as soon as possible after being killed, and in a cool, dry place well protected from flies, and suspended so as to allow free air to ventilate. Do not put game close to other foods which might pick up the gamey flavour. Hang feathered game from the necks, and furred game, such as hares and rabbits, by the hind legs.

Obviously, the question of how long game should be hung is a matter of personal taste. Some game lovers like their birds so high that they almost fall off their hooks. Others prefer a much milder flavour. However, all game must hang until the flesh is tender and a gamey flavour is evident. One way to decide whether a game bird is ready is to pull out a small tuft of feathers above the tail. If it comes away easily, then the bird is ready. However, if there is already a bluish or greenish discoloration of the flesh, sadly it means the bird has been hanging too long. Warm, damp conditions will cause flesh to decompose more quickly. A daily inspection is advisable.

Venison without hanging has less flavour than mutton, and the pheasant less flavour than chicken. If a gamey flavour is not liked, then the only possible way to eat game is straight from the gun, not all that easy.

For perfection game should be shot in the head, thus leaving the body unmarked. However, if the game has been badly shot, hang it for only a very short time and look at the bird every day to make sure it does not become too high. This is especially important if the flesh has been really badly bruised and even broken.

PLUCKING

If buying birds over the counter, plucking is done by the poulterer, but the procedure is the same as for poultry (see page 13).

TRUSSING

Game birds are trussed as for poultry, with the exception of the long-beaked birds, such as snipe and woodcock (see page 161). Very small birds are not usually drawn.

COOKING

Young birds are usually roasted or grilled (broiled), while older birds are casseroled, made into pâtés, pies or a salmi.

AGE

Young birds have soft, pliable feet and their spurs are hardly formed. Old birds have scaley legs and spurs which are long and well formed. The breast feathers and those under the wing should be soft and downy in a young bird and the tips of the long wing feathers pointed ; those of the older bird are rounded. The breast bone of a young bird is pliable and will give slightly when prodded.

FREEZING GAME

All the usual rules of freezing apply to freezing game. They can be frozen either in their natural state (that is, with fur or feathers intact) or plucked, drawn, clean etc., ready for cooking. Unless one is in a hurry, plucking etc. is preferable.

The most important rule for freezing game is that it must be hung before freezing; this cannot be done afterwards. When required it should be thawed and cooked immediately.

SEASON CHART FOR SHOOTING GAME BIRDS IN BRITAIN

Blackcock   This bird is a member of the grouse family; in Devonshire it is called heathpoult. The season varies in different parts of the country. 1 September to 10 December in Somerset, Devon and the New Forest. 20 August to 10 December elsewhere. It is at its best in October.

Capercailzie	20 August to 10 December.
Duck, Wild	August until March.
Goose, Wild	Here again the season varies slightly. It is from 1 September to 20 February on the foreshore; 1 September to 31 January inland.
Grouse	12 August to 10 December, but at its best mid-August to mid-October.
Ortolan	November until January.
Partridge	1 September to 1 February, at their best in October.
Pheasant	1 October to 1 February, at their best from November to January.
Pigeons	These birds have no close season as they are vermin. They are available throughout the year although they are more plentiful in autumn and spring when pigeon shoots are organized.
Plover	October to January.
Ptarmigan	1 September until April.
Quail	Available throughout the year as today most quails are farm hatched.
Rooks	There is no close season for rooks and only the young birds are fit to eat. Rook shoots are held usually in the second week of May in order to thin out the young birds. Only the breasts and sometimes the upper parts of the legs are used.
Snipe	October until February but at their best in October and November.
Squab	These are available throughout the year. There are farms devoted to the rearing of the fat or Belgium squab in Britain.
Teal	October until February.
Widgeon	October until February.
Woodcock	1 October to 31 January, at their best during October and November.

SEASON CHART FOR SHOOTING GAME BIRDS IN THE U.S.A.

In the United States of America there is no 'Glorious Twelfth' and the shooting season varies from state to state. However, broadly speaking the shooting season starts on 1 November and ends on 14 February for upland game, that is birds and small game.

Big game starts on 1 December and, depending again upon the State, lasts 30 to 90 days, but this is a broad statement and not true in every state as each state determines its own time for shooting as well as the limit of the bag.

As far as state control is concerned, the shooting season is therefore state-wise, but for migratory game, such as duck, ring-necked swan etc. it is determined by the Federal Government and varies from year to year, depending on the population of the birds.

Wild Duck

Wild duck are found and eaten all over the world. They should be plucked dry, a chore which may easily be performed by melting a quantity of paraffin wax in hot water and pouring it over the duck. When the paraffin wax hardens, the feathers and down are easily pulled from the carcass. The body is then singed and wiped inside and out with a damp cloth; wild duck should never be washed.

The flesh of wild duck is not to everyone's taste, for it is often fishy in flavour, while estuary duck are often both salty and muddy. Generally speaking, wild duck should not require a marinade, but this is a matter of opinion. Certainly if it is fishy-flavoured, a marinade might rid it of some of this, but if the bird is really fishy, then there is nothing that can be done to improve it. In Turkey cooks drop a really fishy-flavoured duck into a pan with a little water and plenty of salt, cover the pan and cook the duck for 15 minutes, basting fairly frequently with the salty water. The bird is then drained and prepared for cooking and is cooked a great deal longer than most duck fanciers like.

However, the cooking and eating of wild duck is a highly personal matter. Another suggestion for removing a fishy flavour from a wild duck is to push an onion into its cavity, marinate it in red wine and rub it well inside and out with cut lemon or lime.

The breast of the wild duck should be larded to protect it against the heat and to improve the flavour, and the body cavity and the outside rubbed with olive oil or butter and seasoned with salt and pepper. It is best spit-roasted or roasted in the oven. Duck must be basted frequently to prevent drying out. A good basting may be made by melting butter in hot water and adding lemon juice, or by mixing red wine and butter.

Wild duck also benefits from being flambéed in a good brandy or armagnac. Gin is also a most acceptable spirit for flambéeing, as it has a juniper basis.

One note of caution, if the duck is not bled, it should be cooked within 24 hours. This precludes the possible development of dangerous toxins.

Both ducks and appetites vary, but one wild duck, unless large, is sometimes enough for one person only. If serving a number of ducks, it is a compliment to one's guests to roast each duck according to individual tastes.

It is not practical to describe every member of this extensive family of wild fowl, but the following list is intended to be representative of this gastronomically delightful class of bird.

African Yellow-Billed Duck. Generally considered to be the best of the African wild duck for the table, and is found from the Sudan to the Cape. It can be eaten all the year round.

Australian Black Duck. One of the commonest ducks of Australia and New Zealand. It is often referred to as brown duck, grey duck or wild duck, is a surface feeder and almost entirely a vegetarian. All recipes for mallard or wild duck can be used.

Australian Blue-Winged Shoveller. One of the common wild ducks of Australia (except the far north), Tasmania and New Zealand. Also known as spoonbill duck, it feeds on aquatic plants and animals. It is inferior to the Australian black duck or the teal. Cook it as for mallard or wild duck.

Australian Chestnut Teal. One of the smaller wild ducks usually found in small flocks from south-western Queensland to Victoria and in southern South Australia, mid-western Australia and Tasmania. It feeds on aquatic vegetation and animal life, is much prized gastronomically and is cooked as wild duck.

Bahama Duck. A wild duck, native to all regions of the West Indies and further south through the Argentine, it feeds solely on water plants, weeds etc., being entirely vegetarian. The flesh is highly considered gastronomically and during the dry season, when all the ducks are forced to resort to the coastal areas, this species is said to be less oily in taste than any of the others. It can be cooked in all ways of mallard or other wild duck.

Baldpate Duck. Otherwise known as the American widgeon, this bird is a fresh-water marsh duck about 20 in. in length and weighing from 2 to 3 lb. It is grey headed with warm brown flanks and a bluish beak, feet and legs, and it is found from Alaska to Panama. Its food is primarily pond vegetable life, and it is highly prized as a table bird for its delicate but distinctive flavour.

Black Duck. A dark brown duck with white wing linings, called the black mallard in the United States, it ranges from Canada to North Carolina and winters from New England to Louisiana. It is shot as a game bird, and it is highly prized as a food.

Bufferhead Duck. A small, plump duck of North America noted for its beauty of plumage. About 13 in. long, the drake is black and white with a crested head shaped like a puff-ball and surmounted by a green bordered white patch. The species is fairly rare and delicious to eat.

Canvasback Duck. The largest of the American diving ducks, reaching 23 in. in length, and one of the best-known and most sought after ducks in America. The white-belted body gives the bird its name, and the long bill, which tapers and joins the head at such an angle that there is no forehead, is its most distinguishing feature. Highly prized by both the duck shooter and the gastronome, it forms one course of the classic 'Eastern Shore' menu – Maryland terrapin soup, Chesapeake oysters, and canvasback duck.

Cinamon Teal. This is the least numerous of the puddle ducks in the North American continent. Identifiable by its cinnamon-coloured head at close range, but easily mistaken for other teal in flight, this small duck is from 12 to 14 in. in length and seldom exceeds 2 lb. in weight. It flies in small, compact groups and prefers to move about in stormy weather, thus making him a sporty target. A delicious table game bird, his flesh does not have the strong fishy flavour of many of the puddle ducks.

Mallard. This omnivorous duck is found throughout the world. The male is generally brightly coloured with chestnut and blue-green; the female is brown. Its abundance, size, availability and delicate flavour make it possibly the most important of the wild ducks.

Pintail Duck. This beautiful duck is as fine for food as for sport. It is recognized by its long slender neck and pointed tail, which have caused it to be nicknamed 'sea pheasant'.

Teal. Among the smallest of wild ducks, and often called puddle ducks, teal are widespread throughout Europe, Asia and the Americas, and are found in fresh-water streams, ponds and lakes. A distinguishing prefix describes the various species, examples being cinnamon teal, Chinese teal and green-wing teal.

Widgeon. The middleweight of the duck family, this fresh-water pond bird averages 20 in. in length and from 2 to 3 lb. in weight. Its food is mainly pond vegetable life and it is prized as a table bird for its delicate but distinctive flavour.

Wood Duck. The North American Carolina wood duck and the Asian mandarin duck are representative of this genus. They are among the world's most colourful birds and their taste is comparable to their beauty. Wood duck once faced extinction in North America because of over-shooting for plumage and meat, but intensive conservation efforts and careful regulation of hunting have restored them.

GENERAL ADVICE ON ROASTING WILD DUCK

Tastes vary considerably, both in regard to the time and manner of roasting wild duck· It should never be over-cooked, and the general opinion is that too-well-cooked duck is a spoiled duck. Cooking times given in wild duck recipes for roasting vary between 10 and 30 minutes. However, 10 minutes is only for those who like their meat really underdone to almost rare, for in this time the duck is hardly more than barely heated. Thirty minutes gives only a moderately rare meat. For most people 20–25 minutes cooking strikes a happy medium.

Draw the duck (see page 15) and wash it quickly in cold water. Push into its cavity 2 tablespoons (2½) of chopped onion and 1 cup (1¼) of chopped celery. Truss the duck then dredge it with salt, pepper and flour. Put it on a rack in a roasting pan with warm water in the bottom of the pan. Place it in a hot oven and baste with water and duck drippings. When the duck has been roasted to the desired rareness, transfer it to a hot dish and keep hot. Discard the stuffing; it was used only for flavouring and to absorb some of the fishy flavour of the duck. Reheat the gravy, scraping round the sides of the pan, and strain.

Serve the duck with an orange sauce (see page 212), the gravy and a green salad.

WILD DUCK IN BURGUNDY (French)

1–2 servings:

1 wild duck
1 duck's liver
6–8 slices streaky bacon, diced
3 tablespoons (3¾) chopped parsley
salt, pepper

2 oz. (¼ cup) unsalted butter
1½ oz. (6 tablespoons) flour
½ cup (⅔) stock
1 cup (1¼) red burgundy

Preferably the duck should be killed without bleeding it. Clean and singe the bird. Chop its liver with the bacon and parsley, add salt and pepper and stuff this mixture into the cavity. Put on the rack of a roasting pan and roast the duck for 30 minutes in a moderate oven. Heat the butter, add the flour and stir to a brown *roux*. Gradually add the stock and when this mixture is smooth stir in the wine. Take the duck from the oven; pour off the pan juices into the sauce. Return the duck to the oven to keep hot. Stir the sauce and continue cooking for a few minutes. Strain and serve in a sauceboat. Place the duck on a hot serving plate and garnish with watercress. Serve with game chips (see page 206).

ROAST WILD DUCK (Yugoslavian)

2 servings:

1 large wild duck
2 tablespoons (2½) olive oil
juice 1 lemon
½ lb. fat sliced bacon

4 oz. (½ cup) butter
1 cup (1¼) warm water
salt

Clean the duck which, for Yugoslavian taste, should have been on ice for 48 hours. Rub it well with the oil and lemon juice. Cover completely with bacon and leave for 2 hours. Heat the butter and water in a roasting pan, add the duck (on the rack), bake in a moderate oven for 1 hour, basting frequently. When the duck is tender sprinkle it with salt and cut into serving pieces. Strain the liquid in which the duck was cooked and serve as a gravy. Serve with a green salad.

MALLARD DUCK WITH CHERRIES

2–3 servings:

1 mallard duck
lemon juice
salt, pepper
2 tablespoons (2½) butter
2 tablespoons (2½) dry sherry or chablis

1 clove garlic, crushed
½ cup (⅔) pitted black cherries
2 teaspoons (2½) cornflour (corn-starch)
1 bay leaf

The mallard often has a rank and gamey flavour when it has been driven to the coast and feeds on marine mollusks but this is preferred by many people to the flesh of inland grain-fed duck.

Rub the duck with lemon juice, salt and pepper. (It is also a wise precaution to stuff the cavity of the duck as in the following recipe.) Heat the butter in a large but somewhat shallow pan, add the duck and brown it all over. Drain off surplus butter and pour the sherry over the duck. Take it from the pan, put aside but keep hot. Add the garlic, cherries and any cherry juice to the pan; bring to a gentle boil and cook for 3 minutes. Mix the cornflour with water to a thin paste and stir this into the pan. Stir and cook until the sauce is thick and smooth. If it proves too thick, add some more liquid. Return the duck to the pan, add the bay leaf, salt and pepper and cover the pan tightly. Cook over a moderate heat until the duck is tender, turning it from time to time to ensure even cooking. Serve the duck garnished with the cherries, puréed potatoes and other vegetables to choice.

ROAST MALLARD (American)

3–6 servings:

1–2 mallards	butter
salt, pepper	bacon slices
1–2 potatoes	garlic
1–2 onions	sherry and cream to taste

Soak the duck in very strongly salted water for about 3 hours. Dry thoroughly inside and out, then rub with salt and pepper. Peel the potatoes and onions and place one of each inside the duck. (These must be removed before serving as their duty is to absorb as much as possible of the fishy flavour of the duck.) Pre-heat the oven. In a roasting pan heat enough butter in which to cook the duck. Add the duck, cover with bacon and add, if liked, garlic (strictly to taste). Cover tightly and roast in a very hot oven for 20 minutes; reduce the heat to slow and cook for a further 10 minutes. Just before serving add the sherry. Take the duck from the pan, put aside but keep hot, and discard the stuffing. Strain the gravy into a small pan, add the cream and cook gently for 5 minutes. Serve the duck with the sauce poured over it, and rice, a sharp jelly and a watercress salad.

Other vegetables such as carrot or celery, as well as apples, lemon, parsley or strips of bacon are stuffed into wild duck to absorb the fishy flavour. A non-vintage chablis can take the place of the sherry.

WILD DUCK WITH A WINE SAUCE

4 servings:

2 wild ducks	3 tablespoons (3¾) each port and
1 lemon, halved	claret
salt, pepper	1 tablespoon (1¼) brandy
3 oz. (6 tablespoons) butter	3 tablespoons (3¾) cream
1 teaspoon (1¼) flour	

If the ducks have a fishy smell, stuff with a potato, apple or onion before cooking.

Rub the ducks with cut lemon, salt, pepper and two-thirds of the butter. Roast them in a hot oven for about 25 minutes. Baste often. Put aside and keep hot. Knead the remaining butter into the flour then add the port and claret. Pour this into a small pan and cook gently until reduced by half. Cut each duck into halves and place on a hot dish. Warm the brandy, pour this over the duck pieces and set alight. Put aside but keep very hot. Mix the duck blood (if it is available) and the gravy from the pan with the wine sauce. Add a good squeeze of lemon juice, stir, and add the cream. Cook this gently for a few minutes then pour it over the duck. Garnish with croûtons and serve with a green salad, watercress or cooked broccoli.

BRAISED WILD DUCK - 1

2–4 servings:

3 wild ducks
2 cups (2½) stock
salt, pepper
6 shallots
juice 1 lemon

2 oz. (¼ cup) butter
2 tablespoons (2½) flour
½ cup (⅔) red wine or port
cayenne pepper

Put the duck giblets into a pan with the stock, salt, pepper and the shallots. Simmer for 1 hour and strain. Rub the ducks with salt, pepper and half the lemon juice. Half roast the duck in a moderate oven. Heat the butter, add the flour and stir to a *roux*. Add the giblet stock, stirring all the while, and bring to the boil. Add the wine, the remaining lemon juice and a little cayenne pepper. Cut the duck into neat pieces, drop these into the sauce and simmer until the meat is quite tender

The duck can be marinated, if liked, in sufficient port wine to cover, which is then used in the making of the sauce.

BRAISED WILD DUCK - 2

2–4 servings:

1–2 wild ducks
juice 1 lemon
salt, pepper
fat slices bacon
plenty sliced onion and carrot

fresh rosemary, bay leaf and thyme
2 cups (2½) stock
½ cup (⅔) brown sauce (see page 208)
½ cup (⅔) red wine, port or claret

Rub the duck inside and out with half the lemon juice, salt and pepper. Line a shallow earthenware baking dish with bacon, cover with the sliced onions and carrots and lay the duck on top. Add salt, pepper and herbs. Cook gently, covered, until the bacon has rendered its fat then pour this off. Add the stock and the brown sauce together, which should be enough to come half-way up the duck; add the wine and the remaining lemon juice. Cover and continue cooking until tender. Take the duck from the pan, joint it and arrange on a hot platter. Strain the sauce and serve this separately in a sauceboat. Serve the duck with Brussels sprouts and game chips (see page 206), garnished with the onions, carrots and bacon.

'BLOODY' DUCK

This recipe for wild duck is only for those who like their meat red.

1–2 servings:

1 wild duck	**butter**
lemon juice	**salt**

Thoroughly clean the duck and rub it well with lemon juice. Place it uncovered in a roasting pan in a pre-heated hot oven and roast it swiftly, basting frequently with hot water to which a little butter and salt is added, for 18–20 minutes by the clock, no more no less. Take it from the pan. Serve on a hot platter with wild rice (even in the U.S.A. this is rather expensive), redcurrant or other sharp jelly or *sauce bigarade* (see page 208), green salad, and a full-bodied red wine.

WILD DUCK FLAVOURED WITH ORANGE JUICE

2–3 servings:

1 wild but very plump duck	**bacon slices**
fresh orange juice	

Carefully pull off the skin from the breast of the duck and then cut off the breast flesh from the bone. Slice this with the grain into slices as large and as thin as possible. Skin the legs, remove the meat and slice this into equally thin pieces. Have ready a pan of boiling, salted water, drop the pieces of duck into this and cook them for 15 minutes. Take out the pieces, dry them carefully, put them into a dish and cover with strained orange juice. Leave at least 1 hour. Heat a shallow pan and fry several slices of mild bacon until crisp; take these from the pan, put aside but keep hot. Drain the pieces of duck from the orange juice, dry and then fry them for a few minutes only in the bacon fat; they must not over-cook. Serve the duck and the bacon together with a watercress salad, peeled oranges and perhaps a *sauce bigarade* (see page 208) and a platter of brown rice.

If the skinning and slicing seem too much, cut the duck into neat joints and continue as the recipe suggests, but cook the joints longer than 15 minutes in salted water.

SALMI OF WILD DUCK

Duck beyond its first youth can be used in a salmi.

2–4 servings:

1–2 ducks	sauce:
$\frac{1}{4}$–$\frac{1}{2}$ lb. streaky bacon	**2 oz. ($\frac{1}{4}$ cup) butter**
1 oz. (2 tablespoons) butter	**2 tablespoons ($2\frac{1}{2}$) flour**
1 onion, sliced	**2 cups ($2\frac{1}{2}$) strained stock**
bouquet garni	**$\frac{1}{2}$ cup ($\frac{2}{3}$) claret**
6 green olives, pitted	

Dice the bacon and fry it in its own fat until crisp. Remove half and put aside to use for a garnish. Add the butter, onion, bouquet garni and the duck to the pan and cook slowly for 20 minutes. Baste from time to time. Take the duck from the pan and cool it; then cut off as much meat as possible. Skim off the fat from the gravy in the pan and strain the gravy. Put the duck pieces into a casserole and keep hot.

To make the sauce, melt the butter in a pan and add the flour, stirring all the while, to make a *roux*. Add the stock, still stirring, then the gravy and the claret. When the mixture is smooth bring it once more to the boil and cook for 5 minutes. Pour this sauce over the pieces of duck, add the bacon and olives and continue to cook for a further 20 minutes or until the meat is tender.

To this dish can be added mushrooms; port may be used instead of claret. Some cooks add ripe stoned apricots, sliced pineapple rings and Cumberland sauce (see page 209), or the juice and grated rind of an orange. These variations are strictly 'to taste' (canned pineapple rings are rather sweet but ripe apricots are extremely good with poultry and game dishes).

Serve the duck with fingers of fried bread and, if adding mushrooms, apricots etc. use these as a garnish. The duck livers can be simmered in butter, mashed and spread over the breasts of the ducks while cooking.

WIDGEON

Hang for three days. Pluck and then cut off the neck close to the body. Draw the skin over the opening. Do not cut off the legs but twist them at the knuckle and lay the feet alongside the breast. Cover with fat bacon or larding and place on the rack of a roasting pan. Add enough hot water to the pan to prevent burning. Lightly roast the birds in a hot oven for 25 minutes, by which time the meat will be underdone, as is preferred by most epicures; for well-done meat roast the widgeon another 10 minutes. Five minutes before the bird is ready, take it from the oven, remove the bacon or larding, baste the breast well, dredge with flour, again baste and then return the widgeon to the oven to continue cooking for another 5 minutes. The flouring and basting will give the bird an attractive frothing. Allow one bird per two people.

TEAL

Teal are smaller than widgeon and one per person should be allowed. Hang them for 3 days and then pluck and dress as for widgeon.

ROAST TEAL – 1

1 teal per serving:

teal	**lemon juice**
butter	**flour**
cayenne pepper	

Brush the teal generously with butter; sprinkle with cayenne pepper and lemon juice. Place on a rack in a roasting pan and roast in a hot oven for 20 minutes, basting often with the drippings. Five minutes before it is ready sprinkle with flour, baste again and continue cooking until the flour looks frothy. Garnish with slices of lemon and watercress and serve with a thin gravy and an orange salad (see page 206).

ROAST TEAL – 2

Roast the teal in the same manner as for Roast Teal–1 but stuff each bird with a peeled and split orange. When the teal are cooked serve them garnished with orange slices, watercress and a gravy made by adding red wine to the drippings. Tangerines are also used instead of oranges and if the latter are too sweet then add a little lemon juice. Two or 3 teaspoons ($2\frac{1}{2}$–$3\frac{3}{4}$) of Cointreau or Grand Marnier could also be poured over the teal and would not go amiss.

STEWED TEAL

1–2 teal per serving:

teal	cornflour (cornstarch)
flour	1 glass claret
unsalted butter	orange juice
salt, cayenne	fried bread

Preserve the hearts, livers and gizzards of the teal. Dredge the birds with flour, put them into a pan with plenty of unsalted butter and brown them all over. Take them from the pan and reserve the gravy. Let the teal become quite cold; if possible leave until next day. Carve the birds in such a way that the wings and legs are taken off each piece with a portion of the breast adhering to it. Break the bodies of the teal into small pieces and put them into a pan with the livers, hearts and gizzards. Stew them gently with as much water as to cover them until the gravy is quite strong. Strain the gravy, season with salt and pepper, return it to the pan, thicken with a little cornflour and water paste, then add the claret and a little orange juice. As soon as this mixture begins to boil add the pieces of teal and let them simmer until thoroughly reheated but do not let the gravy boil after the teal has been added. In the meantime make the fried bread, each piece large enough to hold 1 piece of teal. Arrange the bread on a hot plate, place on each piece of bread 1 portion of teal and pour the sauce over them. Garnish with fresh parsley and wedges of lemon or lime.

Grouse

Grouse are found throughout the colder regions of the northern hemisphere and are related to the pheasant and all of the sub-family *Tetraoninae*. They range in size from 15 to 20 in. in length, are of stocky build and have reddish-brown feathers.

All grouse are extremely palatable as they are principally vegetivorous and are highly prized as a game bird and a table delicacy.

Grouse have a special meaning for the British sportsman, and the opening day of grouse shooting, 12 August, means really the 'Glorious Twelfth'. The principal species found in North America are the ruffled grouse, considered to be one of the finest of game birds, the prairie chicken and the ptarmigan. In Europe the family is further represented by the capercailzie, the black (black cock) and the red grouse.

In North America the large blue grouse, dark slate in colour and living in coniferous forests up to the timber line, is found from the Yukon Territory to New Mexico, and is shot as a game bird. It is relished for its distinctively gamey, dark, sweet flesh.

The Canadian grouse is a game bird occupying woodlands throughout the northern two-thirds of America, from Alaska to Newfoundland, and generally is found in the sparsely settled areas which have been overgrown with conifers. Its overdeveloped sense of curiosity often leads it to invade the camps of hunters or holiday-makers where it is killed with a stick, thus earning its nickname of 'fool hen'.

Grouse are not served high and can be eaten within 24 hours of killing, although it can if necessary be hung for a short period.

Major Pollard maintains that grouse and kindred birds should hang from a minimum of three days to over a fortnight, according to the weather and larder, but this is not usual. Its rich gamey flesh needs only brief cooking to bring it to the perfect state of doneness, that is slightly under-done, not raw or blue but pink. They must be well larded to make up for the natural leanness of their flesh. A plump grouse weighing about 1¼ lb., its correct weight, will serve one or two people.

The late Professor George Saintsbury wrote: 'While nearly all the game birds are good, grouse seems to me to be the best, to possess the fullest and at the same time the violent flavour . . . .'

ROAST GROUSE (for young birds only)

Grouse are by nature dry birds and need a little assistance if they are to be roasted. In their cavities insert a piece of butter the size of a walnut or a slice of neatly rolled bacon. A small onion stuck with cloves is another suggestion; one might three-quarters fill the cavity with rice. The real secret, though, lies in liberal basting, which must be done at the beginning of cooking, for once the bird has become dry no amount of basting will moisten it again.

2 servings:

2 grouse
butter, fat bacon
olive oil

flour
2 slices fried bread or toast

Prepare the grouse in any way as suggested above. If the grouse are not already larded, cover them generously with strips of fat bacon. Place them on a rack in a roasting pan and roast in a hot oven for 15 minutes. Reduce the heat to moderate and continue cooking until the birds are almost tender, another 15–20 minutes. Baste often. Take the birds from the oven, remove the bacon or larding, rub with olive oil and dredge with flour. Return the grouse to the oven, baste well and let them brown. Collect the drippings from the pan, pour these over the pieces of fried bread and put the birds on top, one bird to each piece of fried bread. Serve at once garnished with watercress and accompanied by fried breadcrumbs, bread sauce (see page 209) and a redcurrant, cranberry or black grape jelly. Generally speaking the only vegetable permitted with grouse is potato, either as game chips or straw (see page 206).

OLD GROUSE FOR ROASTING

Generally old grouse are not for roasting but if they are so high that their feathers can be pulled loosely from the 'apron' they can, with care, be roasted. Put a piece of bread inside the cavity but remove and discard this before serving. Prepare and roast the old grouse as in the previous recipe but allow longer cooking time and be extra generous with the basting. If the grouse is not too old it will prove an acceptable dish. Serve as for young grouse but with a thick gravy as well.

ROAST GROUSE (Scottish)

Scotland has a red grouse not to be found elsewhere except in parts of northern England, and it has been honoured in its Latin scientific name, *Lagopus scoticus*, by the sub-title *scoticus*. It is of exquisite flavour, weighs about 19 ounces and is perhaps the most highly regarded and expensive game bird in the world. It should hang from 3 to 10 days, according to its age and the weather, and be carefully plucked to avoid breaking the delicate skin. Draw but do not wash the grouse, instead simply wipe inside and out.

grouse
butter
lemon juice, salt, pepper

red whortleberries or cranberries
fat bacon
1 piece toast per bird

Mix 1–2 oz. (2–4 tablespoons) of butter for each grouse with a little lemon juice, salt and pepper and stuff this into each bird. Add whortleberries or cranberries, as both bring out the flavour of the flesh and help to keep it moist. Wrap each bird well in bacon and then wrap in greaseproof paper or aluminium foil. Roast in a moderate oven for 15 minutes, remove the paper and continue roasting to brown the birds. The complete roasting time is between 20 and 40 minutes, according to the size and age of the birds. Grouse must be taken from the oven in the nick of time, neither overdone nor underdone, so care must be exercised.

Boil the livers for 10 minutes and then mash them with a little butter, salt and pepper and spread this over the pieces of toast. Put this into the roasting pan during the last few minutes of cooking but do not let it become sodden in the fat. Serve the grouse on the toast with game chips (see page 206).

SPATCHCOCK OF GROUSE (For young birds)

1 serving:

Take a young plump grouse and split it in two through the back but without separating the halves. Season well on both sides and rub generously with sweet oil. Open it out quite flat and thread it on a skewer. Grill (broil) it over or under a brisk heat for 7 minutes on each side. Baste frequently, adding a trace of lemon juice at the last moment and coarsely ground pepper to the dripping. Take from the skewer, spread with *maître d'hôtel* butter (see page 211) and serve garnished with watercress or thin slices of crisply fried bacon and a sharp jelly such as cranberry, rowanberry, elderberry or black grape.

CASSEROLE OF GROUSE

For old birds.

2–4 servings:

2–4 grouse
white wine or draught cider
1 white onion, thinly sliced
freshly ground pepper
salt
flour

olive oil
1 clove garlic, sliced
4–8 oz. mushrooms, peeled and
 sliced
pinch cayenne pepper and thyme

The grouse should be prepared as for roasting. Put them into a bowl and cover with the wine or cider – for this recipe the one is as good as the other. Add the onion, pepper and salt and leave to marinate for 24 hours. Take the grouse from the marinade, dry them well and roll in flour. Heat sufficient oil to brown them and as they brown put them into an iron casserole into which they will fit neatly. Add enough marinade to cover, the garlic, mushrooms, cayenne pepper and a sprinkling of thyme. Bring this to the boil on top of the stove, cover, lower the heat and simmer until the meat is so tender that it lifts easily off the bone.

Most of the autumn vegetables marry with this dish but red cabbage cooked with apples, red wine and brown sugar is one excellent accompaniment, plus creamed floury potatoes or game chips (see page 206).

SALMI OF GROUSE

This salmi is not made, as so often is the case, from odd bits of rewarmed meat but of freshly cooked grouse.

2–3 servings:

2–3 grouse
butter
2 cups (2½) stock
bouquet garni
1 cup (1¼) claret or port

pepper and small strip mace
3 very small onions, finely sliced
1 tablespoon (1¼) tomato purée
fried bread

Fry the birds in hot butter until brown. Cool, cut each bird into halves and transfer to another pan. Add the stock, bouquet garni, claret, pepper and mace. While this is cooking, reheat the butter and fry the onions until soft but not brown. Add the tomato purée and mix well. Pour this sauce over the grouse and simmer for 30 minutes or until tender. Somewhat older birds require longer cooking. Serve on triangles of fried bread with a watercress salad and game chips or straw potatoes (see page 206).

MAYONNAISE OF GROUSE

cold cooked grouse
mayonnaise
hard-cooked eggs (optional)

crisp lettuce leaves
fresh tarragon

As the flavour of grouse is very strong, a not too ripe grouse is best for this recipe. The mayonnaise should be home-made and preferably made with a fine olive oil and tarragon vinegar. If using hard-cooked eggs, they should be sliced. Use the lettuce leaves as a base, add only the flesh of the grouse and the sliced egg, if wanted, cover with mayonnaise and sprinkle with finely chopped tarragon.

POTTED GROUSE

Potted grouse made from the meat of the grouse with ham and a little tongue is perfect. It can be eaten at any meal either in a sandwich or with toast. It does need some care in its preparation, especially in its flavouring. The addition of a little lemon juice and a few drops of Tabasco sauce to sharpen the flavour makes a great difference.

cold cooked grouse
a little ham and tongue
unsalted butter, softened

salt, pepper, pounded mace
lemon juice and Tabasco sauce
clarified butter

Use only the breast meat of the grouse and strip off the skin and any fat. Pound the meat in a mortar with the ham and tongue until it is smooth; then add the butter, ½ lb. to every lb. of pounded meat. Add salt, pepper, a pinch of mace, a few drops of lemon juice and Tabasco sauce. Pass all this through a wire sieve or the finest cutter of a mouli-grater and put into a pot, pressing it down with the back of a spoon. Put the pot into a slow oven to heat the contents, press down again then, while still warm, cover with clarified butter. Let this get cold.

Pheasant and partridge can be potted in the same way. A liquidizer (blender) can be used instead of pounding. One pound of potted meat is usually sufficient for 6–8 servings.

PTARMIGAN

The smallest member of the British grouse family, the ptarmigan or mountain grouse, differ from the common grouse in that the legs have feathers down to the claws. It is seldom seen below a height of 1,500 feet as it is a bird of the snows and the wind; otherwise it can be distinguished by its white wings and white underparts of its body, and has earned such romantic names as 'Child of the Mists' and 'Wraith of the Snows'. In winter it adopts a pure white plumage.

It is by no means a rare bird and there are many more of these snow grouse than is realized. Because they prefer to live at such high altitudes and in inaccessible places, few people in England ever manage to see a ptarmigan, but they are certainly exciting birds to find and to hear their harsh grating call which has been described as sounding like two pieces of granite being rubbed together. It is keenly sought after by many sportsmen.

In the northern hemisphere they are represented by about eight species. They feed on buds, berries, mosses and lichens, making the meat sweet and tender, with a delicate but definite aroma.

Other members of the family include the American willow grouse, the rock ptarmigan (found from Alaska to Labrador) and the red grouse (see page 108).

Ptarmigans, which are about the same size as red grouse, should be well hung before being dressed.

ROAST PTARMIGAN

All recipes for grouse are suitable for ptarmigan. They make very good eating although inferior to the true grouse. The flavour of ptarmigan varies greatly and quite often they are dry and too strongly flavoured with juniper. Major Pollard says that one way to abate both these faults is to cook them in two successive boilings of milk, throwing the first lot of milk away.

4 servings:

2 ptarmigan	1 cup (1¼) red wine
2 slices fat bacon	salt, pepper
4 oz. (½ cup) butter	2 slices toast, buttered

Hang the birds as long as possible. Pluck and draw them carefully and truss in the same manner as for poultry (see page 16). Wrap each bird in a slice of bacon and secure this firmly. Heat the butter in a roasting pan, add the ptarmigan and roast in a hot oven for 40 minutes, basting frequently after the first 10 minutes. Ten minutes before the birds are ready, remove the bacon to let the birds become nicely browned. Warm the wine, pour it over the birds and baste them well with it. When the ptarmigan are tender, take them from the pan and keep hot.

Put the pan on top of the stove, bring to the boil and reduce the gravy by about one-third. Add salt and pepper to taste. Serve the ptarmigan on the buttered toast, the gravy (separately) a sharp sauce and fried breadcrumbs (see page 25).

CAPERCAILZIE or CAPERCAILLIE

The capercailzie is a large bird of the grouse family often known as the wood grouse. It is a bird of the Scottish Highlands but is comparatively rare these days, although its numbers are increasing. It is a handsome bird with a fine plumage, the legs being feathered down to the toes as with the mountain grouse. The male of the species are Beau Brummells, and their hens correspondingly dowdy. Unfortunately the eating habits of the capercailzie, feeding on the young growths of pine trees, do tend to give the flesh a turpentine flavour.

Capercailzie should be allowed to hang for a considerable time to make them really tender. For the connoisseur they are at their best when high. Major Pollard, my mentor, says that some epicures keep them until amputation is required and only the deep breast portion can appear. He also recommends that to abate a too strong turpentine flavour, the capercailzie should be steeped in milk for 2 to 3 hours before plucking. Another trick is to stuff the bird with raw potatoes which are discarded before serving.

ROAST CAPERCAILZIE

For the following recipe the capercailzie is not meant to be quite as high as the epicures might like, but certainly high. Capercailzie must be drawn, washed and thoroughly dried before roasting.

4–6 servings:

1 capercailzie
softened butter
salt, pepper
several slices fat unsmoked bacon
2 oz. ($\frac{1}{4}$ cup) butter

1 cup ($1\frac{1}{4}$) stock or water
1 cup ($1\frac{1}{4}$) cream
1 tablespoon ($1\frac{1}{4}$) cranberry or
  rowanberry jelly

Truss the capercailzie, rub it with softened butter, sprinkle with salt and pepper and cover with bacon. Heat the butter in a roasting pan, add the stock and place the bird on the rack in a roasting pan. Roast in a moderate oven until tender, basting frequently. Take out the bird, put aside but keep hot. Strain the gravy into a small pan, scraping carefully round the sides of the roasting pan. Add the cream and the jelly. Test for seasoning. Serve with game chips (see page 206), a green salad and a tart jelly.

Allow 20–25 minutes per pound for roasting capercailzie, and if a stuffing is preferred, a chestnut or chipolata stuffing (see pages 208, 220) could be used.

Guinea-fowl

This is a family of crested West African birds (Numididea), related to the pheasant and with several species, to be found starting in the Ethiopian region, extending south-east to Madagascar, and south-west to Natal.

Guinea-fowl were brought to Europe by the Greeks, and they became popular later among the Romans, for a dish of guinea-fowl was part of the upper class Roman menu by Varro's time. They suffered a decline then reappeared in the sixteenth century when the Portuguese returned with them from the Guinea coast of West Africa. In its wild state the flesh of the guinea-fowl can be tough and exceedingly dry, and is best cooked gently in a casserole. It has at no time made any great impact on Mediterranean cooking, although in Sicily I have eaten roast guinea-fowl served with ripe figs.

Guinea-fowl are now domesticated and have been reared in many parts of the world for several hundred years. In France it is still wild and considered a game bird; the flesh of these birds is prized for its tenderness, delicate flavour and slight hint of gameyness. Naturalized and domesticated as they are, they prefer a warm climate and also thrive better in a farm-yard than in a poultry yard, as they are inclined to be quarrelsome.

They are valued not only for their flesh, but also for their eggs. One of the most popular of the species, the common pintado, has dark grey plumage finely spotted with white and grows to the size of a large pheasant. It is sometimes called 'come-back' from its frequent harsh cry. Guinea-fowl are mostly gregarious ground eaters but like to roost in trees.

Guinea-fowl are common in shops today and reasonably priced. They can be cooked in many of the ways of cooking pheasant and also prepared for the table in any manner suitable for chickens. However in general guinea-fowl are barded or larded to be roasted in an oven or on a spit. They can also be stewed in a *cocotte* and take kindly to gentle braising.

In the sixteenth century in Britain, guinea-fowl was called turkey, and many literary references to the turkey in early English writing usually meant the guinea-fowl (see page 82).

ROAST GUINEA-FOWL

2 servings:

1 guinea-fowl, trussed and drawn	**1 cup (1¼) stock**
thin slices bacon	**watercress**
butter or other cooking fat	

Place the guinea-fowl on a rack in a roasting pan. Cover it with slices of bacon and fix these with toothpicks or small skewers. Roast in a moderate oven for 35–45 minutes. Baste it liberally with butter while cooking. Guinea-fowl, even when domesticated, is naturally dry. When the bird is tender, take it from the pan, discard the trussing strings and place it on a hot dish. Pour off surplus fat from the pan. Add the stock and scrape around the sides of the pan to get all the flavoursome sediment. Bring to the boil, stir well and cook for 2–3 minutes. Strain. Garnish the guinea-fowl with watercress and serve with the gravy, fried breadcrumbs, bread sauce (see pages 205, 209), and grape jelly. Game chips, straw or match potatoes go well with guinea-fowl.

Before trussing, the guinea-fowl can be stuffed with pared tart apples and herbs.

GUINEA-FOWL PIE WITH GRAPES

2 servings:

1 guinea-fowl, halved	**powdered cloves**
8 slices streaky bacon	**brown sugar**
salt, pepper	**paprika**
1 lb. seedless grapes	**½ lb. short pastry**
rosemary	**1 egg yolk, beaten**

Fry the bacon in a heavy casserole until the fat runs but do not let it become crisp. Take the bacon from the pan and put aside. Add the guinea-fowl to the pan and fry until brown; if the bacon has not produced sufficient fat, add a little butter. Add salt and pepper. Arrange the guinea-fowl halves, skin-side up, on the bottom of the pan and surround with grapes. Sprinkle with the rosemary, powdered cloves, a very little sugar and paprika. Cover with the bacon and then with pastry, rolled out to a square. Brush with the egg yolk and bake in a hot but not fierce oven until the pastry is a golden brown.

Serve with game chips (see page 206).

ROAST GUINEA-FOWL WITH JUNIPER BERRIES

6 servings:

3 guinea-fowl each weighing 2 lb.	**3 tablespoons (3¾) brandy**
softened butter	**¼ cup (⅓) stock**
2 tablespoons (2½) juniper berries, crushed	**salt, pepper**

Truss the wings and legs of the guinea-fowl close to the body. Brush liberally with softened butter and roast on a rack in a roasting pan in a hot oven for 10 minutes, basting frequently with the drippings from the pan. Add the juniper berries and roast for a further 20 minutes or until the guinea-fowl are tender, adding more butter if required (guinea-fowl are extremely dry birds and need a lot of basting with fat). Take the birds from the pan and put aside for a moment. Pour off the fat from the pan, return the guinea-fowl and pour the brandy over them. Add the stock. Stir, scraping well around the sides of the pan. Cook on top of the stove, stirring for 5 minutes, then remove the birds to a hot serving dish and halve them lengthwise (large guinea-fowl can be cut into more pieces). Test the gravy for seasoning and strain it over the birds.

Serve with fried breadcrumbs (see page 207), watercress, apple purée or redcurrant jelly.

BRAISED GUINEA-FOWL

2–3 servings:

1 large guinea-fowl
3 medium-sized onions, cut into rings
2 sticks celery, trimmed and chopped
¼ lb. mushrooms, peeled and sliced
¼ lb. seedless grapes
fresh thyme, parsley and marjoram
   to taste, finely chopped

salt, pepper
1 oz. (2 tablespoons) melted butter
flour
1 cup (1¼) white stock
1 cup (1¼) white wine
1 tablespoon (1¼) flour, arrowroot
   or potato starch

For this recipe a large, deep casserole with a tightly fitting lid is required. Arrange the onions, celery, mushrooms, grapes, herbs, salt and pepper in a layer on the bottom. Rub the guinea-fowl with butter, place it on the bed of vegetables, sprinkle with flour, add the stock and wine and cover. Put into a moderate oven and cook for 45 minutes. Uncover, liberally baste the bird with its own liquid and continue cooking for a further 10–20 minutes, basting frequently until the bird is brown and tender. Raise the temperature of the oven a little. Take the bird from the casserole, place it on a hot plate and surround with the vegetables and grapes. Keep hot. Mix the measured flour with enough water to make a thin paste and stir this into the liquid in the casserole. Bring this to the boil and cook, stirring all the time, for at least 5 minutes. Strain the sauce through a sieve and pour it over the guinea-fowl. Serve with boiled potatoes sprinkled with parsley.

CASSEROLE OF GUINEA-FOWL

2–3 servings:

1 large guinea-fowl
salt, pepper
6 peppercorns
¾ cup (1) milk
1 blade mace
1 small onion, coarsely chopped

1 small carrot, thinly sliced
2 sticks celery, chopped
fresh herbs to taste, finely chopped
2 oz. (¼ cup) butter
2 tablespoons (2½) flour
4 tablespoons (5) cream

Put the guinea-fowl into a casserole with sufficient hot water to cover; add salt and peppercorns. Bring to the boil on top of the stove, lower the heat and cook gently until the fowl is tender. Take it from the pan and let it cool. Measure out $\frac{3}{4}$ cupful (1) of the liquid in which the fowl has cooked and pour this into a pan. Add the milk, mace, vegetables, herbs, salt and pepper and bring this slowly to the boil. Lower the heat and cook until the vegetables are tender. Rub through a sieve. Heat the butter, add the flour and stir this to a roux. Gradually stir in the sieved vegetables and cook slowly for 10 minutes. Add more salt and pepper if required. At the last moment add the cream. Keep hot. Cut the guinea-fowl into neat pieces and put these into a shallow casserole; pour the sauce over the top and reheat until the fowl is hot (but do not reboil). Serve in the casserole.

GUINEA-FOWL HUNTERS' STYLE

2–3 servings:

1 large guinea-fowl

dried thyme

rosemary

olive oil and brandy

6 large mushrooms, chopped

1 small onion, chopped

1 large sprig parsley, chopped

$\frac{1}{2}$ clove garlic, crushed

salt, pepper

1–2 slices fat bacon

1 oz. (2 tablespoons) butter

$\frac{1}{2}$ cup ($\frac{2}{3}$) stock

12 small mushrooms

a little garlic and onion, minced

parsley, finely chopped

Wipe the guinea-fowl inside and out with a damp cloth. Mix together a little thyme and rosemary with a few drops of olive oil and brandy. Rub the inside of the bird with this mixture. Make a stuffing with the liver of the guinea fowl, the large mushrooms, onion, parsley, garlic, salt and pepper. Fill this into the body of the guinea-fowl. Truss the bird and sew up the opening.

Dice the bacon and blanch it in boiling water for half a minute. Drain and dry. Heat the butter in a heavy casserole, add the bacon, let this begin to cook, then add the guinea-fowl. Brown it on all sides, turning it from time to time. Add the stock, cover the pan and bake the guinea-fowl in a moderate oven for 45 minutes, basting from time to time. Remove the cover and let the guinea-fowl cook for another 15 minutes. Peel the small mushrooms. Heat about $\frac{1}{2}$ cup ($\frac{2}{3}$) olive oil, add the minced onion and garlic, fry for 1 minute then add the mushrooms. Sprinkle with salt and pepper.

Serve the guinea-fowl on a hot dish generously sprinkled with parsley, surrounded with the small mushrooms, and with game chips (see page 206), served separately.

Partridge

'A Partridge I was born, and such must die,
          Where'er I come within the Power of Man . . .'

Rev. Charles Coxwell of Abbington,
Glostershire, 1773

There are several species of the partridge in both Europe and northern Asia. The common or grey partridge, as it is called in Britain, is found in Britain and continues eastwards as far as the Dnieper. When we talk of the partridge in Britain we usually mean the common partridge, of which Major Pollard wrote, ' . . . the plump delicate partridge, your true British bird (*Perdix perdix*) not your coarse, red-legged French infantry . . .', by which he meant the red-legged partridge which came from Europe and is often referred to as French partridge.

While the common partridge is found throughout the British Isles, the red-legged is found mainly in Essex and Hertfordshire, although these areas are not its sole habitats.

Gastronomically the common partridge has the edge on the red-legged, although the latter is a bird of no mean flavour and, in fact, there are game lovers who consider it as tasty as the grey bird.

European partridges have been introduced into the United States and have settled down in the northern and western areas of that country, as well as in Canada, and is known as Hungarian partridge. The Chukkar partridge from Asia also flourishes in the United States.

The common partridge is a rotund, orange-brown little fellow, with a grey neck and underparts, and its rufous tail cannot be missed in flight. However, in flight it is not easy to distinguish the hen from the cock.

There is an old saying, 'good farming and partridges go hand in hand', and this is not far from the truth, for they are birds of corn-growing country, although they like hedgerows and gorse or scrub for cover.

In culinary French, a partridge up to the age of six months, of either sex, is always *perdreau*; after six months both sexes are called *perdrix*. It is easy enough to recognize the young birds; their first flight feather is rounded at the tip and not as blunt as with older birds. Also, their feet are a yellowish brown.

Provided the birds are young (and this is important), the most usual way of cooking them is to roast and serve them simply with a watercress salad and game chips (see page 206) or straw potatoes (see page 206).

Old birds, again to quote the Major, 'which occur plentifully both in nature and in gift game', are best turned into a salmi or cooked slowly with sauerkraut which gently moistens them. Partridge pie, pudding or soufflé are country recipes for dealing with aged birds, and a partridge can even be boiled and then covered with a thick, well-flavoured onion sauce.

The higher or gamier the partridge, the longer cooking it can suffer, and one must take care not to mask the flavour of the flesh of the young bird with too heavy or too rich extraneous sauces etc. Such richness can be applied to older game or, to bring the Major into the matter again, 'the less tasteful French partridge'. When dealing with Asian partridges, a certain richness does no harm at all.

A partridge should weigh not more than 1 lb., and when plucked its flesh should be light coloured. Its bones should be small, in fact, it should be almost all breast, and its age preferably be between 6 weeks and 4 months.

ROAST PARTRIDGES – 1

2 servings:

2 partridges	**butter**
salt, pepper	**2 slices crustless bread, fried**

Place the prepared partridges in a roasting pan, sprinkle with salt and pepper and rub them liberally with butter, for they are very dry birds. Roast them in a hot oven for 25–30 minutes, basting frequently in the butter and the juices which have oozed from the birds. Put the fried bread on to a hot serving dish and place a bird on each piece. Garnish with watercress and serve with straw potatoes, fried breadcrumbs, bread sauce and a brown gravy (see separate entries).

If the partridge livers are available, make a liver paste. Fry a little finely chopped shallot or onion in butter and add the livers. Fry together for a few minutes, then rub through a fine small sieve. Add salt, pepper and a little butter. Spread this over the birds just before serving.

If the partridges are not very young and the flesh seems dry it helps to put a lump of butter, seasoned with salt and pepper or a few pieces of juicy steak inside the body cavity.

ROAST PARTRIDGES – 2

4 servings:

4 partridges	**butter**
salt, pepper	**chicken stock**
4 slices streaky bacon	**1 cup (1¼) cream, beginning to sour**
4 thin slices lemon	

Rub the partridges inside and out with salt and pepper and tie over each breast a slice of bacon. Inside each bird place a slice of lemon. Butter a baking pan, add just enough stock to cover the bottom then add the partridges. Roast in a moderate oven for 25 to 30 minutes, basting frequently. When the birds are tender and their gravy a rich brown pour the cream over them and continue cooking until the cream bubbles, basting twice. Serve the partridges hot with the gravy (scraping well round the sides of the pan to collect it all, a bread sauce (see page 209), and, if possible, parsley jelly (this can be made with a mint jelly recipe, substituting parsley for mint).

ROAST PARTRIDGES WITH APPLES (French from Normandy)

2 servings:

2 plump partridges
butter
salt, pepper
3–4 cooking apples

2 slices bread
foie gras
4 tablespoons (5) calvados or
  brandy

Rub the partridges generously with butter, sprinkle with salt and pepper and roast for 25–30 minutes in a moderate oven with a few tablespoonfuls of water in the pan. In the meantime pare and core the apples, cut into halves, and place them in a buttered baking dish, flat side down. Dot generously with butter and bake in a moderate oven until they are soft but still retain their shape. Heat enough butter to fry the bread on both sides until crisp and a light brown. Take the partridges from the pan, remove their livers, mash these and mix with a small quantity of *foie gras*. Spread the toast with the liver paste, then place this on a hot platter. On each piece put a partridge. Sprinkle with calvados and ignite. When the flames die down garnish the dish with apples.

SPATCHCOCK PARTRIDGE (for young birds only)

1 partridge per serving:

This is a simple but splendid dish. Split each partridge down the back, press it flat and stretch it out on a skewer. Rub it with a fine olive oil and sprinkle with salt and freshly ground black pepper. Grill (broil) over or under a quick heat, turning it twice during the cooking process in order to seal the juices on both sides. Lower the heat and finish cooking rather more gently in order to cook the bird right through. In all, 20 minutes should be sufficient. Turn on to a hot platter. Spread with *maître d'hôtel* butter (see page 211) and serve with a remoulade sauce (see page 214) and watercress.

PARTRIDGES WITH CABBAGE (for elderly birds)

4 servings:

4 partridges
2 large onions
2 large carrots
7 slices streaky bacon
salt, pepper
bouquet garni

2 small white cabbages, blanched
4 small onions each stuck with 1
  clove
stock, preferably game
white wine or cider

Slice the onions and carrots, dice 3 slices of bacon and put all into a heavy casserole. Add the salt, pepper and bouquet garni. Shred both cabbages and with half cover the ingredients in the casserole. Truss the birds (see page 96) as for roasting and fix a slice of bacon over the breasts. Into each partridge push one onion stuck with a clove. Arrange them on the cabbage, cover them as snugly as possible with the remaining cabbage, add enough stock to barely cover and cook gently on top of the stove for 2 hours or until tender. Just before serving add a little wine.

To serve, arrange the cabbage (with the onion, carrot and bacon) on a hot platter to form a bed. Place the partridges, their onion stuffing discarded, on the top. Strain the gravy, bring this to the boil and pour it over the partridges.

There are several versions of this recipe. Some cooks add pork or sausages to the casserole, others a little garlic and about 6 juniper berries. Alternatively, serve the partridges on the cabbages surrounded by fried chipolatas and with boiled potatoes.

PARTRIDGES IN CREAM (Norwegian)

2 servings:

2 partridges	salt
4 oz. ($\frac{1}{2}$ cup) butter	6 tablespoons ($7\frac{1}{2}$) cream
2 tablespoons ($2\frac{1}{2}$) butter	butter for frying
2 tablespoons ($2\frac{1}{2}$) flour	2 slices fried bread or toast

Take the livers from the birds and put them aside. Heat the first quantity of butter in a pan, add the partridges and let them cook gently for 20 to 25 minutes, turning from time to time to brown all over. Blend the 2 tablespoonfuls of butter with the flour and add salt to taste. Add the cream and cook the mixture over a low heat, stirring all the while, for 5 minutes. Remove from the heat and let the sauce stand covered for 5 minutes. Heat a very little more butter and gently fry the livers until soft enough to mash; spread over the toast. Place the partridges on these. Strain the sauce through a very fine sieve and pour this over the top.

BRAISED PARTRIDGES

6 servings:

6 partridges	1 sprig thyme
salt, pepper	1 cup ($1\frac{1}{4}$) red wine
4 oz. ($\frac{1}{2}$ cup) butter	6 slices streaky bacon
1 each carrot and onion, sliced	1 heaped teaspoon ($1\frac{1}{4}$) flour
2 bay leaves	$\frac{1}{4}$ cup ($\frac{1}{3}$) cream

Truss the birds and rub them lightly with salt and pepper. Heat the butter in a large pan and add the vegetables, bay leaves, thyme, partridges, salt and pepper. Cook for 10 minutes over a good heat. Add half the wine, cover the pan, lower the heat and cook very gently. Chop the bacon finely, add this to the pan (plus the remaining wine) and continue cooking until the birds are tender, adding just a dash of water now and again. When the birds are tender, take them from the pan, untruss, put aside and keep hot.

Strain the liquid. Sprinkle the flour into the pan, gradually return the liquid, stirring all the time to prevent lumps. Add, if required, a little water to thin the sauce. Bring this to the boil, add the cream, stir and pour the sauce over the partridges. Serve with a thick and smooth lentil purée or a thick celery purée (see page 205).

PARTRIDGES IN A PIQUANT SAUCE

4 servings:

4 partridges
½ lb. mushrooms, peeled and coarsely chopped
6 slices streaky bacon
1 each large onion, carrot and parsnip, peeled and thinly sliced
1 tablespoon (1¼) finely chopped parsley
1 teaspoon (1¼) brown sugar
1 tablespoon (1¼) flour
¼ cup (⅓) red wine
1 tablespoon (1¼) capers
juice ½ lemon

Stuff the mushrooms into the partridges. Line the bottom of a large pan with the bacon, cover with the sliced vegetables and parsley, and add the partridges and about 1 cup (1¼) of water. Cover and cook gently on the top of the stove until the partridges are tender. Take them out and place on a hot dish; put aside but keep hot.

Add the sugar to the pan and continue cooking until the sugar dissolves, stirring continuously to prevent burning. Sprinkle in the flour, stir this well, then add the wine, ½ cup (⅔) of water, capers and lemon juice. Bring to the boil, lower the heat and cook gently for 15 minutes.

Rub the bacon and vegetables through a sieve or mouli grater or purée in a liquidizer (blender), then strain. Scoop out the mushrooms from the partridges and arrange these as a garnish round the birds. Pour some of the sauce over the partridges and serve the rest in a sauceboat. Serve with straw potatoes (see page 206) or game chips (see page 206) and a watercress salad.

SALMI OF PARTRIDGES

4 servings:

4 partridges
1 oz. (2 tablespoons) butter
¼ lb. streaky bacon, cut into pieces
2 shallots, chopped
fresh herbs, finely chopped
salt, pepper
blade of mace
1 medium slice ham
stock
½ cup (⅔) claret
fingers of dry toast
sauce:
1 oz. (2 tablespoons) butter
1 tablespoon (1¼) flour
about 1 cup (1¼) stock
juice ½ lemon

Heat the butter in a shallow pan; add the bacon and fry until it begins to change colour. Add the partridges and fry them for 10 minutes, turning them until they are brown all over; add more butter if required. Take the partridges from the pan and cool. With a sharp knife carve off the wings, legs and breasts; skin and trim the pieces. Break up the carcasses and put them with the trimmings into the pan, adding the shallots, herbs, salt, pepper, mace and ham. Cover all this with stock (preferably game stock) and cook it slowly for about 2 hours. Skim off surplus fat and strain the stock. Return the strained stock to the pan, add the claret and the partridge meat; let this cook very gently until the meat is tender.

Meanwhile, prepare the sauce. In a small pan heat the butter; add the flour, stirring this to a *roux*, and then enough stock to make a sauce of medium thickness. Add the lemon juice and pour the sauce over the simmering partridge meat. Pile all this in the centre of a hot dish and surround with fingers of very hot and dry toast. Serve with creamed potatoes.

PARTRIDGES – HUNTERS' STYLE (Portuguese)

6 servings:

6 partridges	1 bay leaf
1½ cups (scant 2) olive oil	2 cloves garlic, crushed
½ cup (⅔) wine vinegar	2 shallots, peeled and coarsely
1 cup (1¼) white wine	chopped
parsley, coarsely chopped	salt, pepper
bouquet garni	fried bread

Put the partridges into a bean pot with the rest of the ingredients except the fried bread. Cover and cook for 3 hours over a very low heat. By this time the birds will be truly tender, even the most elderly of their species. Drain and place each partridge on a piece of hot fried bread. Pigeons can be cooked in the same way.

A bean pot is a deep, plump, earthenware, lidded baking dish much used in certain parts of the United States. Similar earthenware pots are available in Britain.

PICKLED PARTRIDGES

3–6 servings:

3 partridges	fresh thyme to taste
oil for frying	1 cup (1¼) red wine
3 tablespoons (3¾) wine vinegar	12 small onions
handful fresh parsley	4 carrots, peeled and cut into rounds
1 stick celery, cut into rounds	3 cups (3¾) water
2 bay leaves	lemon slices as garnish
salt, pepper	

This dish can be served hot or cold. Heat a fair quantity of oil in a pan until it begins to smoke, add the partridges and fry them until brown all over. Transfer the partridges to a casserole, add the vinegar, parsley, celery, bay leaves, pepper and thyme. Cover and cook slowly until the vinegar is absorbed, then add the wine. Cook for a further 10 minutes. Add the onions, carrots and water. Bring to a gentle boil, add a little salt, lower the heat and simmer for 1 hour, skimming the top of the gravy from time to time. Serve the partridges on a hot dish surrounded by the onions and carrots, and garnished with sliced lemon. Strain the gravy into a hot sauceboat. If serving the partridges cold, immediately they are cooked put them into a large glass jar or casserole, strain the liquid over them and cover the surface with a thin layer of olive oil. Leave until quite cold, then cover and keep in a cool place until required.

PARTRIDGES WITH GRAPES

2–3 servings:

2–3 partridges
1 lb. seedless green grapes

**4 oz. ($\frac{1}{2}$ cup) larding or very fat
  mild bacon**
salt, pepper

Prepare and trim the birds, put a few grapes in each and truss (see page 96) for roasting. Cover the bottom of a *cocotte* or heavy pan with the larding cut into very small pieces. Put the partridges on top and add the remaining grapes, salt and pepper. Cover the pan and cook over a moderate heat until tender. Serve the partridges in their sauce on a hot serving plate and garnished with uncooked grapes.

PARTRIDGES IN VINE LEAVES

Fat young pigeons and squabs can be cooked in the same manner.

4 young partridges
salt

8 vine leaves
8 thin slices fat green bacon

Rub each bird lightly with salt inside and out. Cover each breast with 2 vine leaves and 2 slices of bacon and tie firmly with string or thick thread. Have ready a large pan filled with boiling unsalted water. Drop the birds in, cover the pan, reduce the heat and boil gently for 25 minutes. Take them out and plunge immediately into a bowl of iced water and leave until quite cold but no longer. Discard the vine leaves and serve the partridges with a green salad.

Pheasant

The pheasant lives in woodland borders and in rush reeds near water, and on park and farm-land. Its diet is varied, but nuts, berries, fruits, bulbs, grass, weeds etc. are favourite foods. It is the only game bird which is bred for shooting.

The common pheasant is a hybrid, and although not indigenous to Britain, no one knows when or by whom it was introduced. Pheasants were first introduced into the United States (it is said) by Judge Denney during the presidency of General Grant. It carries in its veins the blood of many sub-species. Probably the first pheasants came to Britain with the Romans (possibly the species *Phasianus colchicus*) who knew a great deal about the rearing of them. Later came the ring-necked pheasants which mixed freely with the earlier inhabitants. Since then many other species have been introduced, including the large and desirable Mongolian, with its rich red flanks and green gloss plumage. But British pheasants are mongrels and no two seem to have the same plumage, making any detailed description pointless. However, whatever their colour, pheasants may be distinguished from all other game birds by their long tails and the large red wattle surrounding the eyes.

There is almost unanimous consent that the pheasant is the finest eating of the game birds – but everything depends on the treatment of the bird. In the past, pheasants were hung either from the head or tail feathers until they fell with a plop. This surely carried the axiom 'the wilder the pheasant, the better the flesh', rather too far. The time that the real pheasant flavour takes to develop by hanging is variable. If it is too fresh, it is no tastier than a chicken, but less tender (see Hanging).

Hen pheasants are superior to the cock, and Colonel Hawker, the famous British sportsman of some 150 years ago, advised his fellow sportsmen to keep the hens and give away the cock pheasants to his friends. This advice, says Major Pollard, a sportsman of equal dedication, sounds rather mean but can be justified by counsels of expediency.

The age indicators of a cock pheasant are his spurs, which are rounded in a young bird, short but pointed in a two-year-old, and both long and sharp in older birds. In old hens and cocks, the general tone of the plumage is dark, the feet hard and roughened. Aged birds should be cooked by stewing methods, not roasted.

Pheasants are dry-breasted birds and it is generally wiser to bard them well with strips of larding pork, pounded flat and tied securely. Rubbing the bird with butter and putting a large knob of it in the cavity also helps.

The pheasant is an obliging bird which lends itself to a variety of dishes, and its flavour is well-matched with such items as apples, grapes, raisins etc. If, however, it is to be served plainly roasted, then it must be well hung; otherwise it can prove both dull and tasteless. Although a really good-sized bird will serve four or even five people, I prefer to suggest one pheasant for three people.

However, if you have only one pheasant and more than three people to serve, roast a chicken along with the pheasant, in the same roasting pan, and when the two birds are cooked and served it will be remarked that the chicken has cunningly taken on some of the flavour of the pheasant.

ROAST PHEASANT-1

3 servings:

1 young pheasant	**1 slice lemon**
salt, pepper	**3–4 slices streaky bacon**
1 bay leaf	**butter**
1 clove garlic	**flour**

Sprinkle the pheasant inside and out with salt and pepper. Slip the bay leaf, garlic and lemon into the cavity. Cover the breast with bacon and a piece of foil smeared with butter. Put the pheasant, breast up, on a rack in a roasting pan and into a hot oven. Roast until tender, basting frequently with melted butter. Roasting time should be between 40–45 minutes, according to the size and age of the bird. Just before the pheasant is ready, take it from the pan, take off the foil and bacon, baste the breast, dredge with flour, and return the bird to the oven to brown the surface and give it a frothy appearance. Remove the trussing skewers or strings. Return the tail feathers to their original position.

Serve with madeira sauce (see page 211), game chips, Brussels sprouts, watercress salad or with boiled rice, the bacon as a garnish and a sharp jelly, such as cranberry, redcurrant or elderberry.

ROAST PHEASANTS-2

6 servings:

2 young pheasants	**2 slices streaky bacon**
3 oz. (6 tablespoons) butter	**flour**
2 shallots	**watercress**

Put half the butter and 1 shallot into each pheasant, cover the breast with a slice of bacon and wrap each bird separately in foil. Put the pheasants, breast up, on a rack in a roasting pan and roast them for 40–45 minutes in a hot oven or until tender, but the flesh should remain somewhat rare. Take the pan from the oven, open up the foil, remove the bacon, dredge the birds well with flour and return them to the oven still in the foil but with the breasts exposed. After 5 minutes baste well and continue cooking until brown. Place the birds on a hot serving dish and return the tail feathers to their original position, garnish with watercress.

Serve with a bread sauce (see page 209), cranberry, grape or redcurrant jelly and puréed or straw potatoes (see page 206).

If shallots are not available, use an equivalent quantity of mild onion.

ROAST PHEASANTS WITH CHESTNUT STUFFING

6 servings:

2 young pheasants	**1 oz. (2 tablespoons) butter**
salt, pepper	**1 egg, beaten**
green herbs to taste, chopped	**$\frac{1}{4}$ cup ($\frac{1}{3}$) red wine**
$\frac{1}{2}$ lb. cooked chestnuts, peeled and	**3–4 slices streaky bacon**
coarsely chopped	**sour cream**
1 bread roll, soaked in milk and	**1 oz. (2 tablespoons) melted butter**
squeezed dry	**2 tablespoons ($2\frac{1}{2}$) redcurrant jelly**

Rub the outsides of the pheasants with salt and insides with herbs. Finely chop their livers and gizzards and mix with the chestnuts, bread roll, salt, pepper, the first quantity of butter, egg and wine. Blend this mixture thoroughly and fill the cavities of both birds with it. Lift the skin away from each carcass and insert pieces of bacon between the skin and the flesh. Smooth the skin down again. Place the pheasants on a rack in a roasting pan, cover with foil and roast in a moderate oven for 20 minutes. Remove the foil, brush the birds generously with sour cream and return them to the oven. Roast for another 20–30 minutes basting twice with melted butter. Take the birds from the oven, put aside but keep hot. Make a gravy from the liquid in the pan, collecting the sediment clinging to the sides. Strain through a fine sieve. Bring to the boil and mix with the redcurrant jelly. Test for seasoning and pour into a sauceboat. Return the tail feathers to their original position. Serve the pheasant with game chips (see page 206), watercress salad and a sharp jelly.

ROAST PHEASANT STUFFED WITH GRAPES

3 servings:

1 pheasant	**1 oz. (2 tablespoons) melted butter**
salt, pepper	**1 cup ($1\frac{1}{4}$) stock**
$\frac{1}{2}$ lb. white grapes, peeled and	
stoned	

Wipe the pheasant and sprinkle it lightly inside and out with salt and pepper. Fill the cavity with grapes then sew up the opening. Put the pheasant on a rack in a roasting pan, breast upwards. Brush with butter. Heat the stock, pour this over the pheasant and into the pan. Roast the pheasant in a moderate oven until it is tender but slightly underdone, basting every 10 minutes. The usual cooking time is 40–45 minutes. Take the pheasant from the pan; put it aside but keep hot. Heat the gravy on top of the stove, scraping round the sides of the roasting pan to collect all the drippings. Bring this to the boil, strain through a fine sieve and test for seasoning. Pour a little of the gravy over the pheasant and the rest into a sauceboat. Return the tail feathers to their original position. Serve with game chips (see page 206), a green salad and a tart jelly.

ROAST PHEASANTS WITH SOUR CREAM SAUCE

6 servings:

2 young pheasants
1 cup (1¼) soft breadcrumbs
sherry or madeira
½ cup (⅔) hazel-nuts, shelled and
   crushed
12 juniper berries, crushed
1 teaspoon (1¼) grated orange peel

salt, pepper
melted butter
2 tablespoons (2½) onion pulp*
½ cup (⅔) sweet white wine or cider
1 cup (1¼) sour cream
dill or fennel, finely chopped

Mix the breadcrumbs with enough sherry to thoroughly moisten them. Add the hazel nuts, 6 juniper berries, orange peel, salt and pepper. Stuff the cavities of the birds with this mixture, then sew up the openings and truss (see page 96). Put the birds on a rack in a roasting pan, brush liberally with melted butter and sprinkle with salt, pepper and the remaining juniper berries. Put the pan into a very hot oven for 10 minutes, baste the pheasant twice with melted butter then lower the oven heat to hot and continue roasting the pheasants until tender and a golden brown. Take the birds from the pan and keep hot while making the sauce.

Add the onion pulp to the pan, scrape round the sides of the pan, mix and fry all this together for a few minutes; then stir in the wine and gradually the sour cream. Continue cooking, adding dill to taste and stirring all the while until the sauce is hot. Test for seasoning. Strain and pour some of the sauce over the pheasants and serve the rest in a sauceboat.

Serve the pheasant with straw potatoes (see page 206), Brussels sprouts and a tart jelly.

*One way in which to make onion pulp is to finely chop an onion and either pulp it in a liquidizer (blender) or mince it and then rub it through a sieve.

PHEASANTS STUFFED WITH APPLES

6 servings:

2 young pheasants
salt
pinch of marjoram
2 fairly large tart apples, pared,
   cored and halved
¼ lb. mushrooms, finely chopped

grated onion, parsley, garlic, chervil
   mixed to taste
4 slices streaky bacon
butter or other fat
¼ pint (½ cup) red wine
½ cup (⅔) sour cream

Rub the pheasants all over with salt and the insides with marjoram or wipe them with a cloth soaked in brandy. Hollow out the apple halves leaving a thick 'shell'. Stuff the mushrooms and some of the onion and herb mixture into the apple shells and then rejoin the halves, tying them together with cotton. Put a stuffed apple inside each pheasant. Tie 2 slices of bacon over the breast and legs of each bird. Grease the bottom of a roasting pan with butter, add the pheasants and cover the pan with foil. Roast in a moderate oven. After 20 minutes cooking, remove the foil, pour half the wine over the pheasants and, basting frequently, roast them another 30 minutes. Take the birds from the pan, put aside but keep hot. Mix the remaining wine with the sour cream and stir this into the gravy in the pan. Bring to the boil on top of the stove, stirring constantly and scraping the sides to catch all the sediment. Strain into a sauceboat. Serve the pheasants with the gravy, straw potatoes (see page 206), a sharp jelly and boiled rice.

PHEASANT EN CASSEROLE (Italian)

12 servings:

4 young pheasants	$\frac{3}{4}$ tablespoon (1) cocoa
salt, pepper	$\frac{3}{4}$ tablespoon (1) potato flour
4 slices streaky bacon	2 cups (2$\frac{1}{2}$) white wine
oil	2 tablespoons (2$\frac{1}{2}$) wine vinegar
1 onion, chopped	$\frac{1}{2}$ oz. (1 tablespoon) butter
1 stick celery, chopped	1$\frac{1}{2}$ tablespoons (2$\frac{1}{4}$) blanched orange
1 carrot, chopped	rind, cut into thin strips
4 tablespoons (5) sugar	12 slices fried bread

Sprinkle the birds with salt and pepper. Wrap a slice of bacon around each. Heat a little oil in a pan and fry the onion, celery and carrot until a golden brown. Add the pheasants and brown these quickly over a high heat. Transfer the birds to an earthenware casserole. Rub the vegetables through a sieve and pour the sieved result over the birds. Cook in a moderate oven for 45 minutes basting frequently.

Meanwhile boil the sugar with $\frac{1}{4}$ cup ($\frac{1}{3}$) of water until it lightly caramelizes. Stir in the cocoa, potato flour, half the wine and all the wine vinegar. Cook for 5 minutes. Add the butter, the remaining wine and the orange rind, stirring all the time until the sauce is smooth and of medium thickness.

To serve, transfer the pheasants to a hot serving platter. Strain the gravy into the sauce, mix well and reheat. Pour the sauce over the pheasants and serve garnished with very hot triangles of crisply fried bread. A tart jelly and some dark green vegetables could accompany this dish, with plainly boiled potatoes.

PHEASANT À LA SAINTE-ALLIANCE
(Faisan à la Sainte-Alliance)

No book on game would be complete without this recipe evolved by the great Brillat-Savarin in his *Physiologie du Goût* and described as a dish fit for a king. But, as Major Hugh Pollard, sportsman and writer, wrote: 'the onward march of democracy, and the havoc their ideals play with the domestic budget, are slowly making it a legendary dish'.

'Take a pheasant, hung until it is perfect to eat. Pluck it and interlard it carefully with the freshest and firmest pork fat you can find.

Take two woodcocks. Bone and draw them and make two piles, one of the meat, the other of the entrails and livers.

With the meat, make a stuffing by chopping it with steamed beef bone-marrow, a little grated pork fat, pepper, salt, *fines herbes* and a quantity of good truffles, enough to stuff the pheasant completely.

Take good care to put in the stuffing in such a way that none falls out. This is sometimes difficult when the bird is rather old. Nevertheless, there are various ways of achieving this end. One is to cut a slice of bread and tie it on to the bird with a string so as to seal its breast.

Cut a slice of bread which overlaps the laid-out pheasant from neck to tail by two inches. Next take the liver and entrails of the woodcock. Pound in a mortar with two large truffles, an anchovy, a little grated pork fat and a piece of good fresh butter.

Toast the bread and spread this paste evenly on it. Put this under the pheasant, prepared as indicated above, so that the bread will be thoroughly impregnated with the roasting juice.

When the pheasant is cooked, serve it, elegantly couched on the slice of bread. Surround with Seville oranges, and look forward with an easy mind to the outcome.'

PHEASANT NORMANDY STYLE

3 servings:

1 pheasant
1½ lb. cooking apples
4 oz. (½ cup) unsalted butter
1 cup (1¼) cream

Pare, core and thickly slice the apples. Heat the butter in a pan, add the pheasant and brown it all over. Take it from the pan and put aside. Add the apples to the pan and let these brown lightly. Put a layer of apples in a casserole, add the pheasant and arrange the rest of the apples around it. Pour the cream over the top. Cover and cook in a moderate oven for 40 minutes or until the pheasant is quite tender.

Serve the pheasant with the apples and breadcrumbs fried in butter (see page 205).

PHEASANT WITH POMEGRANATE JUICE

3 servings:

1 pheasant
3 tablespoons (3¾) unsalted butter
½ lb. large black grapes
sections 1 small seedless orange
¾ cup (1) pomegranate juice
3 tablespoons (3¾) brown sauce
(see page 208)

The pheasant should be trussed (see page 96) as for roasting. Heat the butter in a pan, add the pheasant and brown it on all sides. Transfer it to an earthenware casserole and pour the butter over it. Peel and seed the grapes, add these to the pheasant, then the orange sections, the pomegranate juice and the brown sauce. Cook this in a moderate oven until the pheasant is tender and serve the bird in the dish in which it was cooked, accompanied by hot buttered breadcrumbs (see page 205).

Pomegranate juice will darken the gravy and give it a tart flavour so if serving a sauce choose a sweet one.

The pomegranate juice is obtained either by breaking a large pomegranate and putting the seeds in a liquidizer (blender) and straining the juice or by pounding an unscathed pomegranate until soft, making a hole in the skin and draining out the juice.

PHEASANT IN RED WINE (Italian)

4 servings:

1 pheasant, cleaned	3 bay leaves
1 onion, chopped	salt, pepper
3–4 carrots, chopped	2 cups (2½) dry red wine
1 stick celery, chopped	1 tablespoon (1¼) olive oil
2 cloves garlic	4 slices bacon, chopped
a little rosemary	1½ tablespoons (scant 2) flour

The pheasant should hang for no fewer than 5 days. Joint it into 4 serving portions; place it with its liver and innards, in a deep earthenware casserole. Add the onion, carrots, celery, garlic, rosemary, bay leaves, salt, pepper and wine. Cover and leave in a refrigerator for 2 days.

Take the pieces of pheasant from the marinade and dry them thoroughly. Heat the oil in a heavy casserole, fry the bacon, add the pieces of pheasant, brown and sprinkle with flour. Strain the marinade and pour it over the pheasant. Cover and cook slowly until the bird is tender. Take it from the pan, put aside but keep hot. Skim off the fat, bring the gravy to the boil and strain it over the pheasant.

Serve with an apple compôte and straw potatoes (see page 206) or game chips (see page 206).

BOILED PHEASANT

This little curiosity is for those who are not overfond of game-flavoured birds. It sounds unenterprising but it was described by an epicure as being 'remarkably good and like boiled fowl with a spark of genius'.

3 servings:

1 hen pheasant, trussed	salt, pepper
1 onion, carrot and stick of celery	bouquet garni

Put the pheasant into a pan, cover with water and add the remaining ingredients. Cook gently for 1 hour. Take the pheasant from the pan, discard the trussing strings and bouquet garni, and serve on a hot dish smothered with celery sauce and with braised celery as a vegetable accompaniment.

If preferred the pheasant may be stuffed with oyster forcemeat (see page 221) or with chestnut purée (see page 218). Sew up the opening and wrap the pheasant in foil before immersing it in water. When cooked it can be served with either a port wine or poivrade sauce. Pour some of the sauce over the pheasant and the rest in a sauceboat.

SMOTHERED PHEASANT (for a not so young bird)

4 servings:

1 pheasant	**butter**
flour	**2–3 sticks celery**
salt, pepper	**$\frac{1}{3}$ cup ($\frac{1}{2}$) red wine**
4 large onions, coarsely chopped	**$\frac{1}{3}$ cup ($\frac{1}{2}$) consommé**
thyme, marjoram and parsley,	
** chopped**	

Cut the pheasant into serving pieces, shake these in a bag containing seasoned flour until each piece is thoroughly coated and place them in a roasting pan or Dutch oven. Surround with the onions and sprinkle with thyme, marjoram and parsley. Dot liberally with butter. Lay the celery on top (leaves as well if these are fresh), add the wine and consommé. Cover, put into a hot oven and cook for about 1 hour. Baste frequently and test to see if the pheasant is tender. It may be necessary to add more wine should it appear to be dry. Remove the cover approximately 10–15 minutes before the pheasant is ready, to let it brown. Take out the pheasant, onions and celery and arrange all on a hot platter. Put the roasting pan on top of the stove over a moderate heat, add a little more red wine, scrape round the sides of the pan to loosen any particles that adhere and, when the gravy is hot, strain it over the pheasant and serve.

Serve with redcurrant or grape jellies, croûtons, creamed potatoes and fried parsley.

PHEASANT À LA RUSSE

Any kind of feathered game can be cooked in this fashion.

3 servings:

1 pheasant, trussed	**streaky bacon**
milk or buttermilk	**1 cup ($1\frac{1}{4}$) cream**

Put the pheasant in enough milk to completely cover it and leave in a cool place for 3 days, adding to the milk from time to time. Take the bird from the milk, dry it, then cover it with bacon, fixing the bacon with tiny skewers to make sure it is secure. Place the pheasant on a rack in a roasting pan, adding a little of the milk in which it was marinating. Roast it in a hot oven for 30–45 minutes, basting frequently with some of the cream to give it a glaze. Take the pheasant from the pan. Remove the trussings and the bacon. Put the pheasant on to a hot plate and keep it hot. Pour the rest of the cream into the pan, blend it well with the gravy, scraping round the sides of the pan. Bring the gravy almost to the boil, strain and pour it over the bird. Serve very hot.

The use of milk makes the flesh tender and more delicate. Serve with buttered breadcrumbs (see page 205), an orange salad (see page 206) and a tart jelly.

CHARTREUSE OF PHEASANT

Chicken or partridge may be used in the same manner.

4 servings:

1 lb. cold, cooked pheasant
½ cup (⅔) brown sauce (see page 208)
1 large mushroom, peeled and chopped
1 egg yolk
½ cup (⅔) flour panada
2 whole eggs
1 tablespoon (1¼) cream
salt, pepper to taste

sauce:
1 oz. (2 tablespoons) butter
1 tablespoon (1¼) flour
2 cups (2½) stock
tomato sauce for colour
1 small onion, chopped
fresh herbs to taste, finely chopped
mushroom trimmings
sherry to taste and a little lemon juice

Grind a quarter of the pheasant meat and mix with the brown sauce, mushroom and egg yolk. Put aside. Pound the remainder of the pheasant meat with the panada and 2 whole eggs. Rub this through a mouli grater. Add the cream, salt and pepper. Pour some of this mixture into a greased charlotte mould (or similar mould) and leave a well in the centre. Put the ground pheasant into this. Spread with remaining pheasant. Cover the mould with greased paper and steam gently for 1 hour. Turn out to serve.

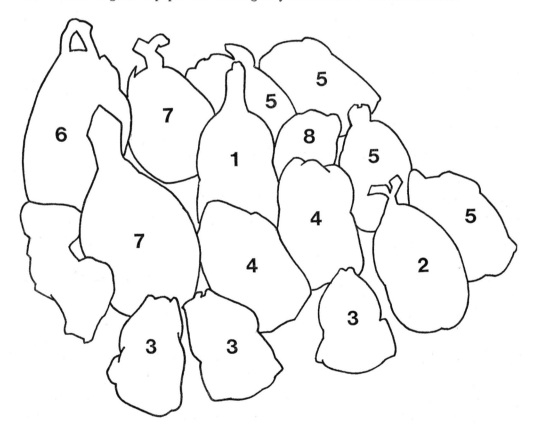

Assorted small birds: 1 wild duck, 2 teal, 3 quail, 4 wood pigeon, 5 rock pigeon, 6 partridge, 7 red-leg partridge, 8 woodcock, with straw potatoes and gravy. Quail eggs in the foreground.

While the chartreuse is cooking, prepare the sauce. Heat the butter, add the flour and stir this to a *roux*. Gradually add the stock and stir until the sauce is smooth. Add the tomato sauce, the onion, herbs and mushroom trimmings. Simmer until the sauce is thick and reduced. Strain, return to the pan, stir in the sherry and lemon juice, add salt and pepper, if required, and serve hot.

Serve the chartreuse with fried mushrooms, sliced kidneys and diced cooked ham.

PHEASANT À LA MODE D'ALCANTARA

This is a very famous and ancient recipe, one of many said to be from the monastery of Alcantara in Spain, the cuisine of which was celebrated throughout the Middle Ages. Versions of it vary slightly and Escoffier includes it in *La Guide Culinaire*. It is said to have survived the sacking of the library of the monastery by Napoleon's soldiers. As may be imagined there are no exact ingredients for such a dish but for those who like to cook with imagination and expense it should prove worthwhile.

3 servings:

1 young pheasant	4 oz. ($\frac{1}{2}$ cup) unsalted butter
$\frac{1}{2}$ lemon	salt, pepper
1 duck liver and its weight in	port wine
truffles	6 small black truffles

Clean the pheasant, carefully remove the breastbone and otherwise prepare it for roasting in the normal way. Rub inside and out with lemon. Simmer the duck liver in a little butter, add salt and pepper and when tender rub it through a fine sieve. In the meantime simmer the weighed truffles in port wine. Mix the duck liver with the truffles and stuff this mixture into the pheasant. Sew up the opening and leave it in a bath of port wine, happily marinating for 3 days. Turn frequently. Take the pheasant from the marinade, drain and wipe it dry. Heat the remaining butter in a casserole, add the pheasant and roast it in a moderate oven until tender, basting it frequently and remembering to keep it rare. While the pheasant is cooking, take 2 cups ($2\frac{1}{2}$) of the port wine marinade and cook this over a good heat until it is reduced by half. Add the truffles (I have another recipe which suggests 18 not simply 6) and simmer for 15 minutes. Pour this sauce over the pheasant while it is still hot and continue cooking another 10 minutes. Serve the pheasant in a deep heated platter with its sauce – if there is too much for the dish serve the rest in a sauceboat. Game chips (see page 205) and a watercress salad are the only accompaniments suggested.

SALMI OF PHEASANT

3 servings:

1 roasted pheasant	$\frac{1}{2}$ cup ($\frac{2}{3}$) sherry
1 oz. (2 tablespoons) butter	pinch cayenne pepper
sprig thyme and 1 bay leaf	juice $\frac{1}{2}$ lemon
1 cup ($1\frac{1}{4}$) brown sauce (see page 208)	

Roast saddle of hare with sour cream sauce, game chips and parsnips.

Cut the pheasant into neat joints and carefully remove all the flesh. Put the bones with the trimmings into a pan with the butter and herbs and stir these over a low heat until browned; then add the brown sauce and the sherry. Cook gently for 15 minutes, strain, return the sauce to the pan and add the cayenne pepper, lemon juice and the pieces of pheasant meat. Let these heat gently but do not allow them to boil.

Serve on a round dish bordered with mashed potatoes and garnished with stoned, braised green olives, sliced and fried mushrooms or truffles simmered in butter.

PHEASANT SOUFFLÉ WITH MADEIRA SAUCE

This type of soufflé can be prepared with any game even the humble pigeon, hare or wild rabbit – but not tame rabbit as its flavour is too bland.

2–3 servings:

1 lb. cooked pheasant meat	2 egg whites, stiffly beaten
¼ lb. fat bacon	butter
pheasant stock	sauce:
2 egg yolks, well beaten	game gravy or stock
½ cup (⅔) madeira	madeira
salt, pepper	meat glaze (optional)

Put the pheasant meat and bacon twice or thrice through the finest plate of a grinder. Moisten with some of the liquid from the pheasant or other game stock; add the egg yolks, the measured quantity of madeira, salt and pepper. Mix thoroughly and fold in the egg whites. Pour this mixture into a well-buttered mould and place in a bain-marie. The water should not be allowed to boil or the mixture will curdle. Cook on top of the stove or in the oven with a moderate heat until the mixture sets. While it is cooking prepare a sauce.

Mix some game gravy or stock with madeira and, if available, a little meat glaze for extra flavour. Bring to the boil. Serve this in the sauceboat – 1 good tablespoon (1¼) per person should be sufficient.

CASSEROLE OF PHEASANT (Georgian, U.S.S.R.)

Pigeons are cooked in the same manner.

3 servings:

1 pheasant	1 cup (1¼) seedless raisins
2 oz. (¼ cup) butter	juice 3 oranges
salt, pepper	strained strong green or Orange
½ cup (⅔) walnuts, shelled and blanched	Pekoe tea

Heat the butter in a casserole, add the pheasant, salt, pepper, walnuts, raisins, orange juice and enough tea to barely cover. Cover the casserole and cook the pheasant slowly until it is tender. Beware of over-cooking. The pheasant should be served in its own sauce, which is fairly dark and sweet, with a purée of potatoes or rice.

Pigeon & Squab

The term pigeon includes any of the species belonging to the Columidae, the doves and pigeons, there is no sharp distinction between the two names. Pigeons are found wild in most parts of the world and are reared domestically in some countries as pets, and for sport and the table.

Nowadays pigeons are available almost throughout the year as they are no longer shot only after the spring sowings. Considered by most farmers as pests, they are shot as and when the farmer feels tormented enough, and are therefore very cheap.

Domestic pigeons should be kept without food for 24 hours before killing, and should be hung head downwards in order to bleed correctly and thus keep the meat pale in colour. They should be plucked while still warm and must never be scalded as this toughens the skin.

Pigeons are easy to cook and full of gamey flavour. Their flesh, like that of most small birds, is dry, but this is something easily remedied. The birds can be well larded or they can be marinated for a while in herb-flavoured oil. A knob of butter can be placed inside the cavity, or they can be roasted well wrapped in buttered foil. If they are young (and a good poulterer can tell this at a glance), they can be roasted; otherwise braising on a bed of moist vegetables is the best way of cooking them; alternatively, they can be turned into an aromatic ragoût. Really tough birds can be made into a stock for a soup. Pigeon pies are old country favourites, although I prefer to use the breast meat only for these, as I find most people do not like dealing with the bones which are covered with pastry.

Wood pigeons, all too plentiful in corn-growing areas and plump from stolen corn and other produce, technically come under vermin, not game. They make good eating as they are meaty little birds, and shooting men like them because they are extraordinarily astute and fly high and fast, a characteristic usually praised in a game bird. Unhappily wood pigeons have large appetites, eating simply for the sake of eating. When shot, they should be plucked very close and then rubbed with a stiff brush dipped in oil. If well larded, they can be stuffed and roasted like chickens, for they are often so plump as to look like tiny brown chickens.

In Paris restaurants it is not unknown to discover pigeon listed as one of the most expensive items on a menu. These are not the pigeons of our cornfields or public buildings but birds especially reared for the table; the Bordeaux pigeons or squabs, *pigeoneau*. These birds are plump and broad-breasted.

During the 'thirties there were three or four squab farms in Britain; now (at the time of writing) there appears to be only one farm, and many people are not aware of the existence even of this farm.

Pigeons and squabs are trussed in the same way as chicken (see page 16) except that their feet, scaled and scraped, are left on, folded across the rear of the bird. Cooking time in all pigeon recipes depends entirely on the age and the size of the bird.

GRILLED (BROILED) PIGEON

1–2 pigeons per serving:

Pigeons may be grilled whole or split open and flattened with a cleaver. They are more easily grilled when flattened, but retain their juices better when left whole.

Wash the pigeons, dry them thoroughly and dip in oil; season them with salt and pepper and grill (broil) under a good heat until browned all over. Baste once or twice. Grilling time is roughly 10–15 minutes on each side. Serve the pigeons as hot as possible with a *sauce tartare* (see page 214) and a watercress salad. Other suggestions are a mushroom or tomato sauce (home-made), a simple parsley sauce or any of the piquant sauces.

CASSEROLED PIGEONS WITH CABBAGE

4 servings:

4 pigeons	**6 juniper berries or a good pinch**
1 large firm white cabbage	**cumin seed**
4 oz. ($\frac{1}{2}$ cup) butter	**salt, pepper**
2–3 slices streaky bacon, diced	**$\frac{1}{2}$ pint ($1\frac{1}{4}$ cups) stock**
1 large onion, finely chopped	**$\frac{1}{2}$ cup ($\frac{2}{3}$) red wine**
1 large hard cooking apple, pared	
and chopped	

Cut the cabbage into quarters, remove the hard core and shred the rest. Sever the pigeons into halves down the backbone. Heat the butter in a deep fireproof casserole. Add the bacon, then the onion and cook until the onion begins to change colour. Add the pigeon halves or as many as will go into the pan at one time and brown each piece on both sides. As the pieces brown, take them from the pan and put aside but keep hot. Add the shredded cabbage to the pan and stir this round and round until it is coated with fat. Continue cooking for a few minutes or until the cabbage begins to soften. Add the apple, juniper berries, salt and pepper. Let this cook gently. In the meantime heat the stock and wine together, and pour it over the cabbage. Lay the pigeons on top, cover with foil and the casserole lid and place in an oven of a moderate to low heat. Cook for 2 hours or until the pigeons are tender. Serve in the casserole.

COMPÔTE OF PIGEONS

6 servings:

6 pigeons
2 oz. (¼ cup) butter
¼ lb. bacon, cut into small cubes
bouquet garni
salt, pepper
pinch sugar
½ lb. small onions, peeled

¼ lb. fresh mushrooms
3–4 carrots, peeled and diced
2–3 turnips, peeled and diced
1 cup (1¼) stock
1 cup (1¼) white wine
1 teaspoon (1¼) cornflour (cornstarch)

Melt the butter in a large pan, add the bacon and then the pigeons, stir them in the fat and fry until they brown. Add the remaining ingredients, except the cornflour, and let the whole cook gently until the pigeons are tender. Take the pigeons from the pan and place them down the centre of a serving dish. Strain off the bacon and vegetables and arrange these on either side of the pigeons. Put all this into a hot oven to keep warm. Skim off any surplus fat from the stock and bring it again to the boil. Mix the cornflour with enough water to make a thin paste. Stir this into the stock and continue cooking until it is thick. Strain this sauce over the pigeons. Garnish the pigeons with watercress and serve with straw potatoes (see page 205), peas or green beans.

CASSEROLE OF PIGEONS

4 servings:

4 pigeons
salt, pepper
8 slices streaky bacon
1 teaspoon (1¼) butter or other fat

¾ cup (1) red wine
juice ½ lemon
½ cup (⅔) sour cream or yoghourt

Rub the inside of each pigeon with salt, cover with 2 slices of bacon and sprinkle with pepper. Grease the bottom of a casserole into which the pigeons will fit tightly and place them inside. Mix the wine and lemon juice together and pour it over the pigeons. Cover and cook in a moderately hot oven for about 45 minutes. Uncover, spoon the sour cream over the pigeons and continue cooking, uncovered, for 10 minutes to let the flesh brown. (Instead of sour cream, yoghourt, fresh cream or buttermilk may be used.) Serve with rice and mushrooms.

POT ROASTED PIGEONS

6 servings:

6 pigeons
salt, pepper
6 thin slices streaky bacon
4 oz. (½ cup) butter
1 pint (2½ cups) stock or cream

sauce:
1 tablespoon (1¼) flour
1 cup (1¼) stock
½ cup (⅔) cream
1 teaspoon (1¼) redcurrant jelly

Sprinkle the pigeons with salt and pepper and cover each pigeon with a slice of bacon. Heat the butter in a deep pan and put the pigeons into this, breast side down. Sear the birds, then add the stock or cream or a mixture of both (buttermilk may be used instead of cream). Cover and cook over a gentle heat. When the pigeons are tender take them from the pan, put aside and keep hot. Skim and strain the gravy. Return this to the pan. To make the sauce, mix the flour with the stock, add this to the gravy in the pan and, stirring all the while, bring to the boil. Add the cream, stir well, add the jelly and, still stirring, cook until the sauce is thick. If it is not sufficiently smooth pour it quickly through a sieve. A little madeira may also be added to the sauce. Place the pigeons on a hot plate, pour a little of the sauce over them and serve the remainder in a sauceboat. Serve the pigeons garnished with watercress and with a sharp jelly.

FRICASSEE OF PIGEONS

4 servings:

4 pigeons	**¼ lb. mushrooms, peeled and sliced**
salt	**1 tablespoon (1¼) flour**
4 oz. (½ cup) butter, heated	**1 heaped teaspoon (1¼) finely**
1 cup (1¼) white wine	**chopped parsley**
freshly ground black pepper to	**½ cup (⅔) stock**
taste	**½ cup (⅔) sour cream**

Chop the pigeons in half lengthwise, sprinkle each piece with salt and leave for 30 minutes. Arrange the pieces in a shallow, wide pan, add the hot butter, pouring some over each half of pigeon. Add the wine and pepper, cover the pan, cook very gently until the pigeons are just tender and then add the mushrooms. Cook for a further 10 minutes. Take out the pigeons and put aside but keep hot. Sprinkle in the flour, stir gently and add the parsley and the stock. Cook over a low heat for 5 minutes, stirring gently all the while; add a little more stock if the sauce seems to be too thick. Return the pigeon pieces to the pan, stir them into the sauce, then add the cream and mix this in gently. Serve the pigeons in their sauce in a deep dish. Accompany with puréed or straw potatoes (see page 205) and such vegetables as peas, carrots and thinly sliced green beans.

STEWED PIGEONS

4 servings:

4 pigeons	**salt, pepper**
2 oz. (¼ cup) butter	**port**
2 cups (2½) stock	**mushroom ketchup**

Heat the butter and fry the pigeons until brown. Add the stock, salt and pepper. Cook until the pigeons are tender; cooking time depends on age and size. Take the pigeons from the pan but keep them hot. Skim off surplus fat from the gravy, add port and the mushroom ketchup in equal quantities (to taste) and bring gently to the boil. Pour the sauce over the pigeons before serving. Serve with potatoes, carrots, turnips etc.

CASSEROLE OF WOOD PIGEONS

6–12 servings:

6 pigeons
1 oz. (2 tablespoons) butter
¼ lb. lean bacon, cut into strips
1 onion, coarsely chopped
salt, cayenne pepper
bouquet garni
1 tablespoon (1¼) chopped parsley

1 small piece lemon rind
1 blade mace
1 bay leaf
2–3 cups (2½–3¾) stock
1 tablespoon (1¼) flour
½ cup (⅔) marsala

Cut the pigeons into halves or keep whole, as preferred. Heat the butter in a casserole, add the bacon, let this cook until the fat runs, then add the onion, salt, pepper, bouquet garni, parsley, lemon rind, mace and bay leaf. Fry all this for about 5 minutes. Add the stock; if the pigeons are halved 2 cups (2½) is enough, otherwise use 3 (3¾) and bring this to boiling point. Add the pigeons, cover the casserole tightly and cook gently until they are tender; not less than 1 hour and probably longer, as the timing depends entirely on the age of the pigeons. When the pigeons are tender add the flour mixed to a thin paste with cold water. Stir this well into the stock and bring to the boil. Cook until the stock is thickened. Add the wine, test for seasoning, correct this if necessary and serve the pigeons in the casserole.

WOOD PIGEONS COOKED IN AN IRON POT

6 servings:

6 pigeons
1–2 onions, thickly sliced
draught cider, beer or red wine
flour
salt, pepper
3–4 slices fat bacon

3 medium-sized onions, thinly
sliced
4 cups (5) hot stock (preferably
game) or water
1 tablespoon (1¼) arrowroot or flour

Pack the pigeons, necks down, in an earthenware casserole and place a thick slice of onion on each. Add cider to cover and leave overnight to marinate. Take the pigeons from the casserole, dry them well and roll in seasoned flour. Put aside. Fry the pieces of fat bacon in a heavy iron pot until the fat runs. Take the bacon from the pan, add the thinly sliced onions and cook these until they soften but do not let them brown. Place the pigeons on top of the onions, cover the pot and cook them slowly for 15 minutes. Turn them over and then add the stock. Strain the cider marinade, bring it to the boil and pour it over the pigeons. Cover the pot and simmer for 2 hours over the lowest possible flame. Thicken the gravy with a thin paste made from the arrowroot mixed with water. Stir this well into the liquid in the pot, then continue cooking for a further 30 minutes. Just before serving a glass of port may be added; it gives a slight sweetness to the dish.

Serve green beans, Brussels sprouts, Savoy cabbage and creamed potatoes or rice with this dish.

CASSEROLE OF WILD DOVE (American)

Pigeons may also be cooked in this manner.

Wild or wood doves, according to Henry Buttes, Master of Artes, in his book: *Dyets Dry Dinner* (1599), live for 30 years. They 'cure the palsie, excite Venus. It is the emblem of sincere and simple meaning, also of pure love, voyd of all malice. It was the good Angell to Noah.'

6 servings:

6 prepared doves	6 large carrots, thickly sliced
2 tablespoons (2½) each butter and bacon fat	1 large onion, diced
1 hard white cabbage, cut into 8 pieces	1 cup (1¼) cooked Lima beans (optional)
	salt, pepper

The birds can be cut in halves or left whole.

Melt the butter and bacon fat in a pan and fry the doves until brown. Put the cabbage into a large pot and add the carrots, onion, beans, salt, pepper and finally the doves. Then add the fat from the frying pan and enough water to come at least 2 in. above the birds. Cover and simmer for 1½–2 hours. Arrange the doves on a hot platter with the vegetables as a garnish. Serve with rice.

Instead of using white cabbage, pre-cooked red cabbage may be used and produces an equally delicious dish. Lima beans are of South American origin; they are flat and slightly kidney shaped. In the United States the pale green Lima beans are preferred and along the coastal regions of California more Lima beans of this kind are grown than anywhere else in the world. In Britain they are sold in cans. Failing these, the best substitute would be broad beans.

SQUAB

Squabs are young pigeons just fledged to the point where they are about to leave the nest. They are never more than 4 weeks old and weigh no more than 14 oz. At this stage they are fat and delicate. They can be cooked in any of the ways of cooking pigeons but they are best split and fried in a good olive oil or an oil and butter mixture. There is not a great deal of meat on such young birds but what they have is good and nourishing. Squabs are considered excellent for invalids.

When purchasing squabs, which are in the markets all the year round, look for their plumpness and light flesh. As squabs their flesh is light and even milky but once the squab has learned to fly or walk around a little they lose their special squab characteristics, become lean and are in fact pigeons.

FRIED SQUAB

Split the squabs into halves lengthwise and fry in either olive oil or oil and butter mixed. Brown on both sides. Put aside (but keep warm) and make a sauce. Add enough flour to the fat in the pan to make a *roux*; add to this sufficient stock to make a medium-thick sauce (a little wine may be added as well). Serve the squabs with this sauce and a watercress salad. As there is not much meat on squabs, they can be reinforced with fried mushrooms and hard-cooked eggs, deep fried to a golden brown. Serve 2 squabs per person.

STUFFED SQUABS WITH A RED WINE SAUCE

Pigeons and doves can also be stuffed and cooked in the same manner.

6 servings:

6 squabs of equal size
salt
1 lemon
butter
6 slices fried bread
stuffing:
butter
½ **lb. streaky bacon, diced**
½ **lb. lean pork, diced**

6 chicken livers
¼ **lb. mushrooms, sliced**
salt, pepper
sauce:
¼ **bottle red burgundy**
a little meat glaze (see page 243)
lemon juice
salt, pepper
butter

To make the stuffing, heat a heavy pan, put in very little butter, add the bacon and cook until its fat runs; then add the pork and chicken livers and cook gently for 10 minutes. In another pan heat enough butter to fry the mushrooms until soft. Combine the contents of the 2 pans and rub all through the fine blade of a mouli grater. Test for seasoning.

Wash and dry the squabs, then rub the insides with salt and cut lemon. Remove the breast bones and stuff the squabs loosely with the stuffing; sew up the opening and truss (see page 96). Spread softened butter on the breasts and legs to prevent scorching or burning and place the birds on a rack in a roasting pan and roast in a slow oven for about 1 hour. Baste frequently with hot water in which a little butter has been melted. Take the squabs from the pan, place one on each piece of fried bread and keep hot.

Scrape the sides of the pan in which the squabs were cooked in order to get every scrap of flavour from the drippings. Stir in the wine, add the meat glaze, a good squeeze of lemon, salt and pepper. Bring this gently to a boil, add a small knob of butter and pour it all through a sieve. Return it to the pan to reheat and then pour the sauce over the squabs.

For those who are not very adept at removing breastbones, simply stuff the squabs as they are.

Quail

Technically the quail is a migratory bird related to the partridge family in the Old World, and to several gallinaceous birds found in the New World. However, the quail is more than simply another game bird. It is both the sportsman's and epicure's delight, being as tasty on the table as it is honest in the field. Many members of the family are found throughout the world, but representative of the family are the European common quail, the blue quail of Africa and the American quail.

In the United States, the names quail and partridge are used interchangeably in different parts of the country. It is also known as the 'bob white' from the sound of its call. Generally, however, the various species carry a descriptive word as part of their nomenclature, such as, for example, California quail, mountain quail and the crested quail.

In Britain it is rarely, if ever, caught in its wild state. Many are sent alive from the Middle East and fattened before they are brought to the market. In the spring quail cross the Mediterranean in their thousands—covering the whole distance without pausing—and arriving exhausted in France. Here they are caught, trapped alive and kept in cages for fattening. Although these carefully reared birds are not without flavour they do not have the same flavour as the wild birds.

James Beard says that although the quail in the United States is probably the most plentiful of the game birds, it is beyond question the most poorly cooked. Quail are subjected, he complains, to very complicated forms of cooking, but they are at their best just plainly cooked. Both in the United States and Britain there are quail farms, which means that quail are available almost all the year round.

The weight of a quail is between 2 and 6 oz. and when plucked, with its light coloured flesh, it looks like a small ball of fat. One quail is usually reckoned a serving, but for lovers of this delicious little bird, two or three are not considered too many. In both China and Japan quail is considered a great delicacy.

Quail should be eaten not later than the day after being killed. They must be dry plucked, singed and drawn from the neck. The head and neck are removed and the wings trussed.

ROAST QUAIL

2 quail per serving:

quail
1 large vine leaf per quail
1 slice streaky bacon per quail

1 piece crustless toast per quail
melted butter

Wrap the quail first in a vine leaf and then in a slice of bacon. Tie with thread and place on the rack of a roasting pan. Roast in a hot oven for 10–12 minutes. Serve on toast which has been spread with the drippings from the quail and with melted butter. Garnish with wedges of lemon and watercress.

Alternatively, the quail can be roasted on a spit before a lively heat from 12–15 minutes. If fresh vine leaves are not available, canned ones may be used.

QUAIL WITH A PORT SAUCE

2 servings:

4 quail
4 each vine leaves and slices bacon
4 thick slices crustless bread

butter
½ cup (⅔) port
foie gras or a good liver paste

Truss the birds for roasting and wrap each one first in a vine leaf and then in a slice of bacon. Tie securely with thread. Roast in a hot oven for 12–15 minutes. While the quail are cooking, fry the bread in butter until crisp and brown on both sides. Each piece should be just large enough to take one quail. Keep hot in the oven. Take the quail from the pan; put it aside but keep hot. Pour the port into the pan in which the quail were cooked, add a small piece of butter and cook for a few minutes, swirling the port around the pan to collect all the drippings and sediment. Spread the fried bread with *foie gras*, arrange one quail on each piece, strain the sauce over the top and garnish with watercress. Serve at once.

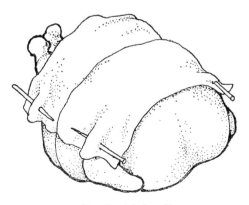

Quail with barding.

GRILLED (BROILED) QUAIL

2 quail per serving:

Split open as many quail as required and beat lightly to flatten. Sprinkle each quail generously with salt and pepper. Place the quail on a rack in a grill pan close to the heat and brown slightly on both sides. Dot with butter, lower the heat and turn frequently, brushing with butter each time. Grill gently for about 20 minutes until brown and tender. Serve with watercress or a green salad.

QUAIL HUNTSMAN STYLE

3 servings:

6 quail
6 tablespoons (7½) brandy
3 oz. (6 tablespoons) butter
1 bay leaf
pepper and fresh herbs

1 teaspoon (1¼) flour
½ cup (⅔) white wine
2–3 tablespoons (2½–3¾) stock,
strained

Warm the brandy, pour this over the quail and ignite. Heat the butter in a casserole on top of the stove, add the quail, bay leaf, pepper and herbs. Cook the quail over a good heat, turning them frequently. When the quail are tender, add the flour and, still turning them round and round, add the wine and stock. As soon as the sauce is blended and bubbling hot, take the quail from the pan, discard the herbs and bay leaf, pour the sauce over the birds and serve accompanied by a green salad or watercress.

STUFFED QUAIL

6 servings:

12 quail
salt, pepper
2 cups (2½) red wine
1 small piece fresh ginger, sliced
½ cup (⅔) seedless raisins

3 cloves
1 cup (1¼) cooked rice
grated rind and juice 1 small orange
½ cup (⅔) melted butter

Rinse and dry the quail and rub with salt and pepper inside and out. Mix the wine, ginger, raisins and cloves. Bring to a gentle boil, lower the heat and cook gently for 5 minutes. Discard the cloves and the ginger. Strain off the raisins. Mix together the raisins, rice, orange rind and 1 tablespoon (1¼) of the melted butter. Blend thoroughly and stuff a little of this mixture into each quail. Put the birds on to a rack in a roasting pan and brush liberally with butter. Roast for 5 minutes in a hot oven and then cook a further 25 minutes in a slow oven. Baste frequently with the remaining butter, orange juice and the wine. Place the quail on a hot dish. Stir the gravy in the pan, add salt and pepper to taste, strain and pour some of it over the quail. Serve the rest in a sauceboat.

Craig Claiborne (*The New York Times Cook Book*) has a similar recipe but he finishes cooking his quail in a chafing dish and pours the liquid over the top. When the liquid begins to steam, he pours a liberal dose of warmed brandy over the quail, ignites it and serves it at once – a splendid refinement if one has a chafing dish.

With quail, serve straw potatoes or game chips (see page 206) or one can serve creamed potatoes and tender green peas. If fresh ginger is not available, use ginger preserved in syrup.

I have also cooked squabs in this manner. As these are larger, the quantity of stuffing needs to be increased.

QUAIL À LA CRAPAUDINE (French)

À la crapaudine is French for cut open and grilled (broiled).

2 servings:

4 quail	a few slices onion
salt, pepper	juice 1 lemon
pinch mixed spice	2 tablespoons (2½) olive oil
1 bay leaf	browned breadcrumbs
fresh parsley and thyme	a little melted butter

Split open the birds (lengthwise along the breastbone) but do not cut them into two. Flatten them and place in a flat dish. Sprinkle with the salt, pepper and mixed spice. Add the herbs and onion. Mix the lemon juice with the oil and pour this over the top. Leave the quail in this marinade for several hours, turning them frequently. Take the quail from the marinade, dry and roll them in the breadcrumbs.

Grill gently, turning from time to time and moistening with melted butter. Serve with a green salad or watercress and, if liked, with a sharp sauce or jelly.

QUAIL WITH GRAPES

2 servings:

4 quail	½ cup (⅔) brandy
4 vine leaves	2 tablespoons (2½) light gravy
4 slices streaky bacon	stuffing:
2½ oz. (full ¼ cup) butter	livers from the quail
salt, pepper	2 tablespoons (2½) diced bacon
½ lb. large white grapes, peeled and seeded	4 tablespoons (5) breadcrumbs
	a little brandy

To make the stuffing, mash the livers and mix with the remaining ingredients using just enough brandy to moisten.

Wrap round each quail a vine leaf and slice of bacon. Tie with thread. Fill the birds with stuffing. Heat the butter and fry the quail in this for approximately 8 minutes. Add salt and pepper. Take the quail from the pan and put into a shallow casserole. Add the grapes and cook uncovered in a moderate oven for 5 minutes. In the meantime stir the brandy and gravy into the butter in which the quail were fried, cook gently until it thickens to form a demi-glaze and pour it over the quail just before serving. Serve with a green salad.

A refinement to this recipe is to soak the vine leaves in brandy before wrapping them round the quail.

BRAISED QUAIL WITH MADEIRA

3 servings:

6 quail	**1–2 sticks celery, cut into rounds**
3 oz. (6 tablespoons) butter	**1 tablespoon (1¼) flour**
1 small onion, sliced in rings	**½ cup (⅔) stock**
1–2 carrots, diced	**½ cup (⅔) madeira**

Heat the butter in a braising pan and lightly fry the quail until they are brown. Add the onion, carrots and celery and continue cooking until these are lightly coloured. Sprinkle with flour, stir to blend, add the stock and the madeira, lower the heat and continue cooking until the quail are tender. Serve with creamed potatoes or boiled rice.

QUAIL IN CREAM (American)

2 servings:

4 quail	**salt, pepper**
4 slices streaky bacon	**1½ cups (2¼) veal or chicken stock**
2 oz. (¼ cup) butter	**1 cup (1¼) cream**
8 shallots or equivalent in mild onion	**3 tablespoons (3¾) pickled grated horse-radish**
1–2 tablespoons (1¼–2½) brandy	

Thoroughly clean the quail and cover the breasts with bacon. Tie this securely. Heat the butter in a heavy pan, add the quail and shallots and brown them. Warm the brandy, pour it over the quail and set this alight. Sprinkle with salt and pepper. Add the stock and cook uncovered in a moderate oven for 15 minutes. Add the cream and the horse-radish, gently stir everything to blend and continue cooking for a further 15 minutes. Arrange the quail on a hot platter and pour the sauce over them. Serve with triangles of fried bread and a watercress salad.

RAGOÛT OF QUAIL

6 servings:

12 quail	**bouquet garni**
2 oz. (¼ cup) pork or duck fat	**½–1 lb. fresh small mushrooms**
1 tablespoon (1¼) flour	**12 small artichokes**
1 cup (1¼) consommé	**juice 1 orange**
salt, pepper	

Clean the birds and wipe them dry. Heat the pork fat in a casserole, add the quail, sprinkle in the flour and cook for a few minutes, turning them from time to time. Add the remaining ingredients, except the orange juice and cook slowly on top of the stove until the quail are tender. Just before serving add the juice and stir.

Serve with a grape jelly, boiled rice and a green salad. Failing quail, 6 pigeons can be used.

SPATCHCOCK OF QUAIL

2 quail per serving:

quail	onion or shallots, finely chopped
olive oil	butter for frying
fresh herbs	soft breadcrumbs
bay leaf	clear, slightly thickened gravy
salt, pepper	sauce Périgueux (page 213)
lemon juice	

Split the quail open down the back and flatten them well. Make a marinade of olive oil, herbs, bay leaf, salt, pepper, lemon juice and onion. Leave the quail in this for about 1 hour, turning them frequently. Take from the marinade 20 minutes before cooking. Dry them and heat sufficient butter in which to fry the birds, let them become brown, sprinkle with breadcrumbs, add salt and pepper and then finish off cooking under a grill (broiler). Serve hot with a gravy and the *sauce Périgueux* separately.

If preferred, instead of grilling the birds, after they have browned simply add a little stock or wine and continue to cook them gently until tender.

Serve with chestnut purée.

QUAIL À LA GOURMANDE

2 quail per serving:

quail	chicken stock
butter	truffles as garnish, thinly sliced
lean ham	large mushroom caps, peeled and
truffles	cooked in butter
champagne	salpicon of foie gras (see below)

There are no exact ingredients for this recipe, which is for those who can cook, like to eat luxuriously, and can afford quail, truffles, *foie gras* and champagne.

Prepare the quail as for roasting without any blanket of larding, simply cleaning and trussing them. Stuff each one with butter, chopped lean ham and chopped truffles. Heat sufficient butter in which to cook the quail on top of the stove until tender. Take them from the pan but keep hot.

Stir into the butter and quail drippings enough champagne and chicken stock to make a sauce – in what proportion is a matter of taste (and pocket). Add some sliced truffles. Fill the mushroom caps with the *salpicon* of *foie gras*. Arrange these on a round or oblong hot platter, put the quail in the centre and cover with the sauce, which must be very hot. Serve immediately.

Salpicon is a Spanish word and in French cooking parlance is a preparation made of one or more ingredients cut into dice and bound with a sauce. A *salpicon* of *foie gras* is *foie gras* mixed with a madeira, port or sherry sauce, if served hot; if served cold, mixed with a tart jelly.

QUAIL À LA GREQUE

2 quail per serving:

quail	**currants**
butter	**pistachio nuts**
rice pilau	**lean ham, diced**
salt, pepper	**game stock**

Truss the quail as for roasting and cook them in butter on top of the stove until tender. Have ready a rice pilau flavoured with salt and pepper, a few currants, pistachio nuts and ham. Arrange this on a platter to make a 'bed' for the quail. Add the quail. Scrape round the pan in which the quail have cooked, add enough game stock to this to make a **sauce** and cook it quickly until it thickens. Pour the sauce over the quail and serve.

QUAIL AUSTRALIAN STYLE

1–2 quail per serving:

The quail season varies in different parts of Australia, according to the run of the quail. In most states, if not all, it is a protected bird, with a limited bag of 12 birds on the opening day's shoot. The usual methods of cooking quail are applied in Australia but the outdoor cook has one method which he prefers above all. This is it:

Clean the quail but do not remove the feathers. Make a mud or clay pack and cover the birds thickly, at least half an inch thick. Bury the clay package in the embers of a very hot wood fire and leave it for an hour or so, fanning the embers from time to time to keep them alive. When ready to eat, pull off the clay covering and the feathers will come with it. The bird is all ready for serving, beautifully tender with all its natural juices retained. This recipe can be applied to other game birds as well and even domestic fowl.

Roast duck with baked apples and peas

A Mixed Bag

A mixed bag – but how mixed? This section of the book could be extended indefinitely. There are few land birds which are not edible and, in the field of game animals, the British certainly need to become as adventurous as the Americans, who are prepared to eat anything, if properly cooked, from the squirrel (classed in Britain as vermin) to the giant moose. And yet, with the advent of deep freezing plants, there is no reason why we should not be buying and eating game from all parts of the world the year round.

In France and Italy more small birds are shot and put into the pot than in either the United States or Britain. In Corsica blackbirds are cooked in various ways and also made into a *pâté* (perfumed with the shrub and brushwood of the Scented Isle) which is as much sought after by connoisseurs as that from Strasbourg and Périgord.

Once we ate peacocks and some still do in other parts of the world, although I feel it is overrated as an eating bird for its flesh is very dry. Swan was considered one of the medieval dishes *par excellence*, although again this is not one of the finest eating birds. The Americans consider the flesh of a young wild squirrel delicious, and in the East the flying bat is served and eaten with French-style sauces. There was a time when the seal and the porpoise were choice *pièces de resistance* in Britain. The Romans ate hawks, and it is recorded that Hippocrates equated the flesh of puppies to that of birds.

Alexandre Dumas the Elder was a gifted cook, and in his dictionary of the kitchen he gave recipes for fillets of kangeroo and elephant's feet, casseroled and flavoured with madeira, garlic and other aromatic spices.

All of which shows how mixed indeed this bag could have been and according to those searching for new foods to feed us, should be.

BECFIGUE À LA BROCHE

The *becfigue*, or in English the figpecker, figeater or fig-bird, is a small bird which feeds largely on figs and is much eaten in France and the Mediterranean area generally. They are caught and cooked in much the same manner as ortolans and are so small that several can be consumed at a sitting.

Game pie and game pâté.

P.A.G.—K

3 servings:

12 becfigue	**12 strips streaky bacon**
12 juniper berries	**12 vine leaves**
12 peppercorns	**12 slices toast or crisply fried bread**

Clean and prepare the *becfigue* and into each put 1 juniper berry and 1 peppercorn. Cover each with a strip of bacon and wrap in a vine leaf. Thread on to 3 spits and grill (broil) under or over a good heat. Serve the *becfigue* on slices of toast and over them pour the drippings. Serve at once and without any accompaniments.

ROAST BLACKCOCK

blackcock	**vine or cabbage leaves**
thin slices streaky bacon	

Cover each bird with 2 thin slices of bacon and vine leaves. Roast in a moderately hot oven, basting frequently. Serve on thick slices of buttered toast with bread sauce and a gravy (see pages 209, 244).

Blackcock can also be roasted on a spit.

GRILLED BLACKCOCK

2 servings:

2 blackcock	**1 cup (1¼) sauce espagnole (see**
salt, pepper	**page 211)**
3 oz. (6 tablespoons) butter	**1 tablespoon (1¼) sherry**

Split the birds down the back and chop off the legs at the first joint. Skewer as for spatchcock (see page 149), as flat as possible. Sprinkle with salt and pepper. Slightly soften the butter and rub this well into the blackcock. Grill (broil) at a fierce heat for 7 minutes, then reduce the heat and continue cooking for 25 minutes, turning the birds from time to time to ensure they are browned both sides.

Served on buttered toast with the *sauce espagnole* flavoured with sherry. Serve with watercress and bread sauce.

HOW TO ROAST A FAT CYGNET (Extravagant)

Since fat cygnets are not everyday fare one must, I suppose, be extravagant about them. The following recipe comes from Norfolk and was given in the days when, presumably, cygnets were more easily available and beef steak was not expensive.

'Pluck the cygnet as you would either a goose or a duck (see page 13). Take 3 lb. of beef steak, pound this in a mortar until fine (or grind it finely and then pound), adding as you work 1 small peeled and chopped onion, a little mace, grated nutmeg, salt and pepper. Stuff some of this into the cygnet and tie it up very tightly so that none of the meat juices escape. Knead what is left over into a rather thick paste and spread it over the breast of the bird. Cover the cygnet with well-greased cooking paper (foil will do here) and put the bird in a hot oven (or skewer on a spit). Roasting will take at least 2 hours, according to the size of the bird. A 15-lb. bird takes $2\frac{1}{4}$ hours. About 15 minutes before the cygnet is ready to eat, take off both the paper and the beef paste and let the cygnet brown. With the beef make a good strong gravy, strain it and add 1 cup ($1\frac{1}{4}$) of port wine. When the bird is dished up for the table, pour over it the port wine gravy and serve with redcurrant jelly.'

The giblets and neck of the cygnet make a good soup. Unless carefully cooked, cygnet can prove to be, like peahen, dry and tasteless.

HAZEL-HEN

A game bird from the mountain forests of Europe (north of the Alps, but not present in Britain) and northern Asia, it is also called hazel or ruffled grouse and, in French, *gélinotte*. It is esteemed wherever it is available, being a plump-breasted bird (about partridge size) of tender white flesh and a subtle gamey flavour, sometimes of pine. It can be cooked in the same ways as guinea-fowl.

HAZEL-HEN COOKED IN CREAM

1 hazel-hen　　　　　　　　　**juice 1 lemon**
salt, pepper　　　　　　　　　**$\frac{1}{2}$ pint ($1\frac{1}{4}$ cups) cream**
$\frac{1}{2}$ lb. (1 cup) butter

The hazel-hen must be plucked and drawn. Sprinkle lightly with salt and pepper and spread with the butter. Place on the rack of a roasting pan and cook in a moderately hot oven until tender (about 50 minutes). Mix the lemon juice with the cream. Baste the bird frequently with the cream and lemon mixture, plus the drippings in the pan.

Instead of fresh cream, sour cream or buttermilk may be used. Serve with game accompaniments such as game chips (see page 206), watercress salad and a tart jelly.

LANDRAIL

The landrail is known in England as the corn-crake. It is not often found in the sportsman's bag for the landrail lives in the corn and hedgerows and seldom flies to oblige the guns. Even when in flight the landrail is not easy to shoot for its curious cumbersome gait makes it difficult to judge. However, it is good eating and in Belgium is called regally, 'the King of the quails' a title given him by cooks but to the eternal confusion of amateur ornithologists.

ROAST LANDRAIL

Draw, truss and wrap in slices of streaky bacon as many landrail as available. Roast in a hot to moderate oven for 20 minutes, basting often with melted butter. Serve on slices of crisply fried bread or toast with gravy, bread sauce (see page 209) and French beans cooked whole in cream and butter.

ORTOLANS COOKED IN A CASSEROLE

1–2 ortolans per serving:

Butter a casserole lightly. Take a good knob of butter per ortolan, a vine leaf and a thin slice of bacon. Rub each bird in butter and wrap in streaky bacon; finally wrap in a vine leaf. Put the ortolans into a casserole, separate each bird with a slice of bread and butter, sprinkle with salt and pepper, cover and cook in a hot oven from 6–8 minutes. Serve the ortolans in the casserole.

PEACOCK

I have eaten this beautiful bird with the hideous voice only in India where, because it is considered a sacred bird, it is sold clandestinely in northern India as Punjabi turkey and eaten frequently by foreigners and Indian Christians instead of the traditional Yule-tide turkey. It required a lot of care in its cooking for it is a dry tough bird, straight from the jungle and shot in circumstances which were dubious to say the least.

It has gone out of fashion in Europe generally but there was a time when a feast was not a feast without a peacock or two. (The Romans in their greedy search for the exotic in eating used to serve a dish of peacock brains.) A tariff of provisions fixed by the City of London authorities in 1271 giving fair prices for meat, poultry and game (which proves that nothing in this world changes) lists the price for peacock as one penny. How much of the peacock was got for this penny is not stated but it was a halfpenny dearer than best hen and threepence cheaper than best coney with skin.

In the days of the Plantagenets, cooks were almost as anxious to please the eye as the palate. Many of their finest dishes were decorated with gold and silver foil (as many northern Indian dishes still are today) and the peacock (with the swan) appeared handsomely adorned at every royal feast.

Sir Walter Scott writes, in his *Lay of the Last Minstrel*:

> 'The mighty meal to carve and share.
> O'er capon, heron-shew, and crane,
> And princely peacock's gilden train . . .'

And with the mention of carving, one should note that etiquette and good breeding in the seventeenth century demanded the employment of niceties of the language when reference was made to the carving of game or fowl. One 'disfigured' a peacock.

The peacock was 'the food of lovers and the meat of lords', and was cooked and served with much ceremony in the days of noble knights and ladies fair. In the kitchen the peacock was skinned, stuffed with spices and roasted. While it was being cooked, a continually wetted cloth was kept round the bird's head to save it from being burnt by the roaring fire. When the bird was cooked it was allowed to cool, after which the skin was neatly sewn on again, the feathers spread out, the comb gilded and a piece of cloth dipped in spirits or wine stuffed into its mouth to be set alight while it was served at table. The serving was accompanied by much ceremonial and performed by ladies most distinguished for rank and beauty; indeed, beauty for the serving of the peacock was rated even higher than rank. The ladies followed the dish to the table in procession to the music of minstrels, who placed the peacock in front of the guest most famed for courtesy or, if it were after a tournament, the victorious knight, who took the chivalrous oath of valour on its head.

But after all this, adds one chronicler, the peacock remained a tough and tasteless bird.

Cassell's *Dictionary of Cookery* (1904) lists two methods of preparing peacock, with recipes intended for peafowl as the latter's flesh is somewhat pleasanter than that of the peacock which Cassell describes as 'coarse and ill-coloured'.

'Peafowl Trussed. These are trussed in the same manner as pheasants excepting that the head should be left attached to the skin of the breast unplucked. It should be carefully covered with buttered paper and fastened under the wing. When the bird is sufficiently cooked, and before it is dished, the paper should be removed and the plumage trimmed.

'Choose a young bird, lard it closely over the breast and legs, fill it with a good veal forcemeat, truss it firmly and roast it before a clear fire for an hour and a half, according to the size of the bird. When done, take off the buttered paper which was round the head, trim the feathers, glaze the larding and serve the bird on a hot dish with a little clear brown gravy under it. Garnish the dish with watercress and send bread sauce to the table in a tureen.'

Well, in India we treated our peafowl in somewhat the same fashion except that we did not keep its head or feathers but had it dressed and trussed as one does a turkey. It was well larded and stuffed variously with any of the usual turkey stuffings, including a good sausage forcemeat which gave it flavour and fat. It was then roasted in the oven in the manner of a turkey and finally 'disfigured' by the cook which was precisely what he did with the unfortunate bird whose sacredness never seemed to be remembered at Christmas time.

PLOVER

Wading birds of the subfamily Charadriinae and related to the phalarope and sand-piper, the plovers include approximately 60 species, distributed throughout the world. They are plump-bodied, with a large head, thick neck and strong, short bill; the legs are shorter and thicker than those of the average wader. They are migratory birds and are capable of flying great distances, but cannot swim well. Gastronomically, the best known are the lapwing and the golden plover.

Plovers are plucked and trussed but are not usually drawn. In Norfolk, where plovers are more plentiful, they are made into pies.

ROAST PLOVER

2 servings:

2 plovers	**flour**
2 slices toast	**melted butter**
gravy	

Pluck the plovers without drawing them and wipe them well outside with a damp cloth. Truss them with the legs close to the body and the feet pressing upon the thighs;

157

bring the head round under the wing. Place the plover on a rack in a roasting pan with the pieces of toast underneath to catch the drippings and roast for 25 minutes, basting frequently. Make sure the trail is caught by the toast as the birds cook.

A few minutes before they are ready, sprinkle with flour and let them froth nicely. Serve the birds on the toast with melted or drawn butter sauce; or instead of melted butter, make a sauce with equal amounts of olive oil and lemon juice with a dash of cayenne pepper or a drop or so of Tabasco sauce added. Alternatively, a madeira sauce (see page 211) may be served. Serve garnished with watercress.

PLOVERS FRIED WITH TRUFFLES

4 servings:

4 plovers, cleaned and trussed	**1 tablespoon (1¼) flour**
4 oz. (½ cup) unsalted butter	**2 cups (2½) stock**
truffles, thinly sliced	**¼ cup (⅓) sherry**
2 cloves	**juice 1 lemon**
1 bay leaf	**1 lump sugar**
salt, pepper	

Lay the plovers breast downwards in a pan with the butter, truffles, cloves, bay leaf, salt and pepper. Cook and stir over a gentle heat for 10 minutes. Mix the flour carefully into the stock, add the sherry and simmer in another pan for 20 minutes. Place the birds on a hot dish and keep hot. Bring the sauce to a quick boil, then flavour it with the lemon juice and sugar. Pour this over the plovers and serve at once, with cooked spinach.

ROCK CORNISH GAME HEN

A delicious small eating bird developed in the United States in the early nineteen-fifties by a Connecticut breeder who crossed a rock Cornish game cock with a Plymouth rock hen. These little birds are marketed when only six weeks old, usually weighing between 1 and 1½ lb. They are short legged, plump breasted with a white succulent flesh full of flavour. A similar bird, with the same name, is also marketed but this is larger and not of the same cross.

6 rock Cornish game hens	**12 sheets aluminium foil or parch-**
6 oz. (¾ cup) unsalted butter	**ment 6 × 10 in.**
salt, pepper	**butter for greasing**
1 teaspoon (1¼) finely grated	**12 slices streaky bacon**
dried orange rind	

Split the birds into halves. Heat the measured quantity of butter in a frying pan (skillet) and fry the birds on both sides for 10 minutes or until just browned. Take from the pan, leave until just cool, then sprinkle each half with salt, pepper and orange rind. Rub the foil sheets with butter and on each place a slice of bacon. Place a halved bird on top, fold over the foil to make a neat package, taking care the edges are firmly sealed.

Place the packages on a large lightly greased baking (cookie) sheet and bake them in a moderate oven for about 20 minutes or until tender. If in doubt, cautiously unwrap one package and test the flesh with a fork. Serve the birds at once, in their packages, with a watercress or green salad, game chips (see page 206) and a tart jelly.

SNIPE

This is a name often applied to any member of the Scolopacidae family of waders, characterized by long bills and streaked plumage. It includes the common snipe, Jacksnipe, great-snipe and red-breasted snipe. The so-called common snipe is found far and wide, from Ireland through to Japan, from the frozen north of Russia to warm South Africa. They like to feed on marshy ground, using their bills to probe for worms and snails, a diet which gives this prized table bird its distinctive flavour and slightly fishy quality.

A North American cousin of the snipe, is Wilson's snipe, *Galinnago delicata*, so named for its delicate flavour. Throughout the northern hemisphere snipe are in season from November to February but are at their most abundant and fattest in frosty weather.

Although the tastiest method of cooking snipe, say the experts, is roasting, they can be prepared in the same manner as woodcock. The thigh of the bird is the most highly esteemed.

Both snipe and woodcock are highly prized by gastronomes, and the former is not unlike the latter to look at, only smaller. Traditionally they are plucked, head and all, the head being twisted round and the birds skewered with their own beaks (see page 161). They are not drawn, but the eyes are removed. After this they are rubbed with butter, wrapped in bacon and roasted. Traditional or not, there are those who find this method of dealing with snipe aesthetically displeasing, insist it makes a fine bird look stupid and prefer them drawn. However, all snipe lovers agree that snipe should be rare. The weight of a snipe varies from as little as 2 oz. to as much as 10 oz.

Snipe must be handled carefully as they have a delicate skin. If the feet are hard and thick, the bird is old; when soft and tender, the birds are both young and freshly killed. If the bill is moist and the throat muddy, the bird has been dead for some time.

Snipe are often rank, and it is advised in such cases to skin the birds, as the rankness lies just under the skin. To skin a snipe, cut off the wings and the head and rub the skin away from the breast. The skin and feathers will then come away like a glove.

Snipe are rarely sold over the counter. The Great Snipe, *Capella media* is cooked in the same manner as snipe.

ROAST SNIPE

The best way in which to roast snipe, say the shooting men, is on a skewer for 15 minutes, with the breast of each bird covered with a slice of fat bacon. Serve them with melted butter and a squeeze of lemon and with redcurrant jelly or a wine sauce. However, in this recipe, which is more explicit, the snipe is roasted in a hot oven. The preparations for the snipe apply to both methods of roasting. Snipe are plucked, trussed and roasted undrawn.

1–2 snipe per serving:

snipe	**stock**
salt, pepper	**1 slice fried bread for each bird**
1 slice streaky bacon per bird	**a little brandy**
butter for roasting	

Make a small hole in front of one leg and take out the stomach and intestines. Leave the remaining entrails intact. Pull off the claws, scald the feet and pull off the outer skin. Skin the head and take out the eyes. Rub the birds with a damp cloth then dry them well and rub in salt and pepper. Bend the necks round and push the beak through the thigh – as for preparing woodcock (see page 161). Blanket the snipe with fat bacon and truss them. Brown the butter in a roasting pan, then add the snipe, breast downwards. Sear them for a few minutes in a hot oven, moisten with stock, lower the heat and roast the uncovered birds until tender. Baste 2 or 3 times and do not overcook; 10 to 15 minutes will see them ready.

While they are roasting prepare some fried bread. When the snipe are ready (they can be tested for tenderness with a skewer), pull out the entrails and chop these finely. Skim and strain the gravy, add the entrails, pour into a small pan, add the brandy and bring to the boil. Pull out the beak and split each bird into halves. Serve the snipe, 2 pieces on each piece of fried bread, with sauté potatoes and a green salad.

BRAISED SNIPE

2 servings:

4 snipe	**salt, pepper**
2 oz. ($\frac{1}{4}$ cup) unsalted butter	**grated nutmeg**
1 small onion, minced	**stock and sherry**
1 tablespoon (1$\frac{1}{4}$) finely chopped fresh parsley	**juice $\frac{1}{2}$ lemon**
	grated bread crust

Prepare the snipe as for roast snipe (see page 159), but without the bacon. Heat the butter in a pan, lay the birds side by side, breast downwards, in the pan, add the onion and parsley and fry the birds until brown, moving them around so that they brown evenly. This will take about 7–8 minutes. Add salt, pepper, a scraping of nutmeg and enough stock or sherry or a mixture of both to barely cover them. Add the lemon juice and a little grated bread crust. Simmer until the snipe are tender; about 10 minutes should be sufficient. Serve the snipe immediately, with their gravy poured over them and with redcurrant jelly.

POACHED SNIPE WITH A BUTTER AND LEMON SAUCE

2 snipe per serving:

snipe, prepared for cooking (see page 159)	**toast**
salt	**butter and lemon juice**

Have ready a pan with plenty of boiling salted water. Drop the prepared snipe into this and cook them for 12–15 minutes. Toast some large slices of bread, 1 piece for 2 snipe. Drain the snipe and place them on toast. Heat enough butter to make a sauce, add a little lemon juice, stir well, and pour it over the snipe. Serve at once.

SNIPE FLAMBÉE

See Woodcock Flambée (page 163).

WOODCOCK

This game bird, prized for its unusually good flavour and considered by many as superior to the snipe to whom it is related, is one of the waders. It is about the size of a grouse and is in season from 1 October to 31 January. It is partially migratory and numbers of Continental woodcock join the British population during the winter months. Woodcock of various kinds are found all over the world.

Its diet is a mixed one of heather shoots, worms, insects and all forms of life hiding in the mud. As a result of its omnivorous habits, the woodcock carries much meat in proportion to its size, a 12 oz. bird being enough for one person of normal appetite. Also woodcock are good only when they are fat. The most delicate parts are the legs and the intestines for a roast and the wings for a ragoût or salmis.

Traditionally woodcock are plucked head and all. Pick and singe it; take the bone out of the neck, leaving the skin and head attached to the body. Twist the skin of the neck round the wing and put the bill through the wing and body, using this instead of a skewer. Neither woodcock nor snipe require drawing as there is almost nothing there to draw. The eyes are removed from the head.

There are several ways in which to cook the woodcock. Fillets of woodcock are only for those who really like the flavour of the flesh, for these can be somewhat tough and even without savour. Woodcock is made into a salmis or the flesh cooked and puréed for patties. Devilled woodcock is an old-fashioned method of cooking them, and when or where they are plentiful one finds woodcock pie, potted woodcock, and even woodcock

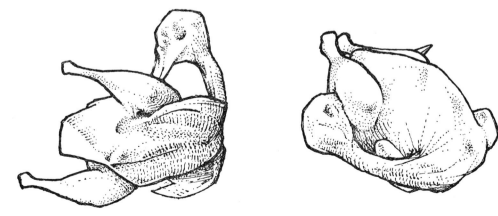

Trussing a Woodcock.

pudding. I have come across recipes in which the tiny birds are stuffed before being roasted; and terrine of woodcock was at one time quite popular.

To truss woodcock the legs are crossed, the head is brought down toward the flanks and the beak pushed sideways into the leg flesh to keep the legs in position.

American woodcock is a game bird of mottled brown and white colouring, found in damp sections of wooded areas, distinguished by its long, flexible beak and known only to sing or 'whistle' during initial flight stages or when courting. Its diet is primarily of worms and berries. It is not a wading bird but does not mind damp feet. When excited or fleeing from danger, it takes off almost vertically, thus making a difficult target.

The flesh of the woodcock is light-coloured and, unlike most 'wet-footed' birds, does not have a strong or fish taste. Care must be taken in preparation as, if slightly over-cooked, it can be dry. When properly prepared it is delicate and delicious.

ROAST WOODCOCK

1 woodcock per serving:

Brush each bird generously with butter. Place on the rack of a roasting pan and under each bird place a slice of toast. This is to catch the trail while they are roasting. A woodcock takes from 15 to 25 minutes to roast in a hot oven, according to the state of rareness desired. Serve the woodcock on the slices of toast, pour the gravy over the top and serve with buttered crumbs (see page 205) and parsley as a garnish.

WOODCOCK STUFFED AND ROASTED

Pluck the woodcock and, contrary to the usual custom, draw it. Remove the gizzards, then mince the trail finely with half its weight in fat bacon and add as much finely chopped parsley as desired, a little pepper and salt, and if liked some finely minced shallot. Fill this mixture into the woodcock, truss it, brush generously with butter and roast as in the previous recipe.

WOODCOCK ALEXANDRE DUMAS

1 serving:

1 plump woodcock	**2 tablespoons (2½) butter**
1 pat butter	**1 cup (1¼) cream**
salt, black pepper	

Clean and singe the bird, removing what intestines it has but reserving the liver. Sew up the skin of the neck so that the opening is tightly closed. Place the liver and the pat of butter in the cavity of the bird; add salt and pepper. Sew up the opening and truss the bird (see page 161). Place on a rack in a roasting pan and roast in a moderate oven for 20 to 25 minutes. After the first 10 minutes add the remaining butter and cream to the pan and baste the bird constantly with this mixture. Serve the bird on a hot platter. Strain the sauce, scraping round the sides of the pan to get all the sediment. Pour a little of the sauce over the woodcock and garnish it with triangles of fried bread. Serve the remainder of the sauce in a sauceboat.

WOODCOCK FLAMBÉE

1 woodcock per serving:

Roast the woodcock for 15 minutes, joint, carve off the meat and pile it into a silver dish. Crush the carcass and strain all the gravy and the trail from it. Pour this into a pan, add salt, pepper, butter and a little mild paprika, stir well and then thicken with a little cream. Pour over the woodcock meat some warmed brandy, set this alight and let it burn out, then cover the whole with the sauce. Serve with a green salad and, if liked, a jelly.

This recipe applies equally to snipe which are prepared whole but opened and basted with the trail before being served hot, flambéed as above.

WOODCOCK À LA PÉRIGUEUX

If the sight of a woodcock skewered with its own head is unpleasant, and it is even to hardened shooting men, then try this method of preparing them. Pluck, draw and truss the woodcock (without head), cover each with a slice of bacon and tie securely with string. Put them into a pan, add as much well-flavoured stock as will barely cover them and as much madeira or sherry as liked. Simmer until the woodcock are tender. Drain, remove the string, place them on a hot platter and pour over them some *sauce périgueux* or truffle sauce (see pages 213, 215). Serve with watercress and buttered crumbs (see page 205).

BAT

A name that covers all flying mammals of the order Chiroptera. In the Bible bats are named among the unclean animals which the Hebrews were not allowed to eat. In India and elsewhere there is the large fruit bat which is edible but taboo to the Hindus (but then, so is most other meat). The fruit bat or flying fox, with its rat-like face and bat-like wings, is a clean animal living exclusively on fruit. I have seen it in action appearing every night swooping through the open doors making for a bowl of fruit, the bananas in particular. Finally the fruit was covered but the thief still came each night in search of an evening meal. It took him one week to discover his nightly raids were fruitless.

The fruit bat is eaten by some. The following instructions for its treatment come from Mauritius, where it is reported that its flesh is a cross between chicken and hare, much depending on the manner in which it is cooked.

'First catch your fruit bat or flying fox. Skin it and clean it as a rabbit. Joint it into serving portions and place these in an earthenware bowl with some chopped onion, bay leaves, thyme, salt, peppercorns and vinegar. Leave it to marinate for three days.

Heat some butter in a pan. Drain the pieces of flying fox and fry them until brown. Cover the bottom of a casserole with bacon, add some chopped onion, one large thinly-sliced tomato, chopped parsley, the pieces of flying fox and a good glass of red wine.

Cook, covered, in a moderate oven until the pieces of flying fox are tender. 'If', adds the recipe, 'you have sensitive guests who feel they cannot stomach flying fox, add some fried mushrooms to the dish, on top of the meat. This deceives them into thinking they are eating hare.'

SQUIRREL (American)

In the United States, where wild squirrels are classified as game, their white and tender flesh is reckoned delicious, but they are not considered as game in Britain and no one eats them. Squirrels can be cooked like rabbit or even chicken. Old squirrels are usually marinated.

CASSEROLE OF SQUIRREL

6 servings:

2 plump young squirrels, dressed
flour, salt and pepper
2 oz. ($\frac{1}{4}$ cup) fat
4–6 onions, thinly sliced
3 cups ($3\frac{3}{4}$) boiling water
4–6 tomatoes, peeled and sliced
2–3 sweet peppers, cut into strips

fresh or dried thyme to taste
1 lb. Lima or broad beans
1 cup ($1\frac{1}{4}$) fresh corn kernels
1 lb. fresh okra (ladies' fingers)
coarsely chopped parsley
Worcestershire Sauce to taste

Chop the squirrels into serving pieces and dredge with well-seasoned flour. Heat the fat and lightly brown the onions. Turn these into a casserole, add the water, tomatoes. peppers, thyme and finally the squirrels. Cover the casserole and cook gently for about 1 hour.

Add the remaining ingredients, cover the pan and continue cooking until the squirrel meat and the vegetables are tender.

Hare

The hare is a small wild animal of the rabbit family, although much larger than a rabbit and fortunately not quite so promiscuous. Legally classified as game, farmers regard hares as vermin. They are mainly vegetarian and are said never to drink. Young hares or leverets are among the most beautiful creatures in the world, and are born with their eyes open, fully haired and able to hop only a few minutes after birth.

In Britain there are three species of hares, of which the brown lowland hare is the largest. The original hares of Britain were the blue or varying hare, which occurs further north and is probably the same species as the Arctic hare of the extreme North American continent. In northern North America there appears to be no clear distinction between hares and rabbits. Hares are popularly called snowshoe rabbit and jack rabbit, and they are widespread. The commonest hare is the prairie hare, the so-called jack rabbit, the varying hare and the wood hare.

Considering how common hares are, it is rather odd that relatively little is known about them in Britain. Russian scientists appear to have done much more work on them than the British have done. The term 'mad as a March hare' is derived from the curious performance of the male in the spring rutting season.

One or more of the varied species occur naturally on all principal land masses, except Australia, where the European hare was introduced during 1870-1 and is now firmly established. The so-called Belgium hare is one of the many domestic breeds of the European rabbit.

In most European countries, other than Britain, hares are greatly prized for their culinary merit and their rich, gamey flesh which makes good eating. They are at their best for eating when the hare is young, when the 'hare-lip' is only faintly noticeable. In Britain, opinion of the eating merits of the hare is low and many shooting men find it difficult to even give them away. They are sold by poulterers as one of their cheapest items, and yet what a lot the good cook can get from such a hare: a roast from the saddle, jugged hare or a ragoût from the legs, and then all the left-overs gathered together, recooked and turned into a splendid hare soup.

A hare should hang, unpaunched, for six days if possible with its head downwards over a bowl to catch the blood (to be used later). A young hare needs no marinating, but older ones, especially those which are obviously over a year old, most certainly should be steeped in a good marinade for at least a day, longer if possible, but it is a debatable point, for many sportsmen and cooks feel that marinating a hare only spoils its fine flavour. However, marinating serves a dual purpose. It tenderizes and adds to the meat a delicate flavour or aroma which could not be given by the usual process of cooking. Unless a hare is properly cooked it can be stringy. Young hares are good roasted or jugged; older ones are best made into *terrines*, brawns, soups and forcemeat to garnish a soup. All hare meat should be well cooked.

When the hare is hung, it is hung as it is, not drawn. A rabbit is always paunched at once to prevent it going rotten. Why this should be so, is rather a puzzle, but this is how it is. Leave a hare well hung for a week and it becomes more gamey and acceptable; but leave the rabbit for the same time and it becomes rotten.

It is generally considered correct to cook hares without washing to conserve their gamey flavour, but many people find it more satisfactory to quickly rinse it in tepid salted water and then to pat dry in a cloth or better still paper towelling.

Only a young hare is suitable for roasting and preferably should be hung for a week before cooking. If it is not as young as it should be, then use the saddle only and jug the rest. Also, if the hare is too large for one's needs, it is wise to make two dishes out of it. Cut the saddle and the hindquarters away from the front quarters just back of the shoulder blades. The saddle and hindquarters (the rabble) make the roast, the remainder can be jugged or used in a ragoût or salmi. If the hare is freshly killed, give it a sound beating with a rolling pin. It can be an energetic beating, stopping short of actually breaking the bones.

ROAST HARE - 1

6–7 servings: for whole hare
6 servings: for saddle and hindquarters
3–4 servings: for saddle only

1 young hare	**1 cup (1¼) stock**
marinade (see page 204)	**salt, pepper**
dripping	**juice ½ lemon**
¼ lb. sliced streaky bacon	**1 tablespoon (1¼) redcurrant jelly**
flour	

Marinate the hare overnight. Heat sufficient dripping in a roasting pan for roasting. Take the hare from the marinade, drain and dry it thoroughly. Strain the marinade. Cover the meat with the bacon fixing it firmly and put on a rack in the roasting pan with the hot dripping, cover it with foil or greaseproof paper and roast for 1 hour in a hot oven. Remove the foil and bacon and sprinkle the hare with flour. Baste it well in its own fat and continue cooking until the flesh is nicely browned. Take the hare from the pan but keep very hot. Pour off all the fat from the pan and sprinkle in 1 tablespoon (1¼) of flour. Add the stock, salt and pepper to taste, and stir well, scraping round the sides of the pan. Cook the gravy gently until it boils and continue gentle boiling for 5 minutes.

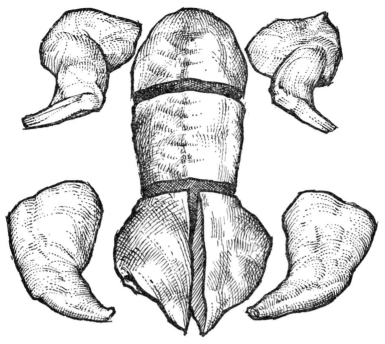

Jointing a Hare

Add the lemon juice, the redcurrant jelly and $\frac{1}{2}$ cup ($\frac{2}{3}$) of the marinade; bring this all to the boil. Strain the gravy and pour it over the hare before serving. If using the liver and the heart of the hare, it should be fried, then minced and sprinkled over the top of the hare.

Serve the hare with forcemeat balls (see page 221), hot buttered beetroots, straw potatoes or game chips (see page 205) and a sharp sauce. Germans add ginger-stuffed cooked pears or quince cooked in brandy as a garnish. Left-over hare can be served cold with mayonnaise or Cumberland or cranberry sauce.

ROAST HARE - 2

6 servings:

1 hare, saddle and hindquarters	**1 cup (1$\frac{1}{4}$) red wine**
marinade (see page 204)	**$\frac{1}{2}$ lb. mushrooms, peeled**
6 slices streaky bacon	**$\frac{1}{2}$ cup ($\frac{2}{3}$) sour cream**
4 oz. ($\frac{1}{2}$ cup) fat, preferably pork	

Wipe the hare with soft white kitchen paper. Cut off the forelegs at the point just behind the shoulders. Leave 12–24 hours in a marinade, then wipe dry. Cover the back of the hare evenly with the bacon and place it on a rack in a roasting pan. Heat the fat to boiling and pour this over the hare. Put the pan into a hot oven and roast the hare for 15 minutes. Reduce the heat to moderate, add the wine and continue basting frequently until the hare is tender. Add the mushrooms after 45 minutes of cooking. Continue cooking for another 15–20 minutes. Take the hare and the mushrooms from the pan, put aside but keep hot. Skim off surplus fat from the gravy, scrape the sides of the pan and stir in the sour cream. Bring this to the boil on top of the stove, stirring all the while.

Serve the hare with some of the gravy poured over it and the rest in a sauceboat, and with a sharp sauce or jelly, straw potatoes or game chips (see page 206), boiled red cabbage and parsnips.

ROAST SADDLE OF HARE

This recipe is designed for a truly young and tender hare which does not require the marinating that an elderly hare so urgently does.

6 servings:

1 saddle of hare
sliced streaky bacon cut into strips
salt, pepper
4 tablespoons (5) port wine

dash cinnamon and nutmeg
4 tablespoons (5) redcurrant jelly
1 teaspoon (1¼) horse-radish sauce

Make slits in the saddle on both sides and push into these the strips of bacon. Sprinkle with salt and pepper. Put on the rack of a roasting pan and bake in a moderate oven, basting frequently with the drippings from the hare and the fat from the bacon, until tender. Place on a hot dish and keep hot. Put the roasting pan on top of the stove, remove the rack and pour off most of the fat. Stir the port, spices and jelly into the fat left in the tin. Bring this to the boil and then add the horse-radish sauce. Pour this over the saddle and serve it with floury boiled potatoes and a green salad.

JUGGED HARE – 1 (British)

There are countless recipes for jugged hare. Some of these, the older recipes, are indeed complicated, involving an extremely early rise for the cook.

Strictly speaking, jugged hare should be cooked in what was called a jugging pot or a stone crock, but today the hare is usually jugged in a modern deep casserole with a tightly fitting lid. The hare can be cooked either on top of the stove or in the oven. Rabbit may be cooked in the same manner.

6–8 servings:

1 hare, weighing between 6–7 lb.
  cut into 8 neat joints (see page 167)
marinade (see page 204)
2 oz. (¼ cup) bacon fat
2 cups (2½) stock
1 large onion stuck with 2–3 cloves
1 bay leaf and bouquet garni
salt, cayenne pepper
1 oz. (2 tablespoons) butter

1 tablespoon (1¼) flour
½ cup (⅔) port wine or claret
1 tablespoon (1¼) redcurrant jelly
blood from the hare
juice ½ lemon and 2 thin strips of the
  rind
garnish:
forcemeat balls (see page 221)

Soak the pieces of hare in the marinade for several hours or overnight. Cook the liver and heart for a few minutes in a little water until tender, drain and put aside. Heat the bacon fat. Take the hare pieces from the marinade, dry them thoroughly and fry in the hot fat until brown. Bring the stock to the boil in the casserole or crock, take the joints from the fat, drain well and add to the casserole with the heart, liver, onion, herbs and seasoning. Cook over a moderate heat or in a moderate oven for 2½–3 hours with the casserole tightly covered so that no steam escapes. By this time the hare should be so tender that the meat falls easily from the bones when prised.

Knead the butter with the flour. Take the hare pieces from the casserole. Strain the liquid into a pan and boil it until reduced to 2 cups (2½). Skim off any excess fat. Add the kneaded butter and flour and stir this until the gravy is thick. Gradually add the wine, jelly and blood, and then the marinade, lemon juice and rind and continue cooking, taking great care that the mixture does not reboil or it will curdle. Correct for seasoning. Arrange the hare pieces in a hot serving dish. Strain the sauce and pour it over the hare.

Forcemeat balls are the correct accompaniment to jugged hare. Any of the winter vegetables will go with this dish, especially leeks, carrots and Brussels sprouts, plus creamed potatoes.

JUGGED HARE – 2

6–8 servings:

1 hare cut into joints (see page 167)
butter for frying
2 tablespoons (2½) flour
white wine and stock
salt, pepper
bouquet garni

dash of nutmeg and ground cinnamon
½ cup (⅔) each seedless raisins and
    stoned prunes
½ cup (⅔) red wine
blood from the hare

If the hare is elderly leave it for 12–24 hours in a marinade (see page 204). Heat sufficient butter to fry and thoroughly brown the joints. (If the hare has been marinated, thoroughly drain and dry before frying.) When the hare is brown, add the flour, stir it well into the fat and let it brown. Add in equal quantities white wine and stock to come half-way up the pan, salt, pepper, bouquet garni and spices. Stir well, add the raisins and prunes and cook covered over a moderate heat until the hare is tender. Just before serving add the red wine and the hare blood.

Other combinations may be used, such as anchovies or dried pears instead of raisins and prunes. If using a marinade, this should be strained and used with the red wine.

Serve with boiled rice or puréed or rice potatoes. If another vegetable seems necessary, try spinach, Brussels sprouts, carrots or white cabbage.

JUGGED HARE – 3 (German – *Hasenpfeffer*)

A similar German recipe also appears under the name *Hasenklein* and then the dish is made with the 'small' of the hare i.e., its head, belly, lungs, heart and breast bones, and is very popular.

6 servings:

1 hare, chopped into pieces	2 large onions, finely chopped
a scraping of freshly ground nutmeg	2–3 tablespoons (2½–3¾) flour
salt, pepper	2 cups (2½) meat stock
4 juniper berries, crushed	2 teaspoons (2½) sugar
½ lb. fat smoked bacon, chopped	1 cup (1¼) red wine

Thoroughly wash the pieces of hare and cook these in boiling salted water with the nutmeg, salt, pepper and juniper berries until tender. Strip the meat from the bones and cut it into small pieces. Fry the bacon in a pan; add the onions and the hare meat. Sprinkle with flour and continue frying for a few minutes. Gradually add the stock and the sugar and cook slowly until the meat is very tender. Add the red wine and bring this to a gentle boil. Serve the hare with rice, creamed potatoes or dumplings.

HARE IN RED WINE (German – Rhineland '*Tippehas*')

6 servings:

1 young hare	1 large onion, chopped
1 large onion, thinly sliced	¼ lb. smoked bacon, sliced and rind
1–2 cloves garlic, chopped	removed
6 juniper berries	½ lb. black breadcrumbs
4 cups (5) red wine	sprig thyme
2 lb. pork, either from stomach	salt, pepper
or neck	hare's blood (optional)
3 oz. (6 tablespoons) butter	

Chop the hare into pieces and put these into a stone jar with the sliced onion, garlic, juniper berries and the red wine. Leave for 3 days. Take out the pieces of hare and strain the marinade. Cut the pork into bite-size pieces. Heat the butter and fry the chopped onion. Line a casserole with the bacon. Add 2–3 pieces of hare, then a layer of fried onion, breadcrumbs, pork, a little thyme and a moistening of strained marinade, salt and pepper. Continue doing this, in layers, until all the ingredients are finished. Cover very tightly and cook in a moderate oven for 2 hours without uncovering, or longer if required. In fact, this dish can hardly cook too long. Add the blood and continue cooking for another 15 minutes.

Serve with noodles or dumplings.

HARE WITH A LEMON FLAVOUR

6 servings:

1 hare	6 cloves garlic
salt, cayenne pepper	bouquet garni
juice 6 large lemons	1 bay leaf
flour	fresh parsley to taste, chopped
½ cup (⅔) olive oil	1 cup (1¼) red wine, warmed

The hare should be jointed as on page 167. Mix together salt, cayenne pepper and lemon juice and marinate the hare joints in this mixture for 12–24 hours, according to the age of the hare. Turn from time to time as there will not be sufficient liquid to cover the pieces. Dry the pieces of hare and sprinkle with flour. Heat the olive oil and fry the pieces of hare until brown. Transfer these to a casserole and barely cover them with boiling water. Add the garlic, bouquet garni, bay leaf, parsley and red wine. Cook this until the meat is very tender and leaves the bone easily. Take the hare from the casserole and arrange on a hot serving dish. Strain the stock into a pan and bring it to the boil; continue boiling for 5 minutes.

Serve the hare with the gravy poured over it and with redcurrant jelly served separately. Serve with almost any vegetable and boiled potatoes.

This method of cooking hare is particularly good for a badly shot-up hare that cannot hang for more than a couple of days.

RAGOÛT OF HARE

A recipe in which commonsense is required and not exact or definite quantities.

6 servings:

1 hare, cut into joints (see page 167)	**8 small onions or 1 large mild onion, coarsely chopped**
seedless raisins and stoned prunes to taste or olives and anchovies	**red wine or cider**
butter	**1 cup (1¼) fresh cream**
	salt

Soak the prunes overnight. Rub the pieces of hare until dry. Heat the butter and fry the hare to a golden brown. Add the raisins, prunes, onions, red wine to cover and fresh cream. Cook gently until the hare meat is tender. If the sauce curdles, it does not matter. Salt should be added rather generously but not pepper.

If using raisins and prunes, then obviously not olives and anchovies. It is strictly a question of 'either/or' and both combinations are good. The anchovies should be filleted if fresh, and the olives (either black or green) must be pitted. Soaking the dried fruit in either red wine or strained tea instead of water naturally adds to their flavour. Serve with boiled rice.

HARE COOKED IN SOUR CREAM (Russian)

6 servings:

1 hare, saddle and hindquarters	**butter or bacon fat**
jugged hare marinade (see page 204)	**2 cups (2½) sour cream**
salt, pepper, aniseed	**flour**
¼ lb. streaky bacon, thinly sliced	

Leave the hare in the marinade at least overnight and preferably for 24 hours. Drain, dry and cut into serving portions and sprinkle with salt, pepper and aniseed. Cut 2 slices of the streaky bacon into small pieces and fry these in a large pan with a little fat until they brown. Place the hare on top and cover with the remaining bacon. Cook for 20 minutes, browning the hare well. Add all but a few tablespoonfuls of sour cream and cook very slowly until the hare is tender. Mix the remaining sour cream with enough flour to make a thin paste. Pour this into the pan and let it cook for 5 minutes, stirring all the time. Serve the hare in its sauce with hot cooked beetroots and boiled rice.

CASSEROLE OF HARE WITH MUSHROOMS

4 servings:

forepart of a hare (see page 167)	1–1½ lb. mushrooms, peeled and
salt, pepper	sliced
1 bay leaf	1 tablespoon (1¼) finely chopped
1 strip lemon peel	parsley
3 oz. (6 tablespoons) butter	½ cup (⅔) fresh soft breadcrumbs
6 slices streaky bacon	¼ cup (⅓) sour cream

Cook the hare in enough water to cover, adding salt, pepper, bay leaf and lemon peel. When tender take the hare from the pan, cool and strip the meat from the bones. Preserve the liquid. In the meantime heat 2 oz. (¼ cup) butter and fry the bacon until crisp. Take it from the pan and in the same fat fry the mushrooms. Add the parsley. Line a shallow casserole with the bacon, then add the mushrooms, parsley and hare meat. Sprinkle with breadcrumbs, dot with the remaining butter and pour the sour cream over the top. Cook in a moderate oven for about 30 minutes. While the casserole is cooking make a thick sauce or gravy in the usual manner from the liquid in which the hare was cooked.

Serve with game chips (see page 206) or creamed potatoes, the sauce, a tart jelly and vegetables to choice.

CASSEROLE OF HARE

6 servings:

1 hare	1 bay leaf
3 slices streaky bacon, chopped	bouquet garni
salt, pepper	1 teaspoon (1¼) brown sugar
4 oz. (½ cup) butter	1 cup (1¼) white wine
6–8 slices streaky bacon	stock to cover
2–3 large carrots, thickly sliced	extra wine
1–2 onions, sliced	redcurrant jelly

Joint the hare (see page 167). Push the chopped bacon under the thin transparent skin and sprinkle the skin with salt and pepper. Heat the butter in a pan, add the pieces of hare and brown them. As they brown take them from the pan. Return half of the hare to the pan; add a layer of sliced bacon, carrots, onions and herbs and all the brown sugar. Add the remaining ingredients in layers in the same order, then add the wine and stock. Cover the pan tightly and cook slowly for about 2 hours or until the meat is tender.

With a solid fuel cooker (such as an Aga) the pan can be left safely on the side of the stove for several hours. Serve with a gravy made from 1 cup (1¼) of the stock mixed with some extra wine and a little redcurrant jelly.

HARE IN A CREAM SAUCE

4–6 servings:

saddle and hindquarters of a young
  hare, jointed (see page 167)
enough cream to half cover
2 tablespoons (2½) red wine vinegar

2 tablespoons (2½) shallots or mild
  onion, minced
salt

Put the hare into a pan; add the cream, the red wine vinegar and the shallots. Cook over a low fire for 1½ hours, stirring often. Add salt (but not pepper) just before serving. The sauce will probably curdle but this does not matter in the least. Serve with rice and either white or red cabbage.

SALMI OF HARE (Italian)

Rabbit may be cooked in the same manner but requires half the time for marinating.

6 servings:

1 hare
1 stick celery, chopped
1 onion, chopped
1 carrot, chopped
1 clove garlic, minced

2 bay leaves
1 teaspoon (1¼) juniper berries
salt, pepper
red wine
4 oz. (½ cup) butter

Cut the hare into pieces and put these into an earthenware dish with the celery, onion, carrot, garlic, bay leaves, juniper berries, salt, pepper and enough red wine to cover. Leave for 24 hours to marinate. Take the pieces of hare from the marinade, dry thoroughly and strain the marinade. Heat the butter in a large pan and quickly fry the pieces of hare until brown. Add the marinade; cover and cook slowly until the hare is tender. Remove the hare to a hot serving dish. Strain half the sauce over the meat. Serve with *polenta* (cornmeal) spread with the remaining sauce.

HARE BRAWN

12 servings:

1 hare
1 rabbit
marinade for hare only (see page
  204)

1 lb. fat ham
shallots and thyme to taste
salt, pepper and cayenne to taste
stock

Leave only the hare in the marinade up to 48 hours. Cut the hare and rabbit into pieces for stewing. Put them both with the ham, shallots, thyme and seasoning into a pot and add plenty of stock. Cook over a moderate heat until the meat is quite tender. Strain, return the liquid to the pan and let this cook until reduced to half. When the hare and rabbit are cool enough strip off the flesh from the bones. Put the meat and ham through the coarse plate of a grinder. Add the reduced stock, then pour all this into a brawn mould, press down well, cover and weight it down.

Leave overnight in a refrigerator until set. If there is any doubt about the stock jelling, add 1 oz. (1 envelope) of gelatine to it, dissolved in the usual way. Turn out to serve with a variety of cold salads, particularly a potato salad prepared with a salad dressing or a plain green salad.

CIVET OF HARE

The French word *civet* applies in the main to a ragoût of furred game cooked in red wine and garnished with small onions, cardoons and mushrooms, and then combined with the blood of the animal concerned. This liaison of blood is essential in the preparation of the dish, the name of which comes from the word *cive* (green onion) with which the dish was originally liberally flavoured.

Although there is a school of thinking which insists that there can only be a *civet* of hare, a *civet* can be prepared with any type of furred, or for that matter, feathered game, and in some areas in France there are such dishes as *civet de mouton*.

CIVET OF HARE (French)

6 servings:

1 hare, cut into 6 pieces (see page 167)	**2 lumps sugar**
marinade (see page 167)	**salt, pepper**
¼ lb. streaky bacon, diced	**butter**
2 onions, finely chopped	**½–1 lb. button mushrooms**
1 tablespoon (1¼) flour	**croûtons**
1 cup (1¼) mixed stock and red wine	

Wash the pieces of hare and drop them into the marinade. Leave for 24 hours. Drain and dry. Put the bacon into a hot pan and fry until the fat runs. Add the onions and let these just change colour. Add the flour and stir this well into the fat. Gradually add the stock and wine to make a sauce, then add the sugar, salt, pepper, half the marinade and finally the hare. Cover the pan tightly and cook the hare until it is tender (2–3 hours), remembering that the hare should be well cooked. Just before the hare is ready, heat enough butter to fry the mushrooms. Add these to the hare and continue cooking for a few minutes. Serve the hare on a hot plate garnished with the mushrooms and croûtons. Serve with creamed potatoes, red cabbage, braised button onions or celery and young boiled carrots.

Additional sauce can be made by pounding the hare liver, mixing it with the hare's blood and adding some finely chopped fresh herbs, a little olive oil, vinegar and red wine stirred into the liquid in the pan and cooked for a few minutes. This should be served separately in a sauceboat.

TERRINE OF HARE

6–8 servings:

1 hare, jointed (see page 167)
2 onions, coarsely chopped
1 bay leaf
mixed fresh herbs
1 lb. fat bacon, cubed

1 tablespoon (1¼) lemon juice
salt, pepper
6 slices streaky bacon
1 cup (1¼) red wine

Put the hare, onions, bay leaf, herbs, fat bacon and lemon juice into a pot with enough liquid to prevent burning and cook the hare until the flesh is so tender that it easily leaves the bones. Remove the hare and the pieces of bacon from the pot and drain them. Strip the meat from the bones and put this, with the bacon, through the coarse plate of a grinder. Add salt and pepper to taste, testing first in case the bacon is salty. Lay 3 of the bacon slices at the bottom of an ovenproof *terrine* or casserole, press the ground meat into the dish, add the wine and cover with the remaining bacon. Put the dish into a pan containing water to cover the bottom and bake in a moderate oven for 3 hours. Take from the oven, apply light pressure on top and leave until the *terrine* is cold.

Rabbit

'Rabettes flesh is best of all wylde beestes, for it is temperate and doth nourissh and is syngulerly prazed of Physiche.'

ANDREW BOORDE, 1552

Before the Second World War rabbit was part of the staple diet of the British, although many professed to despise it. This dislike was quite without reason for rabbits vary greatly and a young rabbit freshly shot in the fields has white flesh like a chicken's and can be similarly treated. Fat elderly rabbits make good stews, pies or casserole dishes. They can be cooked in the same manner as hares, or creamed and curried, or made into a fricassee.

Samuel Pepys, no mean gourmet and gourmand, makes frequent mention of this pretty furry animal and never disparagingly. He notes that he gave 'a grand dinner' offering among the many dishes a 'Friscasse of rabbit', and on another occasion, equally formal, he served after the oysters a 'hash of rabbit'; and again he records that he is 'infinitely pleased' when he met 'William Howe and he spoke to my Lord for me, and he did give him four rabbits . . .'

The rabbit fell into disgrace, not once but often. They were too fertile, breeding from the tender age of six months and annually producing several large litters. Finally statisticians got to work and announced that the average pair of rabbits can be responsible for launching upon the world over a million of their own species. It was their death knell. They were declared a menace and, like Hamelin's rats, rabbits had to be exterminated. The method of extermination was cruel, and one shooting farmer wrote that it was diabolical to infect any animal with a disease such as myxamatosis.

However, the rabbit is making a come-back, and we are beginning to see the once-familiar sight of the stiff, still furred rabbit laid out upon the butcher's marble slab.

Today rabbit farming is big industry and we are able to eat rabbit throughout the year. This rabbit, like our modern chickens, may not have all the flavour our grandparents demanded but nevertheless it makes good eating, especially if properly prepared.

The rabbit has been outlawed not only many times but in many countries. Australia had her rabbit problem and so once did the Balearic Islands, said to be the original home of the rabbit. Pliny records that the inhabitants of these islands wrote in desperation to the Emperor Augustus asking him to send troops to fight against their small but voracious furred enemy who was busy ravaging their land, undermining their houses and becoming

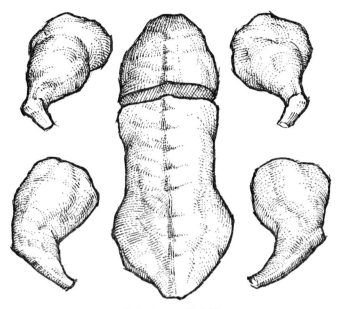

Jointing a Rabbit

a public calamity. The troops arrived armed with ferrets; the fight was fierce, but the ferrets won.

This humble creature, beloved by children probably because of Beatrix Potter, has a long history. In our own records coney is the name by which the rabbit was known, a name which seems to have been derived from a root common to other European languages. Another early British record occurs in the Privy Purse expenses of Elizabeth of York; under the date 24 May 1502 there is an entry of the payment of two shillings 'to a servant of the Abbase of Syon in reward for bringing a present of Rabettes and Quayles to the Quene at Richemount'.

The first rabbits are said to have been discovered in Spain by the Phoenicians who penetrated into southern Spain. The area then called Armonica was over-run by rabbits and the Phoenicians called it Spanija, by which they meant rabbit country. The name seems to have been carried on by the Romans at the time of the conquest also calling it the 'rabbit country' as they changed the name of the Celts into Gaul, Gallis, or the 'country of the cocks'. Athenaeus, the Greek writer, recounts that he first saw a number of these Spanish specimens in A.D. 230 that had been imported into Italy.

To sustain this possibility is the fact that on the reverse side of a medal of the Emperor Adrian, Spain is represented by a woman sitting on the ground with a rabbit squatting on her robe. And again, if we look carefully at the monument to Richard Coeur de Lion in the cathedral of Notre Dame in Rouen we will see the head of a rabbit peering out of a hole with a dog watching it. This is said to allude to that monarch's successful attacks on both Spain and Sicily. Coins of both these countries have representations of rabbits.

At first, of course, it was only the wild rabbit which gained attention and ironically it was protected. During the Norman period in Britain warrens or coningries were established. On the other side of the Channel French nobles were doing the same, peopling the countryside with rabbits, building what were called –*arennes*, hence *garennes* and eventually warrens. The name *varenne* has remained in France and denotes those areas where the original rabbit warrens were established. The plan of the French and Norman nobles was to multiply game and increase the pleasures of the chase. That the rabbit might in turn harass the peasants does not seem to have been considered.

And finally, as I have always noticed, Confucius had something to say. Rabbits, he declared, are among those worthy of being sacrificed to the gods; and for centuries in China rabbits were sacrificed, being especially bred for this purpose.

When rabbits were first domesticated is not quite certain. An early English writer, Tusser, is the first to mention them in *January's Husbandry* in 1580.

In the United States of America distinction is not always made between the rabbit and the hare. In the South it is always called old hare whether it is young or old; while in the West and the North it is rabbit. Rabbits were introduced into the United States; they are not indigenous.

Wild rabbits vary greatly gastronomically and much depends on what they eat. They are vegetarians but not finicky about their food, although farmers may not agree on this point. A rabbit killed after it has been at a diet of garlic is uneatable; another which has been at the bark of young shrubs will be good, but one which has been feeding in a field of maize will be fat and deliciously tender. Domestic rabbits bred for eating, if correctly fed, will have plenty of good white meat, easily digestible and of excellent flavour.

HOW TO DEAL WITH A RABBIT

Much of the following information is becoming academic. However, many of us still manage to live in the country and many more aspire to do so.

Young rabbits have smooth but sharp claws and the small pad under the paws should be well developed. Its ears are soft and thin and tear easily. The cleft in the jaws is narrow and its teeth are small and white. If the haunch is thick, the ears dry and the claws rough and blunt, it is an ancient rabbit, fit only for the stew pot.

Rabbits, like mackerel, must be fresh. Their flesh must be firm, plump and free from discoloration. The wild rabbit is smaller than its tame cousin, its flesh much less fat but its flavour superior.

Rabbits need hanging only for one day in a current of air in a cool, dry place. If it must be kept longer, paunch it as soon as possible after it has been killed. Leave the skin on (as this prevents the flesh from becoming too dry) and hang it up by the hind legs.

To paunch a rabbit, split the skin of the abdomen right down to the tail, take out the stomach and the entrails. Examine the liver; if it looks at all doubtful, blotchy or ragged, discard the rabbit. If the liver is all right, then continue dealing with it, removing with care the small piece of intestine close to the tail and any discoloured pieces; then thoroughly clean the animal.

Now off with the skin. How often I have watched this process as a child and it always seemed to me that the skin came off like a glove. Cut off the ears close to the head, then the tail, then the fore and hind legs at the first joint. Loosen the skin from the body, working it away towards the tail; turn the hind legs inside out and pull off the skin. Draw the skin off, working towards the shoulders and remove it from the forelegs in the same way. Draw the skin off the head, easing it in the same manner, using a sharp, pointed knife. Remove the eyes.

To clean the rabbit, remove its kidneys, the fat in which they are embedded and the heart and lungs. Remove the gall bladder from the kidney. Wash the rabbit well in cold, salted water, changing the water two or three times. Leave it finally to soak in fresh salted water for 30 minutes.

A rabbit should be left to soak for 2 hours or more, even when bought skinned from the butcher. Wipe it dry before using. If its flavour seems very strong, it should be blanched before either boiling or roasting.

One piece of country advice: when cleaning the rabbit, make sure its pelvis is twisted off. Much of what people consider is its unpleasant rabbity flavour is produced by this part of its anatomy.

If a rabbit is to be roasted, it should be trussed. Push whatever stuffing is to be used into the cavity and sew up the opening with coarse cotton thread. Leave a long end so that this can easily be pulled out. Make a small cut on the under surface of the rabbit in the fleshy part of the thighs. This keeps the back straight and not arched. Bring the hind legs forward and the front ones backwards, with the former outside and just overlapping the latter. Fix the legs by passing a skewer through the fore and hind legs from one side to the other, then secure with string. If retaining the head, keep this in position by raising it and running a skewer down the mouth and neck and fixing the head back between the shoulders.

Etiquette and good breeding in the seventeenth century demanded that the roast rabbit be 'unlaced' or as they said, 'unlacing a coney', not carving.

WILD RABBIT STEWED WITH PRUNES (French)

3 servings:

1 wild rabbit	**butter**
½ cup (⅔) vinegar	**2 tablespoons (2½) flour**
1½ cups (2) red wine	**1 cup (1¼) stock**
1 bay leaf	**1 lb. prunes, soaked and pitted**
a few juniper berries	**salt, pepper**
a little garlic or onion	**1 tablespoon (1¼) redcurrant jelly**
3 crushed cloves	

Clean the rabbit and cut it into neat pieces (see page 177). Put the vinegar, wine, bay leaf, juniper berries and garlic with the cloves into a bowl and add the pieces of rabbit. Leave for 24 hours. Drain well and wipe the pieces of rabbit dry. Strain the marinade.

Heat enough butter to fry the pieces of rabbit until a golden brown, add the flour, stir this well into the butter and then gradually add the stock and 1 cup (1¼) of the marinade. Add the prunes, salt and pepper and cook gently until the rabbit is tender.

Take the rabbit and the prunes from the pan and put on to a hot serving dish. Strain the sauce, return it to the pan, add the redcurrant jelly and quickly reheat. Pour the sauce over the rabbit and prunes.

Serve with straw potatoes (see page 206).

Instead of prunes, use half-and-half prunes and Malaga grapes or 1 lb. of large, stoned grapes. It is possible to buy ready pitted Californian prunes. An added refinement is to soak the prunes in port wine.

FRIED RABBIT

Chicken may be cooked in the same manner.

2 pieces tender rabbit per person	**fine breadcrumbs**
oil for deep frying	garnish:
egg, well beaten	**crisply fried bacon, fresh parsley**

Heat a little oil. Wipe the rabbit pieces with a damp cloth. Then thoroughly dry them and fry in the hot oil until almost cooked. Take from the pan, put aside and let the pieces cool. Dip each piece twice into beaten egg and breadcrumbs. Pour enough oil for deep frying into a frying pan (skillet) and heat until boiling. Place the rabbit pieces in a frying basket and slowly drop into the boiling oil. If the oil is sufficiently hot the crumbs will fry instantly and each piece of rabbit will become a golden brown. This will take about 15–20 minutes. Serve very hot on a napkin or simply on a hot plate. Garnish and serve with a *sauce tartare* (see page 214).

RABBIT STEWED IN CIDER

3–6 servings:

1–2 rabbits	**lean bacon or ham, chopped**
juice $\frac{1}{2}$ lemon	**1 lb. tomatoes, peeled and sliced**
$\frac{1}{4}$ cup ($\frac{1}{3}$) olive oil	**salt, pepper**
3–4 large onions, sliced	**1 teaspoon ($1\frac{1}{4}$) sugar**
1 bay leaf	**2 cups ($2\frac{1}{2}$) dry cider**
thyme	

Joint the rabbit(s) (see page 177) and leave for an hour or so in cold water to which the lemon juice has been added. Take the pieces of rabbit from the water and dry them thoroughly. Heat the oil in a pan and fry the pieces of rabbit to a golden brown. Add the onions, let these cook slowly until soft but not brown then add the bay leaf, thyme and a little lean bacon. Let this cook gently for 15 minutes, add the tomatoes and gently stir them into the rest of the ingredients. Add salt, pepper and sugar. Continue to cook gently for a further 10 minutes; then add the cider. Bring to a quick boil for 2 minutes, reduce the heat, cover the pan and continue cooking until the rabbit is tender. Remove the bay leaf and thyme (if using fresh) before serving. Serve with rice, boiled potatoes (preferably somewhat overcooked) or mashed Jerusalem artichokes. An elderly chicken can be cooked in the same manner.

RABBIT IN RED WINE (Belgian)

3–6 servings:

1–2 rabbits, jointed (see page 177)	**$\frac{1}{2}$ lb. prunes, soaked and pitted**
game marinade (see page 202)	**1 cup ($1\frac{1}{4}$) red wine**
flour	**salt, pepper**
oil	**grated nutmeg**

Marinate the rabbit(s) overnight. Strain the marinade and thoroughly dry the pieces of rabbit. Roll these in flour and fry in hot oil until brown. Transfer the browned pieces of rabbit to a heavy pan, add the prunes, red wine and enough marinade to cover the whole. Add salt, pepper and a dash of nutmeg, then cook very slowly for $1-1\frac{1}{2}$ hours or until the rabbit is tender.

Serve with any of the sharp jellies, a green salad and French bread.

RABBIT IN A GRAPE JUICE SAUCE (Mexican)

For this recipe, the grape juice should be prepared with fresh grapes pressed and strained.

3–4 servings:

1 rabbit, jointed (see page 177)
salt
2 tablespoons (2½) butter
2 tablespoons (2½) flour

1 cup (1¼) rabbit stock
juice ½ lemon
1 cup (1¼) black grape juice

Cook the pieces of rabbit in salted water until tender. Take them from the pan, drain (reserving the liquid) and dry thoroughly. Heat the butter, and when it is melted add the flour and stir to a light brown *roux*. Gradually add the rabbit stock, stirring all the time to make a smooth sauce. Stir in the lemon and grape juice, add the pieces of rabbit, test for seasoning and gently cook until the rabbit is reheated.

Serve with potatoes, rice, noodles or spaghetti.

RABBIT IN A DARK SAUCE (Spanish)

3–4 servings:

1 rabbit, jointed (see page 177)
3 oz. (6 tablespoons) butter or
 cooking fat
¼ lb. streaky bacon, diced
1 small bunch spring (green) onions
flour
1 cup (1¼) red wine

1 cup (1¼) water or stock
thyme, parsley, bay leaf
salt, pepper
1 oz. (1 square) dark, bitter
 chocolate
1 tablespoon (1¼) hazel-nuts or
 walnuts

Heat the butter in a large pan and fry the bacon until fairly crisp. Take from the pan, and put to the side. Fry the onions whole but trimmed. Roll the pieces of rabbit in flour and fry them to a golden brown in the same fat. Sprinkle in 1 tablespoon (1¼) of flour and stir well; add the wine and water. Tie the thyme, parsley and bay leaf together and add to the pan. Add salt and pepper and return the bacon. Cook slowly for $1-1\frac{1}{2}$ hours until the rabbit is tender. Crush the chocolate with the hazel-nuts in a mortar or liquidizer (blender) to make a paste. About 15–20 minutes before serving stir this paste into the pan. Serve the rabbit with its sauce in a ring of rice or creamed potatoes. Other vegetables such as young carrots or turnips may be served with it.

RABBIT IN AN ALMOND AND RAISIN SAUCE

3–4 servings:

1 rabbit, jointed (see page 177)
salt
flour
bacon fat
1 sweet pepper, cored and seeded

2 cloves garlic, sliced
1 onion, sliced
2 tablespoons (2½) blanched almonds
2 tablespoons (2½) seedless raisins

Cook the rabbit in salted water until tender. Take the pieces from the pan, drain and dry and roll in flour. Heat some bacon fat (other fat will do) in a deep pan and fry the pieces of rabbit until brown. Take them from the pan, place on a serving dish but keep hot. Cut the pepper into strips, add with the garlic and onion to the pan, lightly brown, add remaining ingredients and enough of the rabbit liquid to make a sauce. Cook gently for 10 minutes and pour this sauce, without straining, over the rabbit.

Serve with boiled potatoes sprinkled with parsley.

RABBIT WITH MUSHROOMS AND BACON (Italian)

4–8 servings:

1–2 rabbits, jointed (see page 177)
olive oil
1–2 onions, coarsely chopped
flour
1 teaspoon (1¼) tomato purée
salt, pepper

meat or game stock
bouquet garni (marjoram or rose-
mary, thyme, 1 bay leaf)
3 slices streaky bacon, diced
1 lb. mushrooms, thickly sliced

Heat enough olive oil in a pan to fry the pieces of rabbit and the onions to a golden brown. Pour off the oil, sprinkle the rabbit lightly with flour, add the tomato purée, salt and pepper and enough stock to just cover, bring this to the boil, add the bouquet garni, cover the pan and cook very gently for 30 minutes. Take out the pieces of rabbit and put these into an earthenware casserole. Strain the sauce. Add the bacon and mushrooms to the rabbit (quartered sweet peppers may be added at this point); cover with the sauce. Cover and continue cooking in a hot oven for another 45 minutes or until the rabbit is quite tender. Serve with rice or potatoes garnished with sprigs of fresh parsley.

BAKED RABBIT DORSETSHIRE STYLE

4 servings:

1 young rabbit
flour
6 slices streaky bacon
salt, pepper
2 cups (2½) soft white breadcrumbs

4 medium-sized onions, finely
chopped
sage to taste, finely chopped
1 teaspoon (1¼) grated lemon rind
1–2 eggs, well beaten
1 cup (1¼) milk

Wash the rabbit, cut it into serving pieces (see page 177) and coat in flour. Put the pieces into a baking dish and cover with the bacon. Sprinkle with salt and pepper. Mix the breadcrumbs, onions, sage and lemon rind together then add the egg(s), milk, salt and pepper. Pour this mixture over the pieces of rabbit. Bake in a slow oven for at least 2 hours. If the top appears to be getting too dry cover it with foil or other kitchen paper. If a dish with somewhat more liquid is preferred, add cider or other liquid to the roasting pan before adding the breadcrumb mixture. Serve the rabbit in the dish in which it was cooked and with almost any vegetables.

RAGOÛT OF RABBIT

4 servings:

1 rabbit	**fresh herbs to taste**
½ lb. streaky bacon, sliced	**3 tablespoons (3¾) flour**
1 each onion and shallot, sliced	**3 cups (3¾) water**
1 carrot, sliced	**salt, pepper**
1 turnip, sliced	

Cut the rabbit into neat joints (see page 177). Fry the bacon in a large pan. Add the vegetables, herbs and the pieces of rabbit and cook until the meat is brown. Sprinkle in the flour and stir for 5 minutes. Gradually add the water, stirring all the time; season with salt and pepper. Simmer for 1½ hours. Discard the herbs and serve the rabbit in its sauce with boiled potatoes and the bacon and vegetables as a garnish.

RABBIT STEW

6–8 servings:

2 rabbits	**salt, pepper**
2 oz. (¼ cup) butter	**1½ cups (2) hot stock**
½ lb. streaky bacon, sliced	**½ cup (⅔) white wine or cider**
3 medium-sized onions, thickly sliced	**bouquet garni**
flour	**8 rounds toast or fried bread**

Chop the rabbits into small pieces. Heat the butter in a deep casserole, add the bacon and fry this until it is crisp and brown. Take it from the pan and put it aside. Add the onions, fry them until brown, then take from the pan and reserve. Add the rabbit and cook for 10–15 minutes, turning often to ensure even browning. Sprinkle with flour, salt and pepper. Blend thoroughly; add the stock and wine. Add the bouquet garni and bring the stew gently to the boil. Return the onions and some of the bacon to the pan. Cook very gently for 1 hour. From time to time skim off any surplus fat. Serve the rabbit on rounds of crisp toast or fried bread, covered with the sauce, garnished with the remaining bacon, and with creamed potatoes.

Instead of stewing the rabbit on top of the stove it can be cooked slowly in a casserole in the oven.

PULLED OR CREAMED RABBIT

3–4 servings:

1 rabbit	**salt**
1 onion, coarsely chopped	**1 oz. (2 tablespoons) butter**
bouquet garni	**1 tablespoon (1¼) flour**
few strips lemon peel	**mashed potatoes as garnish**
6 peppercorns	**parsley, finely chopped**

Wipe the rabbit and put it into a pan with sufficient water to cover. Add the onion, bouquet garni, lemon peel, peppercorns and salt. Bring to a boil over a good heat, lower the heat and continue cooking until the rabbit is tender. Take it from the pan, cool and strip all the flesh from the bones and pull this into strips. Heat the butter in a pan, stir in the flour and blend to a *roux*. Strain and gradually add 2 cups (2½) of the rabbit liquid. Stir and cook over a moderate heat until it thickens to a sauce consistency. Add the 'pulled' rabbit and simmer for 10 minutes. Frame a border of mashed potato on a hot plate and in the centre place the rabbit with its sauce. Sprinkle generously with parsley.

STEWED RABBIT (Portuguese)

4 servings:

1 rabbit	**2 cloves garlic, crushed**
1 oz. (2 tablespoons) butter	**1 teaspoon (1¼) French or German**
2 tablespoons (2½) olive oil	**mustard**
1 cup (1¼) stock	**sprig fresh parsley, finely chopped**
½ cup (⅔) white wine	**salt, pepper**
1 large onion, chopped	**6 tomatoes, peeled**

Cut the rabbit into joints (see page 177), 4 or 6 pieces according to its size. Heat the butter and oil together in a large pan, add the pieces of rabbit and cook until they are browned. Add the stock and the remaining ingredients and cook over a moderate heat until the rabbit is tender.

Serve with boiled rice or potatoes plus any of the green vegetables.

RABBIT CASSEROLE

4–6 servings:

1–2 rabbits, jointed (see page 177)	**2 large onions, coarsely chopped**
1 bottle dry wine or equivalent in	**2–3 carrots, thickly sliced**
cider	**salt, cayenne pepper**
flour	**1–2 cloves garlic, finely chopped**
olive oil	**fresh herbs to taste**

Marinate the rabbit in the wine overnight. Dry the pieces of rabbit (reserving the marinade) and sprinkle them with flour. Heat 2–3 tablespoons (2½–3¾) of oil, add the onions and partially cook them, then sprinkle with flour. Stir and cook until they are soft. Take from the pan and spread at the bottom of an earthenware casserole. Heat a little more oil in the pan, enough to brown the rabbit. When this is hot add the rabbit and fry to a golden brown. Place on top of the onions. In the free spaces put the slices of carrot. Add the wine in which the rabbit was marinating, salt, cayenne pepper, garlic and herbs. Cover, put into a slow oven and cook for about 2 hours or until the rabbit meat is so tender it can be stripped easily from the bones. This dish can be garnished with triangles of fried bread, dumplings, crisply fried bacon, creamed or boiled potatoes, peas, beans or other winter vegetables but requires no extra sauce.

RABBIT WITH GREEN OLIVES (Italian)

6 servings:

1 large rabbit	2 tablespoons (2½) butter
2 large onions, thickly sliced	1 tablespoon (1¼) flour
2 sticks celery, thickly sliced	2 cups (2½) boiling water
2 large carrots, thickly sliced	salt, pepper
1 bay leaf	12 large green olives, stoned
2 tablespoons (2½) dripping	1 tablespoon (1¼) capers

Joint the rabbit (see page 177) and put into a large pan with 2 cups (2½) of cold water; add the onions, celery, carrots, bay leaf and dripping. Cook over a low heat for 30 minutes. Remove the pieces of rabbit and bring the rest to the boil. Mix the butter and flour together and add to the pan; stir and continue cooking gently until the mixture is thick. Add the boiling water and continue stirring until the sauce is smooth. Add salt, pepper, olives, capers and the rabbit and continue cooking for about 30 minutes or until the rabbit is tender.

RABBIT IN A MUSTARD SAUCE

4–6 servings:

1 rabbit, cut into serving pieces (see page 177)	salt, pepper
	a little thyme
2 oz. (¼ cup) butter	parsley, chopped
¼ lb. streaky bacon, diced	1 bay leaf
8 whole small onions or 1–2 large ones, coarsely chopped	½ cup (⅔) white wine
	fried bread
4–5 tablespoons (5–6¼) Dijon mustard	button mushrooms, fried whole

Heat the butter in a large pan, add the bacon, the onions and when the latter begin to change colour, the pieces of rabbit. Fry these until brown all over then take the rabbit, bacon and onions from the pan. Pour off most of the fat, add the mustard, stir this well into the remaining fat, add salt, pepper and herbs and finally the wine. Return the rabbit, onions and bacon. Cover the pan tightly and let it all cook for about 1 hour, it may be left longer depending on the size and age of the rabbit. Do not lift off the lid more than is necessary as the rabbit is cooking in its own steam. Remove the herbs before serving. Garnish the rabbit with triangles of fried bread and button mushrooms.

FRICASSEE OF RABBIT

4 servings:

1 rabbit	2 oz. ($\frac{1}{4}$ cup) butter
1 each onion, carrot and turnip, chopped	3 tablespoons ($3\frac{3}{4}$) flour a little milk
1 bunch parsley, chopped	croûtons
salt, pepper	parsley, chopped

Cook the rabbit in water with the onion, carrot, turnip, parsley, salt and pepper until it is tender. Remove it from the pan and when cool strip off the flesh from the bones.

Make a white sauce: heat the butter, add the flour, stir to a *roux*, gradually add some of the stock from the rabbit and a little milk, and mix to a smooth sauce the thickness of cream. Add the rabbit to the sauce and reheat slowly. Serve with croûtons and garnish with chopped parsley.

RABBIT COOKED IN A RED SAUCE

4 servings:

1 rabbit, jointed (see page 177)	1 sweet pepper, cored, seeded and sliced
flour	
oil	1 teaspoon ($1\frac{1}{4}$) sugar
2 large onions, chopped	2–3 cloves garlic, chopped
1–2 lb. tomatoes, peeled and chopped	salt, pepper
	$\frac{1}{2}$ cup ($\frac{2}{3}$) sweet white wine

Roll the pieces of rabbit in flour. Heat enough oil to fry the rabbit to a golden brown and then add the remaining ingredients. Cook all this slowly for at least 1 hour or until the rabbit is tender. Stir gently from time to time to prevent sticking, although with so much tomato this should not happen. Serve the rabbit in a deep serving dish with the sauce strained over it, accompanied by either creamed or riced potatoes or a plain rice pilau.

RABBIT COOKED IN WHITE WINE

4 servings:

1 rabbit, jointed (see page 177)	thyme to taste
1 small onion, thinly sliced	salt, black pepper
2–3 cloves garlic, sliced	1 cup ($1\frac{1}{4}$) clear stock
1 cup ($1\frac{1}{4}$) white wine	flour
juice $\frac{1}{2}$ lemon	oil for frying

Mix together in a bowl the onion, garlic, wine, lemon juice, thyme, salt, pepper and the stock. Stir well then add the rabbit. Leave overnight to marinate. Next day take the rabbit from the marinade, dry well on absorbent paper and roll in flour. Heat enough oil in a shallow pan to fry the rabbit pieces to a golden brown. Transfer these to a larger pan. Strain and add the marinade. Bring to a gentle boil, lower the heat and cook for about 1 hour or until the rabbit is tender. Take the rabbit from the pan and arrange on a hot plate. Serve the gravy separately in a sauceboat.

Serve with rice or puréed potatoes, sliced turnips and any green vegetables in season. Instead of white wine, a dry cider may be used.

TERRINE OF RABBIT (potted rabbit)

10 servings:

1–2 young rabbits
salt, pepper
$\frac{1}{2}$ cup ($\frac{2}{3}$) brandy
1 cup (1$\frac{1}{4}$) dry breadcrumbs
1 teaspoon (1$\frac{1}{4}$) grated lemon rind

1–2 eggs, beaten
1 lb. streaky bacon, sliced paper-thin
thyme and bay leaves, chopped
a little allspice, ground

Strip the meat from the bones as neatly as possible. Cut the larger pieces of meat into fillets and finely grind the really small bits. Sprinkle the fillets with salt and pepper, put into a bowl with the brandy and leave for 1 hour. Make a forcemeat. Mix the ground rabbit meat with the breadcrumbs, lemon rind, salt and pepper and, if available, some sausage meat. Bind with egg and finally add the brandy in which the rabbit was soaking. Line the bottom and sides of a large *terrine* with strips of fat bacon placing them so close together that they are touching. Spread over this an even layer of forcemeat. Place on top, side by side and lengthwise the rabbit fillets and over these lay some squares of bacon. Press down and spread over this another layer of forcemeat. Sprinkle with thyme, bay leaf, allspice, salt and pepper and cover with long pieces of streaky bacon. Press down the edges and cook uncovered for 1$\frac{1}{2}$ hours in a moderate oven. Leave until cold then cover with foil and a lid. It should keep for weeks. When the *terrine* is cooked the fat will rise to the surface and be quite clear.

Venison

There was a time in Britain and elsewhere when a man could be hanged for poaching deer; yet venison has been used as a food for humans since Biblical days. It was the traditional meat of the households of the medieval lords and large domestic herds were started in private parks as much to provide food as to ornament the surroundings. One English estate, Up Park in Sussex, still has a path made entirely from the bones of deer set vertically in the ground with the knuckles at ground level. This gives us some conception of the vast quantities of deer meat consumed in days gone by. Even today the mention of venison strikes a grand note, although it is sometimes cheaper than beef for roasting.

The word venison itself derives from the Latin *venari*, to hunt, and formerly applied to the flesh of any sort of game or wild beast hunted in the chase and used for food. Today the word is almost entirely restricted to the flesh of the various types of antlered animals. Many people regard venison as a man's meat, probably because it is usually men who hunt the animal for sport and when he has been successful he likes to see the result of his sport on the dining table.

There are three kinds of venison known in Great Britain and Ireland; the stag or red deer peculiar to Ireland; the roebuck known only in the north of Scotland, and the fallow deer common in England. Of these the fallow deer is much the best eating. When it is well kept and properly dressed it is worthy of the high value set on it. Buck venison, which is in season from June to the end of September, is finer than doe venison, which is in season from October to December.

In the United States, all varieties of deer, including elk, moose and reindeer, are popular. The domestication and breeding of reindeer has produced an important new source of meat in Alaska.

Much of the game, both large and small, shot during the open season is privately consumed, so it is as well to know something of its preparation. Like mutton, venison should have attained a certain age before it is killed or it will not have acquired its true flavour. The age of venison may be seen from the cleft of the hoof which is always left on the animal. If this is small and smooth the animal is, or was, fairly young. But no deer destined for venison should be more than three years old, and preferably somewhat younger. If deer is not cleanly shot it will deteriorate rapidly on its journey from the forest or park to the butcher or home.

When it happens that a piece of venison arrives in the kitchen from a known and good origin, it must be wiped dry with a floured cloth and then rubbed with powdered ginger. If there is any suggestion of mustiness in the flesh, wash the meat in lukewarm water, then thoroughly dry and rub with powdered ginger. Wrap it in muslin, inside of which tansy leaves or other suitable green herbs may be tied, then hang the muslin bundle in the coolest place possible.

When choosing venison from the butcher, look carefully. The haunch is the prime joint – all Victorian recipe books give detailed instructions for cooking it, indicating it was frequently served. But this usually is too large for the smaller families of today, so one may prefer a part of the loin and chops. The fat of the meat must be thick, bright and clear; the meat, dark and finely grained. The greater the quantity of fat there is the better the quality of the meat. There are tests such as running a knife or skewer into the shoulder of haunch close to the bone when the resultant smell will indicate all too well whether the carcass is freshly killed or not, but for most of us it is a matter of relying on the butcher and it has been my experience that those who sell game usually know something about it and are willing to advise.

Young deer may be cooked in its fresh state but older game of any kind requires hanging and marinating. Remember when marinating that the longer the meat is left in the marinade the stronger the gamey flavour, so this is left entirely to individual taste. For example, 24 hours of marinating will leave the meat tender but more or less with its natural flavour; 48 hours will bring out its gamey flavour and above this limit the game will be all that much stronger.

Venison is by nature a dry and lean meat and even the best of it tends towards toughness. Hanging helps to tenderize it; marinating venison is another aid, as is larding when roasting. A large piece of fat bacon wrapped round a piece of venison when roasting does it a power of good (or the meat can be wrapped in greased aluminium foil which assists in keeping in all the flavour and moisture). Venison takes a long time to roast and there are many cooks who prefer simply to rely on extensive basting when roasting, eschewing all barding or foil wrapping.

Tougher cuts of venison can be made into stews or casserole dishes, all of which are exceedingly good. Most venison dishes are worthy of a glass of red wine used in their cooking as well as plenty of fresh herbs.

When trimming venison, make sure all the fat and fibres are removed. Deer fat is not pleasant to eat and it spoils the flavour of the meat, giving it a goat-like flavour. Venison chills quickly and then develops a tallow flavour, so when cooking venison steaks they must be served immediately (if they must wait keep them very hot until served).

Venison is regarded by some as a luxury meat. For those who live in areas where it is hunted for sport it is, as James Beard puts it, 'endured as a rather dull and functional substitute for other meats'. Those who buy it over the counter sometimes find to their surprise that it is less costly than the equivalent weight in either beef or mutton. Nowadays good venison is usually found in the larger food stores and the shops of those butchers with a licence to sell game.

ROAST SADDLE OF VENISON WITH CAPER SAUCE

Venison leg can be roasted in the same way.

6–8 servings:

1 saddle venison, about 5 lb.
game marinade (see page 202)
¼ lb. streaky bacon
salt
4 oz. (½ cup) pork fat, suet or butter

1 cup (1¼) sour cream
1 lb. mushrooms
1 heaped tablespoon (1¼) crushed
    capers

Leave the saddle in the marinade for 4–5 days before using. Wash in warm water, wipe and dry thoroughly with a cloth. Remove the skin and sinews with a sharp knife, make incisions at regular intervals, push strips of the bacon into these and rub with salt. Put the meat on a rack in a roasting pan. Heat the fat and pour this while still hot over the meat. Add several tablespoons of the marinade and put the pan into a hot oven. Baste the meat frequently with sour cream until it is tender allowing 15 minutes cooking to each pound. Twenty minutes before the saddle is ready put the mushrooms into the pan to roast under the meat, these should be tender when the meat is ready. Put the meat into a hot dish, garnish with the mushrooms and keep hot while preparing a gravy. Put the roasting pan on top of the stove, scrape round the sides and add 2–3 tablespoons (2½–3¾) of the marinade. Stir well, add the capers and cook over a good heat for 5 minutes. Serve this sauce separately in a sauceboat. Serve the saddle with game chips (see page 206), any of the sharp jellies, watercress salad and possibly glazed baby onions or with noodles or wild or brown rice.

CASSEROLE OF VENISON

6 servings:

3 lb. venison
1–2 cloves garlic
1 bay leaf
6 whole peppercorns
salt, pepper
¾ cup (1) port
4 oz. (½ cup) butter
2 tablespoons (2½) flour

3 cups (3¾) meat or game stock
bouquet garni
1 heaped tablespoon (1¼) finely
    chopped parsley
12 tiny white onions
6 pickled walnuts
½ lb. mushrooms

Cut the venison into cubes (cutting away any skin and sinews) and drop these into an earthenware jar. Add the garlic, bay leaf, peppercorns, a little salt and half the port. Leave the meat in this marinade overnight or longer. Drain and thoroughly dry the meat pieces. Heat the butter in a casserole, add the venison and fry it for 10 minutes, turning to ensure the pieces are evenly browned. Sprinkle in the flour, mix this well then add the remaining port and the stock; stir until the mixture comes to the boil. Take the pan from the direct heat, add the bouquet garni, parsley, onions, salt and pepper and the pickled walnuts. Return the pan to the stove, lower the heat to simmering, cover and continue cooking about 3 hours or until the venison is tender. Half an hour before serving add the mushrooms. Remove the bouquet garni. Strain the marinade, add this to the pan and bring to the boil.

Serve the venison with boiled potatoes or potato dumplings and either redcurrant or grape jelly.

VENISON COOKED IN WHITE WINE

5–6 servings:

3 lb. venison (from a young deer)	bouquet garni
white wine	2 lb. small young turnips
salt, pepper	1½ oz. (3 tablespoons) butter
thin strip each lemon and orange peel	2 tablespoons (2½) flour
	juice 1 orange

Wash the venison, dry it well and cut into serving portions. Put the pieces in a casserole and cover with the wine. Add the salt, pepper, lemon and orange peel and bouquet garni. Bring to a slow boil then cook over a moderate heat for 2 hours. In the meantime thinly pare the turnips and cut them into halves lengthwise. Add these to the pan and continue cooking until they are tender. In another pan heat the butter, add the flour and stir to a *roux*. Add the orange juice and enough liquid from the casserole to make a smooth but thick sauce. Take the meat and the turnips from the pan and put aside. Stir any remaining liquid into the orange sauce. Arrange the venison in a hot, deep platter, surround with the turnips and pour the sauce over the top. Serve with boiled potatoes.

VENISON COLLOPS

6 servings:

2 lb. venison from haunch, neck or loin (from a young deer)	freshly ground black pepper
2 oz. (¼ cup) butter	cayenne pepper, to taste
2 tablespoons (2½) flour	nutmeg, to taste
a little orange or lemon juice	butter
½ cup (⅔) claret	1 cup (1¼) fried breadcrumbs (see page 205)
salt	

Cut the venison into oblong slices considerably thinner than for grilling (broiling). Make 4 cups (5) of stock with the bones and trimmings from the meat. Strain. Heat the measured quantity of butter in a small pan, add the flour and cook to a brown *roux*. Add the stock, stir and cook to a medium-thick sauce. Add the juice, claret, salt, pepper, cayenne pepper and nutmeg. Let this simmer. In another pan heat enough butter to fry the venison on both sides until tender. Arrange on a dish, cover with the sauce and sprinkle with the fried breadcrumbs. Serve hot with any of the tart jellies, i.e. rowan, cranberry or redcurrant.

VENISON COOKED IN BEER

4 servings:

2 lb. venison in 1 piece
1 pint (2½ cups) brown ale
¼ lb. (full ½ cup) brown sugar

2 tablespoons (2½) black treacle or
    molasses
salt, pepper

Marinate the venison in the beer for 24 hours. Put the beer, sugar and treacle into a small pan, stir and cook over a moderate heat until the sugar is dissolved. Put the venison into a larger pan, pour the hot beer over the top, season, cover and bring to a gentle boil. Reduce the heat and cook gently about 1 hour or until the meat is tender. Serve with mashed turnips, cauliflower and boiled potatoes.

CIVET OF VENISON

In this recipe, chestnuts may be used instead of mushrooms.

5–6 servings:

3 lb. venison, cut from the leg
½ lb. pickled pork
oil
2 cups (2½) red wine
stock, preferably game

12 small onions
½ lb. mushrooms, thinly sliced
salt, black pepper
1 clove garlic

Sponge both the venison and the pork, wipe dry, then cut into largish stew-sized pieces. Heat enough oil in a large pan to brown the meat and when browned on all sides add half the red wine and enough stock to cover. Cook gently until the meat is tender. Add the onions after about 1 hour, and the mushrooms about 30 minutes before the venison is ready. Add salt, pepper and garlic. Just before the meat is ready to be served add the blood and the remaining wine. Continue cooking over a low heat until the *civet* is reheated. Serve in a deep platter garnished with croûtons.

Serve with puréed potatoes and any vegetable in season.

VENISON STEAKS IN CREAM SAUCE

6 servings:

6 venison steaks (from a young deer)
6 slices streaky bacon
2 oz. (¼ cup) butter
2 tablespoons (2½) olive oil
1 medium-sized onion, sliced
6 mushrooms, peeled and sliced
2 bay leaves
pinch thyme

pinch caraway seed
½ cup (⅔) dry white wine
1 cup (1¼) fresh cream
1 cup (1¼) sour cream
salt, pepper
dash Worcestershire Sauce
juice ½ lemon

Trim and flatten the steaks a little and wrap each in a slice of bacon. Put aside. Heat the butter and oil in a pan, add the onion, mushrooms, bay leaves, thyme and caraway.

Simmer for a few minutes, stirring from time to time, then add the wine. Continue to cook gently until the onion and mushrooms are tender. Add the fresh cream and continue simmering for 20 minutes over a really slow heat (if the mixture boils it might curdle). Take the pan from the heat, add the sour cream, salt, pepper, Worcestershire Sauce and lemon juice and return it to the stove to simmer gently while separately cooking the steaks. Fry the steaks in a dry pan for 6 minutes on each side. Serve the steaks at once with the sauce poured over them with game chips (see page 206), a chicory (endive) salad and a *sauce poivrade* (see page 213).

VENISON PASTY (Scottish)

Venison pasty, if not food for the gods, has accounted for some high feeding. Keats wrote of the revellers of the Mermaid Tavern:

> 'Souls of Poets dead and gone,
> What Elysium have ye known, –
> Sweeter than those dainty pies,
> Of venison?'

4–6 servings:

2 lb. venison with bone	2 onions, peeled
a little freshly crushed allspice and mace	$\frac{1}{2}$ cup ($\frac{2}{3}$) port or claret
salt, pepper	$\frac{1}{4}$ cup ($\frac{1}{3}$) finest vinegar
mutton fat or butter	$\frac{3}{4}$ lb. puff pastry

If possible make sure the meat has been well hung. Take it from the bones and beat it well. Make a stock from the bones. Rub the allspice, mace, salt and pepper into the meat and rub it lightly with mutton fat. Roll up and tie the meat and sprinkle it with a little more allspice. Strain the stock, return it to the pan, add the venison roll and onions and cook slowly for 3 hours. When the meat is tender untie it and leave overnight in its gravy in the pan in a cool place. The next day skim off the layer of fat which will have formed, cut the meat into small pieces and put into a pie-dish together with some of the gravy, adding the port and vinegar. Put a funnel in the centre of the pie and cover it with rolled out rough puff pastry. Bake in a moderate oven for 30 minutes. Take the pastry from the oven, heat and add the remainder of the gravy through the funnel. Serve the pasty hot, with pickled walnuts.

MARINATED AND SIMMERED VENISON STEAKS

6 servings:

6 fairly thick venison steaks	2 bay leaves
2 large onions, thinly sliced	3 oz. (6 tablespoons) suet or cooking fat
1 bunch parsley, coarsely chopped	
salt, peppercorns	1 gill (full $\frac{1}{2}$ cup) sour cream
1 thin strip lemon peel	

Put a layer of onion at the bottom of a dish, add half the parsley and the steaks. Add the remaining onion and parsley, the salt, peppercorns, lemon peel, bay leaves and enough boiling water to completely cover the meat. Leave in a cool place for 24 hours. Take the meat from its marinade and thoroughly dry each piece. Strain the marinade. Heat the suet in a braising pan until it is very hot; add the steaks, fry quickly on both sides then add half of the strained marinade. Cover the pan and let the steaks gently cook until tender, from time to time adding more liquid if necessary to prevent burning. When the steaks are tender, take them from the pan and arrange them on a hot serving dish. Add the sour cream to the gravy, stir it well, add some more strained marinade and bring all to a gentle boil. Pour most of this over the meat and serve the remainder in a sauceboat. Serve with game chips (see page 206) and any of the tart jellies or a mixed salad and Cumberland sauce (see page 209).

VENISON STEAKS 'NATURE' (Austrian)

The meat for this recipe must be from a young animal and guaranteed tender.

4 servings:

8 small venison steaks, each cut **1 oz. ($\frac{1}{2}$ cup) shredded suet**
   $\frac{1}{2}$ **in. thick** **salt, pepper**

Trim the steaks and pound them gently with the hand. Heat the suet until it is very hot and quickly fry the steaks on both sides until brown but well done. Add salt and pepper to the juice in the pan and pour it quickly over the meat. Serve immediately on hot plates, with straw potatoes (see page 206) and pears simmered in wine or baked apples filled with sour cherries or a chestnut or celeriac (celery root) purée (see page 205).

VENISON STEAKS (Flemish)

6 servings:

6 venison steaks   **1–2 bay leaves**
3 oz. (6 tablespoons) butter   **1 good sprig thyme**
flour   **1 sprig parsley**
brandy   **a little tarragon**
marinade: **1 small onion, sliced**
1 cup ($1\frac{1}{4}$) each wine vinegar and   **4 juniper berries**
   red wine   **1-in. piece cinnamon**
3 tablespoons ($3\frac{3}{4}$) olive oil   **salt, pepper**

Put all ten marinade ingredients into a pan, bring to the boil and boil for 5 minutes. Cool, then pour the marinade over the venison. Turn the meat from time to time and leave for 24 hours. Take the pieces from the marinade and dry each piece. Heat the butter and fry the steaks on both sides until brown. Take from the pan and keep hot. Strain and pour enough of the marinade into the butter to make a gravy. Thicken this with a little flour and at the last moment add 1 tablespoon ($1\frac{1}{4}$) of brandy. Pour the gravy over the hot slices of venison and serve with a sharp jelly and boiled chestnuts or a chestnut purée.

VENISON CUTLETS WITH CELERIAC

4 servings:

4 venison cutlets

1 lb. celeriac (celery root)

2 oz. ($\frac{1}{4}$ cup) butter

$\frac{1}{4}$ cup ($\frac{1}{3}$) cream

salt, cayenne pepper

2 tablespoons ($2\frac{1}{2}$) olive oil

4 slices crisply fried bread

Peel the celeriac and cut it into pieces. Boil in salted water until tender. Strain and mash. Add half the butter and all the cream. Return it to the pan, add seasoning and continue cooking for a further 20 minutes. Stir from time to time. In the meantime trim and lightly pound the cutlets to flatten them. Heat the remaining butter with the oil and fry the cutlets quickly for 10–15 minutes browning them on both sides. Serve the cutlets on fried bread; the celeriac separately. When celeriac is not available, use celery.

HASHED VENISON

This is made from left-overs and cold mutton can be treated in the same manner.

Make a sauce from left-over venison stock, gravy etc. and season it with salt and black pepper. Stir it well, bring to the boil then strain; return it to the pan, add some port wine, mushroom ketchup and redcurrant jelly. When all this is hot, slice the venison left-overs and drop them into the simmering sauce. When the meat is reheated, serve with sippets of fried bread.

This can be served with mashed potatoes, puréed chestnuts, rice, lentil purée or French beans plus redcurrant jelly.

POTTED VENISON (Scottish)

All ingredients are to taste.

cold cooked venison

salt, pepper

powdered cloves, nutmeg and mace

butter

Remove all skin and bone from the meat and pound the flesh, lean as well as fat, in a mortar (or use the liquidizer or blender). Add the salt, pepper, cloves, nutmeg and mace. Clarify as much butter as will thoroughly moisten the venison, mix it well and fill into small pots. Cover with melted butter. Chill before serving with toast.

Boar & Bear

This includes any of the several species of strong, swift-footed and ferocious wild hogs dangerous to the hunter because of their cunning and their formidable tusks. Found today in the moist, forested regions of the continent of Europe and in Asia and North Africa, the beast became extinct in Britain centuries ago as a result of both systematic persecution and the decline of forests. Attempts were made to reinstate the beast but with no success.

The wild boar is not indigenous to North America but the Russian boar (*Sus scrofa*) was imported in the early twentieth century and is now established in some of the hill regions of the South.

The flesh of the boar is lean and pork-flavoured and yet with a distinct 'wild' taste. It is eaten as a delicacy in many parts of the world. Every part of the animal can be eaten, saddle, loin, shoulder, legs and back. Only the head of an old boar is edible and then only when spiced etc.

Many are the legends concerning this dangerous beast. One in Sherwood Forest, of Robin Hood fame, is recorded as having put forty hounds out of action. There is also the story told of a certain scholar of Queen's College, Oxford who, whilst walking, was reading a book of the classics. Suddenly he was attacked by a large boar. It is recorded that he saved his life by ramming the tome down the creature's throat.

Boars are still hunted in many parts of France, where they are still abundant. In France, the boar up to the age of six months is called *marcassin*; when a year old *bête de campagne*, at two years *ragot*, from three to five *sanglier*, and finally *solitaire*. The flesh of the *marcassin* is greatly esteemed for its delicacy.

Wild boar is also popular in other parts of Europe; the germans being particularly fond of it.

Unfortunately wild boar does not often find its way into British kitchens, although probably it is more often seen in an American one. I have given several recipes for its cooking, feeling forever hopeful, for it is really an interesting meat. Both in France and Germany it is eaten with great relish, and the French have numerous recipes for cooking wild boar meat.

BOAR'S HEAD

The ancient ceremonial dish served at Christmas feasts in England was the boar's head and had been so since Norman times, for it was the Normans who introduced it. At banquets and special dinners, a boar's head is still served and it is featured on Christmas shopping lists, but today it is seldom a genuine boar's head. It is all too often simply a brawn which has been set in a boar's head mould. The moulded head is then glazed and decorated. Where a genuine boar's head is used it is often not from a fierce wild boar but something considerably tamer.

However, when a boar's head was a boar's head it was splendidly stuffed, boiled or roasted, placed on a large platter, decorated with laurel leaves and borne in procession and triumph to the dining hall to be greeted by the assembled guests with the singing of the carol, 'A Carol bryngyn in the Bore's head', one of a collection of carols written and published in 1521 by Wynkin de Worde. The tradition of the Christmas boar's head has been kept up at Queen's College, Oxford, since the days when wild boars were found near that ancient university and it is still greeted with the same carol.

Famous though this dish has been throughout the centuries, not many cookery books list it. I have myself used a recipe given in Cassell's *Dictionary of Cookery*, and made my boar's head, not in England but in India, with the help of my cook. He being more artist than cook, produced the most hideously grinning boar's head I have ever seen. However, together we cleaned and boned a local wild pig's head which produced a pretty authentic model. If it is possible to get a wild pig or boar's head, it is worth just once having a go.

'Remove the snout, hair and bones from a boar's head; cleanse it thoroughly, scald and put it into a boiling pot containing vinegar and water; add two ounces of salt, a few peppercorns, some parsley, thyme, eschalot and sage; let it steep for three days, with the tongue and two pounds of the meat. When drained, fill up the cavities made by the removal of the bones etc., with thin slices of the meat and tongue rolled together; fasten up the opening with a strong thread as soon as the head has been filled and the form is good. Put it, tied up in a cloth, into a stewpan with the herbs etc., and add a pint of wine, four cloves, a carrot and an ounce of salt, to simmer from six to seven hours, when it may be taken out and allowed to cool. When quite cold, remove the cloth, undo the fastenings, ornament and glaze the head. Replace the tusks and insert eyes made of white of egg and beetroot.'

WILD BOAR IN A MUSTARD SAUCE (French)

6–8 servings:

3–4 lb. leg of young boar
2 tablespoons (2½) Dijon mustard
salt
2 bay leaves
2 sprigs tarragon
12 peppercorns

1 each carrot, parsnip and onion, sliced
½ head celeriac (celery root) sliced
1 tablespoon (1¼) sharp sauce, such as cranberry
2 tablespoons (2½) sour cream

Bone the leg and spread the mustard evenly in the cavity. Leave for 1 hour. Have ready a large pan with slowly boiling salted water, add the meat and boil gently for 1 hour. Tie the herbs and peppercorns in a piece of muslin, drop them into the pan and at the same time add the vegetables. Continue cooking until the meat is tender. Take the meat from the pan, put aside but keep hot. Strain the stock. Rub the vegetables through a sieve into a small pan, add the cranberry sauce, sour cream and stir this well, then add 1 cup (1¼) of the strained stock. Slice the meat, arrange it on the hot platter, add the gravy and serve garnished with game chips (see page 206) and watercress.

GRILLED (BROILED) WILD BOAR STEAK (American)

6 servings:

6 thick boar steaks	**1 bay leaf**
salt, pepper	**a good sprig parsley** tied
sauce:	**celery tops** together
1 large red onion	**2 cloves**
½ lb. large mushrooms	**1 clove garlic**
1 large sweet pepper	**½ cup (⅔) clear stock**
2 oz. (¼ cup) fat	**salt, cayenne pepper**
1 cup (1¼) claret	**½ cup (⅔) redcurrant jelly**
	1 pony glass brandy

First prepare the sauce and keep it hot. Slice the onion, mushrooms and the green pepper thinly (discarding the seeds and core). Heat the fat, add the sliced vegetables and cook these until soft but not browned, stirring constantly. Add the claret, bay leaf, parsley and celery tops, then the cloves, garlic and stock. Mix carefully and cook gently for 20 minutes. Add salt and cayenne pepper to taste, stir in the redcurrant jelly and finally the brandy. Discard the herbs and keep the sauce hot while the steaks are cooking.

Sear the steaks on both sides over or under a high heat flame, then reduce the heat and grill (broil) to the required degree of doneness. Sprinkle each steak lightly with salt and pepper. Serve the steaks with the sauce poured over them and with grilled tomatoes, creamed potatoes and purple broccoli or simply pickled gherkins.

WILD BOAR, BOHEMIAN STYLE

If wild boar is not available, fresh ham could be treated in the same manner.

4–6 servings:

2–3 lb. wild boar	**1 teaspoon (1¼) kummel**
paprika	**2–3 cups (2½–3¾) light beer**
4 oz. (½ cup) pork fat	**3 tablespoons (3¾) black breadcrumbs**
1 lb. onions, finely chopped	**salt, pepper**

The best part of the boar for this recipe is that taken from the shoulder. Cut the flesh into small pieces and roll these in paprika. Heat the fat in a large pan and fry the onions until they are crisp and brown. Add the meat and fry this for 5 minutes, stirring all the while. Add the kummel, stir, add half the beer, stir again, cover the pan and cook gently for 1 hour. Uncover the pan, add the breadcrumbs and the remainder of the beer. Add salt and pepper, cover and continue cooking until the sauce is thick and brown and the meat is tender. Serve with plain boiled potatoes and pickled gherkins.

WILD BOAR CUTLETS (Alsatian)

If travelling in Alsace do not think only of goose liver and *foie gras* but remember also *Cotelettes de marcassin à l'Alsacienne*. In such a recipe there can be no exact quantities. If wild boar is impossible, try the recipe instead with some pork cutlets. In Alsace they drink Edelzwicker, a dry rather earthy wine with this dish.

1–2 cutlets per serving:

wild boar cutlets in 1 piece
dry earthy wine
few slices of onion
2 cloves

1 bay leaf, 6 juniper berries and
6 peppercorns
butter
sour cream to taste
salt, pepper

Steep the meat overnight or longer in enough wine to cover, adding the onion, cloves, bay leaf, juniper berries and peppercorns. Take the meat from the wine marinade and dry it thoroughly. Strain the marinade. Heat 4 oz. ($\frac{1}{2}$ cup) of butter in a casserole and brown the meat well on both sides; then cover and put into an oven, basting it frequently with the strained marinade. When the meat is tender place it in an ovenproof shallow dish, brush it with softened butter, put it into a hot oven and brown it quickly. In the meantime mix the gravy in a casserole with sour cream, add salt and pepper and bring to the boil. Strain and serve the sauce separately in a sauceboat.

Separate the cutlets and garnish with glazed pearl onions, grilled or baked tomatoes, fried button mushrooms and parsley. Serve with boiled wide noodles and the sauce.

BEAR

The European brown bear, the American black bear and the white polar bear are all considered edible and good eating. The flesh of the smaller black bear is excellent with something of the flavour of the pig. The almost extinct grizzly bear, while edible, has a coarse and tough meat. The really edible bears are those which feed on vegetables, berries and honey. However, one authority warns that the flesh of a bear killed after its anger has been roused will not be pleasant, whatever its feeding habits, since its adrenal glands have been activated and have imparted a very strong unwelcome flavour to its flesh.

Nansen and his companions at the North Pole enjoyed the flesh of the white polar bear. 'We have eaten bear meat morning, noon and night; so far from being tired of it we have made the discovery that the breast of the cub is quite a delicacy.'

Bear steaks should be prepared like beef but should be marinated for two days. Treat it, for example, in the same manner as stewed beef but cook it with the marinade in which it has lain. Thicken the sauce with arrowroot, add some paprika and serve it on a bed of sweet corn and butter.

In many parts of Europe as well as America the bear is still hunted, but it cannot be said to be an everyday delicacy. The most delicious part of the bear, we are told, are the paws which are best cooked in the ashes of a wood fire. However, bears' paws, as far as we in the West are concerned, are becoming of historical interest only but they make one of the earliest recorded dishes of the Chinese. Mencius, a celebrated sage of the pre-Christian era, who lived one hundred years after Confucius, wrote: 'Fish is what I like, so are bear's paws; but if I cannot have both I will forgo the fish and choose the bear's paws'.

Bear's paws are chiefly a delicacy of North China and their cooking belongs to the Shantung or Honan schools. Their flavour is unique, our nearest flavour is fat ham or the German *Eisbein*, not greasy but somewhat gelatinous. It is so smooth that it literally melts in the mouth. In the Far East it is still just possible to find bear's paws but only just so.

However, in America bear is a fairly well sought after animal and the man who shoots the bear usually also cooks it; no one else ever gets a chance.

BEAR COOKED IN BURGUNDY (German)

12 servings:

7-lb. loin bear	salt
strips pork larding	6 juniper berries, pounded
marinade (see page 204)	½ bottle red burgundy
onions, carrots, parsnips, celery	

Cut out the sinews and nerves from the meat; do this carefully, otherwise the meat will be damaged. Lard it well, pushing the strips of pork through the centre of the meat. Put it into the marinade and leave for 5 or 6 days. Peel and coarsely chop the vegetables and put these at the bottom of a roasting pan. Take the meat from the marinade, rub it dry, then sprinkle with salt and the pounded juniper berries. Put the meat on top of the vegetables. Add the wine. Roast for the first 15 minutes in a hot oven, then reduce the heat to low and continue cooking for another 4 hours, basting frequently. Really slow cooking is the secret of cooking bear. Take the meat from the pan, put on a hot platter and keep hot. Strain the vegetables with the gravy through a sieve, return this to the pan and cook it on top of the stove until it is reheated. Pour half the sauce over the meat and the rest into a sauceboat. Serve with sauerkraut or with a garnish of watercress, croûtons, redcurrant jelly and slices of lemon.

BEAR HUNTSMAN STYLE

8–10 servings

6-lb. loin of bear	marinade (see page 204)
¼ lb. fat larding pork cut into strips	1 cup (1¼) cream, scalded

Wipe the meat with a damp cloth and lard it through the centre with the larding pork. Prepare the marinade and put this into an enamel or earthenware bowl. Add the piece of bear meat, cover with a cloth and leave for 10 days, turning the meat daily. Take the meat from the marinade, strain the latter and wipe the meat dry. Put the vegetables from the marinade at the bottom of a roasting pan, add the meat and roast in a hot oven for 15 minutes. Reduce the heat to moderate and roast for another 2 hours, basting frequently with the drippings in the pan. When the meat is quite tender, take it from the pan, put it on to a hot platter and keep hot while a sauce is prepared. Measure off 1 cup ($1\frac{1}{4}$) of the marinade and add this to the pan. Bring to the boil on top of the stove and cook for 15 minutes. Stir from time to time, scraping round the sides of the pan to loosen all the gelatinous bits adhering to the sides. Add the cream, bring it all to a slow boil and then rub through a fine sieve, pressing gently to obtain as much of the vegetable pulp as possible. Pour half the sauce over the meat and the rest into a sauceboat. Garnish with watercress, wedges of lemon and croûtons and serve with redcurrant or a similar jelly.

Marinades

The object of marinating poultry and game is to make the flesh tender and juicy. It is a preliminary to much meat cooking as it relieves the natural dryness of game and meats generally and it reinforces the natural delicacy of meat flavours.

The word marinade comes from the Spanish word *marinada*, to pickle. It is the acid of the marinade which does the work of adding new flavour, softening tough fibres and increasing their natural sapidity through the action of penetration. It ensures a certain preservation and lifts food out of the commonplace.

A marinade, therefore, is a kind of flavoured pickle in which game, meat and fish are soaked before being cooked. Some marinades are used raw and this is better for smaller portions of food; it is a sort of 'instant' marinade. Others are cooked.

In a cooked marinade the liquid and seasonings are boiled together. Sometimes they are used hot and at other times allowed to become cold before being used. It can be used again and again if it is boiled up occasionally.

To use, mix any of the marinades in a fairly shallow bowl or dish and preferably one made of earthenware. There should always be sufficient marinade to completely submerge any food being marinated, otherwise the exposed portion is in danger of becoming decomposed. The marinating meat should be turned frequently to ensure the marinade thoroughly penetrates the meat.

GAME MARINADE – COOKED

4 cups (5) water	1 tablespoon (1¼) salt
1 each carrot and parsnip, thinly sliced	1 cup (1¼) red burgundy
	juice 1 lemon
3 bay leaves	1 teaspoon (1¼) granulated sugar
12 peppercorns	6 juniper berries

Cook the vegetables in the water adding the bay leaves, peppercorns and salt. When the vegetables are tender add the wine, lemon juice, sugar and juniper berries. Put the game into a bowl and pour over it the hot marinade, covering the meat completely. Each day strain off the liquid, reboil it and pour it over the meat again. This can be repeated from 3 to 6 days. The game is then ready to be cooked.

GAME MARINADE – UNCOOKED (American)

1 quart (5 cups) red wine
½ cup (⅔) malt vinegar
2 carrots, sliced
2 onions, sliced
6 shallots, chopped
8 peppercorns

2 cloves
6 juniper berries
pinch thyme
3 sprigs parsley
1 bay leaf

Mix all these ingredients together and leave for 24 hours before using. This quantity of marinade will marinate 3–4 lb. of meat in 24 hours. If a larger quantity of meat is used, then marinate it for 36 hours. Turn the meat every 6 hours if possible.

BUTTERMILK MARINADE (Continental)

This marinade holds the flavour of the meat or game extremely well without adding its own flavour, and also acts as a tenderizer. The shortest period that game should be left in buttermilk is 24 hours; the longest period, 1 week.

Put the game into an earthenware or china bowl and pour over it enough buttermilk to completely cover it. In cold weather add more buttermilk every 2 days, in warm weather add more daily.

When ready to cook the game, take it from the marinade, dry and cook it straight away.

On the Continent game, after being marinated in buttermilk, is often dried and then dropped into a bowl of sour cream and again left for several hours. The sour cream is then made into a sauce and served with the roasted game.

RED WINE MARINADE (German)

Ingredients are all to taste and the quantity 'as required' but there must always be sufficient to cover whatever game is being used.

parsley, finely chopped
carrot, celery and onion, cut into
  rings
whole peppercorns
thyme, finely chopped

a few coriander seeds
a small piece fresh ginger
1–2 thin strips lemon rind
water and wine vinegar
red wine

Put the first 7 ingredients into a pan adding water and wine vinegar in equal quantities; boil for 10 minutes. Now add the wine in exactly the same quantity as the wine vinegar and water combined (i.e. if using 1 cup each of water and vinegar, use 2 cups of wine). Bring the marinade once more to the boil and then pour this over the game. Do not economize on the wine.

MARINADE FOR HARE

3 level tablespoons (3¾) olive oil
1 cup (1¼) white wine
1 cup (1¼) water
4 bay leaves

2 shallots or small onions, sliced
a little thyme
4 cloves
6 peppercorns, crushed

Mix all these ingredients together.

If marinating a truly ancient hare, use port instead of white wine. The hare needs regular turning and should be marinated for at least 12 hours and preferably for 24. The liver and heart do not require marinating but should be parboiled and put aside until required.

MARINADE FOR VENISON – 1

½ cup (⅔) oil
1½ cups (scant 2) red wine
12 white peppercorns, crushed

1 bay leaf
½ medium-sized onion, sliced

Mix the ingredients together. Salt is not added as it draws out too much of the meat juice.

MARINADE FOR VENISON – 2

½ cup (⅔) oil
1 cup (1¼) red wine
1 cup (1¼) water
4 tablespoons (5) mild vinegar

12 white peppercorns, crushed
2–3 cloves
1 bay leaf
½ medium-sized onion, sliced

Prepare as instructed in Marinade for Venison – 1.

MARINADE FOR BEAR

1 cup (1¼) vinegar
1 quart (5 cups) dry white wine
2 onions, sliced
2 carrots, sliced
1 head celery, coarsely chopped
6 shallots, chopped

1–2 cloves garlic, bruised
2 large fresh bay leaves
18 peppercorns, lightly crushed
½ tablespoon (⅔) salt
a little fresh or dried tarragon

Mix all these ingredients together in a pan and bring to the boil. Reboil 2 or 3 times and cool before using.

Accompaniments

BUTTERED BREADCRUMBS

1 cup (1¼) breadcrumbs   **¼ cup (⅓) butter**

Melt the butter in a pan, add the breadcrumbs and stir until all the butter is absorbed.

FRIED BREADCRUMBS

Put 1¼ cups (full 1½) breadcrumbs into a shallow pan with 1 tablespoon (1¼) of butter. Stir with a wooden spoon over a moderate heat until the crumbs are browned. Cool on a sheet of absorbent paper and store in an airtight jar. Fried breadcrumbs will keep for about one week.

CLARIFIED (DRAWN) BUTTER

Cut as much butter as required into pieces and drop these into a saucepan. Cook over a moderate heat. When the butter has completely melted and begun to froth, skim off the foam and strain the clear liquid into a bowl leaving the milk residue at the bottom of the pan. This residue may be used in soups and sauces.

CELERIAC (CELERY ROOT) PURÉE

Celeriac or turnip-rooted celery has an enjoyable flavour. When celeriac is not available, branch celery may be used instead.

1 lb. celeriac (celery root)   **2–3 tablespoons (2½–3¾) cream**
salt, pepper   **1 tablespoon (1¼) butter**

Wash and pare the celeriac (this is necessary as the celeriac skin is stringy) and cut it into small chunks. Cook it slowly in water or stock, adding salt and pepper to taste, until it is tender. Drain and mash, add the cream and butter, return the purée to the pan and continue cooking for a further 15 minutes.

GAME CHIPS

Choose small, even-sized potatoes; wash them well and peel. With a very sharp knife or a French *mandolin* cut into thin slices across the potatoes. Drop into cold water, leave for a short while then drain and thoroughly dry. Have ready some boiling hot oil for deep frying. Put the chips into a frying basket and immerse in the boiling oil. When they are crisp and a light brown take them from the pan, still in the basket. Drain off the fat, reheat the oil to boiling and return the chips. Fry until they are a golden brown then take from the pan. Drain an absorbent paper and sprinkle with salt.

The French *mandolin* is, in Mrs Beeton's day, what used to be called a cucumber slicer and the price of such a practical little instrument has hardly changed since that quoted in my 1880 edition of Mrs Beeton's book of *Household Management*.

ORANGE SALAD TO BE SERVED WITH WILD DUCK

4 large thin-skinned oranges	$\frac{1}{2}$ teaspoon ($\frac{2}{3}$) fine sugar
1 thin-skinned lemon	salt, cayenne pepper
1 tablespoon ($1\frac{1}{4}$) olive oil	fresh parsley or tarragon, finely
1 tablespoon ($1\frac{1}{4}$) brandy	chopped

Peel and thinly slice the oranges and lemon. If a somewhat bitter flavour is preferred, retain the skins. Discard the pips. Arrange the slices of orange and lemon in a salad bowl. Add the oil, brandy, sugar, salt and cayenne. Mix all this thoroughly without breaking up the slices. When ready to serve sprinkle either of the herbs or a mixture of both over the top.

STRAW POTATOES

Wash and peel as many potatoes as required. Grate these using the largest cutter of the grater. Drop them in cold water, leave for 30 minutes then dry thoroughly. Have ready a large, deep pan with plenty of boiling fat and fry the grated potatoes quickly to a delicate brown. Take from the fat and drain on absorbent paper.

Straw potatoes can be prepared in advance. Reheated in a hot oven, their flavour is as good as when freshly fried.

POTATO CROQUETTES DUCHESSE

2 lb. potatoes	2 extra eggs, well beaten
2 oz. ($\frac{1}{4}$ cup) butter	fine breadcrumbs
4 eggs, well beaten	fat or oil for deep frying

Thoroughly mash the potatoes, add the butter and 4 eggs. Leave until cold. Shape into cones, roll in the extra beaten eggs, coat with breadcrumbs and fry in deep fat or oil until a golden brown.

Sauces & Stuffings

APPLE SAUCE FOR COLD GAME (German)

4 tablespoons (5) grated apple　　　　**lemon juice and sour cream**
4 tablespoons (5) redcurrants

Wash and pick over the redcurrants. Mix them with the apple then add lemon juice to taste and enough sour cream to make a sauce. If fresh redcurrants are not available, use canned ones or canned cranberries.

APRICOT SAUCE (Spanish)

For all kinds of game.

$\frac{1}{2}$ **lb. dried apricots, pitted**　　　　**grated peel of 1 large orange**
1 tablespoon ($1\frac{1}{4}$) lemon juice　　　　$\frac{1}{2}$ **cup ($\frac{2}{3}$) sherry**
sugar to taste　　　　**1 tablespoon ($1\frac{1}{4}$) toasted pine nuts**
pinch salt or ground ginger　　　　**1 tablespoon ($1\frac{1}{4}$) brandy (optional)**

Soak the apricots in water until soft, then cook gently to a thick pulp in the liquid in which they were soaked. Rub through a sieve and return to the pan. Add the lemon juice, sugar, salt or ginger, orange peel and sherry. Cook gently until the mixture reaches a thick, cream-like consistency. Just before serving add the nuts and the brandy. Serve hot or cold.

BALBIRNIE SAUCE

A sauce for pheasant mousse or *chartreuse*.

pheasant carcass and giblets　　　　**bouquet garni**
1 oz. (2 tablespoons) butter　　　　$\frac{1}{4}$ **pint (full $\frac{1}{2}$ cup) red burgundy**
2 tablespoons ($2\frac{1}{2}$) chopped shallot　　　　**4 tablespoons (5) meat glaze (see**
2 carrots, thinly sliced　　　　　**page 243)**

Pull off all scraps of meat from the carcass and grind this with the giblets. Heat the butter, add the shallot, carrots and ground meat and cook for 10 minutes. Add the bouquet garni and the wine. Continue cooking until it has reduced a little, add the meat glaze, simmer a further 30 minutes, strain and pour the sauce over the mousse or *chartreuse*.

BEURRE MANIÉ (French)

This is a kneaded butter, used as a thickener for sauces, stocks and gravies.

1 tablespoon (1¼) butter   **1 tablespoon (1¼) flour**

Soften the butter in a bowl with a wooden spoon, then work into the flour to make a paste.

Bring whatever liquid is to be thickened to the boil, take the pan from the heat and gradually add the *beurre manié*, whisking all the time. When it is completely blended, return the pan to the heat and, still stirring, continue cooking until the sauce is thick.

SAUCE BIGARADE (French)

2 bitter oranges   **juice 1 orange**
2 cups (2½) sauce Espagnole (see   **1 teaspoon (1¼) lemon juice**
  page 211)   **salt, pepper**

Peel the rind from the oranges, discarding all pith. Cut the peel into very thin regular strips, put them into a pan, cover with cold water and over a moderate heat let them come to the boil. Drain off the water and add the *sauce espagnole*. Let this cook over a gentle heat until the strips of rind are soft. Just before serving add the orange and lemon juice, a little salt and the pepper.

To this may be added 1 teaspoon (1¼) of redcurrant jelly or a tablespoon (1¼) of madeira or sherry and a few drops of chilli sauce.

BROWN SAUCE

There are variations to brown sauce. The Italians use oil as well as butter, and mushrooms and tomatoes. Other recipes include mushrooms and lemon, some vinegar and capers. The following is a basic method.

1–2 slices lean bacon, diced   **2 cups (2½) clear stock or water**
2 tablespoons (2½) butter   **salt, pepper**
1 large onion, finely chopped   **bouquet garni**
1 tablespoon (1¼) flour

Heat a pan, add the bacon and butter and when the latter is melted and hot add the onion. Cook this until it is a light brown. Add the flour, stir well until the mixture is blended and the flour brown, then gradually add the stock, salt, pepper and bouquet garni. Cook, stirring all the while, until the sauce is smooth and of a medium thickness, about 15–20 minutes. Strain before serving.

BREAD SAUCE (English)

1 cup (1¼) soft white breadcrumbs
1 shallot or small onion
salt, pepper

grated nutmeg, blade mace
1 cup (1¼) milk or cream
½ oz. (1 tablespoon) butter

Put the breadcrumbs, shallot, salt, pepper, a little nutmeg and mace into a pan with the milk or cream or, better still, a mixture of both. Stir well and add the butter. Cook this gently, stirring all the while, for 5 minutes. Take out the shallot and serve the sauce very hot in a sauceboat.

Instead of using mace, some cooks prefer to stick 2–3 cloves in the shallot. When bread is too soft to crumb, and these days much of it is, then break it into the smallest possible pieces, soak it for 30 minutes or so in the milk or cream and rub it through a sieve.

CHERRY SAUCE

For duck or game.

½–1 lb. black cherries
red wine
ground cinnamon and cloves
salt

thin piece lemon rind
1 heaped teaspoon (1¼) cornflour
   (cornstarch) mixed with cold
   water to a thin paste

Stone the cherries, pound them (or use a liquidizer or blender) and put into a pan. Dilute the purée with red wine, flavour with cinnamon and cloves, add salt and lemon rind and cook this until hot. Thicken with the cornflour paste and continue cooking until the sauce thickens. Rub through a sieve and serve hot.

CRANBERRY SAUCE

¾ lb. cranberries
1 cup (1¼) water

2–3 tablespoons (2½–3¾) sugar

Cook the cranberries in the water until soft, rub through a sieve and add the sugar. This sauce should be rather tart.

CUMBERLAND SAUCE (English)

This sauce is especially good with cold venison and other cold game meat, as well as smoked meats.

orange and lemon peel, to taste
4 tablespoons (5) redcurrant jelly
3 tablespoons (3¾) port wine
3 tablespoons (3¾) orange juice

1½ tablespoons (scant 2) lemon
   juice
1 teaspoon (1¼) dry mustard
a little finely chopped shallot

Discard the pith from the orange and lemon peels and cut into the finest possible strips; drop these into a pan, cover with cold water, bring to the boil and drain. Melt the jelly over a low heat, cool, add the remaining ingredients and serve at room temperature.

CRANBERRY RELISH (American)

For turkey, duck and venison.

3 cups (3¾) whole cranberries
1 each orange and lemon

¾ cup (1) sugar
brandy

Wash the cranberries, orange and lemon. Put all (including the rinds) through a grinder. Mix with the sugar. Chill for several hours and when ready to serve add brandy to taste.

SAUCE CHEVREUIL (French)

Especially for venison and a variation of *sauce poivrade*.

1 cup (1¼) sauce poivrade (see page 213)
½ cup (⅔) red wine
½ cup (⅔) strained marinade
1 teaspoon (1¼) sugar
some morsels of venison, diced

mirepoix of vegetables:
1½ oz. (3 tablespoons) butter
1 tablespoon (1¼) diced onion,
  carrot and shallot
1 bay leaf, thyme and parsley
2 tablespoons (2½) diced lean ham

Bring the *poivrade* to the boil, add the wine and the marinade. Bring again gently to the boil, lower the heat and cook for 30 minutes. Add the sugar and continue cooking until reduced to 1 cup (1¼).

Meanwhile make the *mirepoix*. Heat the butter, cook the vegetables with the herbs for 8 minutes, add the ham and continue cooking until the vegetables are tender. Discard the herbs.

Strain the sauce, add the diced venison and *mirepoix* of vegetables, reheat and serve hot.

GERMAN SWEET SAUCE

For venison and hare.

½ lb. dried cherries
1 cup (1¼) red wine
a small piece cinnamon, bruised
2 cloves

thin strips lemon peel
a little brown sauce
½ lb. stewed prunes, stoned

Soak the cherries in the wine, then cook them with the cinnamon, cloves and lemon peel in the wine in which they have been soaked. Add a little more wine if required. Cook for 20 minutes, then pass through a sieve. Return the sieved cherries to the pan, add the brown sauce, then the prunes. Bring to a gentle boil. Serve hot.

GRAPE JUICE SAUCE

Apart from its use with game this sauce is excellent over ice-cream and other sweet dishes. If used as a sweet sauce somewhat more sugar should be added.

2 cups (2½) fresh grape juice
2 tablespoons (2½) cornflour
  (cornstarch)
1 level tablespoon (1¼) sugar

½ teaspoon (⅔) salt
¼ teaspoon (⅓) ground ginger
2 tablespoons (2½) lemon juice

Mix the cornflour, sugar, salt and ginger with enough of the grape juice to make a thin paste. Pour the rest of the juice into a pan and bring it to the boil. Add the cornflour paste and, stirring all the while, bring this again to the boil; continue cooking until the sauce is thick and smooth. Add the lemon juice, stir well, strain if necessary and chill before using.

SAUCE ESPAGNOLE

1 oz. (2 tablespoons) butter
2 medium-sized carrots, peeled
  and sliced
1 medium-sized onion, peeled
1 clove

small pieces ham, chicken, game or
  poultry
1 tablespoon (1¼) flour
2 cups (2½) hot stock
bouquet garni

Put the butter into a pan, add the carrots and onion, with the clove stuck into the onion. Add any scraps of game or other meat and cook over a really low heat until the carrots and onion are a pale brown. Add the flour, blend this into the rest of the ingredients and then gradually add enough hot stock to make a sauce. Add the bouquet garni and let the sauce simmer for at least 1 hour, although some recipes say up to 4 hours. Strain before serving. This sauce will keep for several days if put into a covered jar and kept in a cool place.

LEMON SAUCE

A simple sauce made from a half and half quantity of melted butter and olive oil gently cooked with an equal quantity of strained lemon juice and a good dash of cayenne pepper.

MADEIRA SAUCE

1 pint (2½ cups) brown sauce (see
  page 208)

3–4 tablespoons (3¾–5) madeira

Prepare the brown sauce. Let it cook for 20 minutes and just before serving add the madeira.

MAÎTRE D'HÔTEL SAUCE OR BUTTER

2 oz. (¼ cup) butter
parsley to taste, finely chopped

salt, pepper
lemon juice

Beat the parsley into the butter, add the salt and pepper and only enough lemon juice to moisten.

HOT ORANGE SAUCE

Particularly suitable for serving with wild or farm-yard duck, this sauce may also be used for other game.

2 large oranges	juice 1 lemon
1 cup (1¼) hot, rich, thick, brown gravy	salt, pepper

Cut the oranges into halves and squeeze out all the juice. Put the juice aside. Thoroughly clean the inside of the peels, discarding all the pith, and cut the peel into thin strips. Put these into a pan, pour over them boiling water, cook for 5 minutes and drain. Return the peel to the pan, add the brown gravy, the orange and lemon juices, salt and pepper and bring to a gentle boil, stirring all the while.

SAUCE PIQUANTE (French)

A spicy sauce for chicken, duck or hare.

blood and liver from a chicken, duck or hare	3 cloves garlic, crushed
1 teaspoon (1¼) vinegar	1 clove
¼ pint (full ½ cup) chicken stock	¼ teaspoon (⅓) grated nutmeg
bouquet garni	pinch cayenne and black pepper and salt

Put the blood into a bowl with the vinegar. Mash the liver and then mix it with the blood. Pour this into a pan and simmer over a low heat, adding the stock, bouquet garni, garlic, clove, nutmeg and seasoning; let this simmer for 15 minutes. Strain the sauce, which will be almost mahogany colour, and serve hot.

SAUCE POIVRADE – 1 (French)

This brown game sauce is one of the most popular of the peppery French sauces and used with other marinated meats as well as with game. There are many recipes for this sauce, all basically agreeing but some being more difficult than others to prepare.

2 onions, finely chopped	salt
2 carrots, finely chopped	a little mace or 1 clove
a little ham, chopped (optional)	2 tablespoons (2½) vinegar
1 sprig fresh parsley	4 tablespoons (5) clear stock
pinch dried thyme	2 tablespoons (2½) brown sauce (see page 208)
1 bay leaf	butter
a good pinch coarse pepper	

Put all but the last three ingredients into a pan with half the stock. Cook over a very low heat until the vegetables are soft and the liquid reduced. Add the rest of the stock and the brown sauce. Bring to the boil, let it boil for 2–3 minutes then rub through a sieve. Return it to the pan, bring again slowly to the boil, add a little butter and serve.

SAUCE POIVRADE – 2 (French)

1 oz. (2 tablespoons) butter
1 each carrot and onion, finely
   chopped
1–2 shallots, finely chopped
1 clove or a little mace
1 bay leaf

a pinch thyme
salt
1 teaspoon ($1\frac{1}{4}$) flour
$\frac{1}{2}$ cup ($\frac{2}{3}$) white wine
1 tablespoon ($1\frac{1}{4}$) wine vinegar
pepper

Heat the butter in a pan, add the carrot and onion, shallot, clove, bay leaf, thyme and salt. Cook gently, stirring almost all the time. When the mixture is soft and coloured, sprinkle in the flour. Stir until this is completely blended then add the wine and vinegar. Simmer for 30 minutes. Add a generous quantity of pepper, strain through a fine sieve and serve.

When using vinegar in a sauce it is wise to taste it before serving. If the sauce is rather more tart than liked, add a little sugar to counteract this.

SAUCE PÉRIGUEUX (French)

2 tablespoons ($2\frac{1}{2}$) diced truffles
butter
salt, pepper

1 bay leaf, crushed
3 tablespoons ($3\frac{3}{4}$) madeira
1 cup ($1\frac{1}{4}$) thickened brown stock

Put the truffles into a pan with a little butter and the salt, pepper and bay leaf. Cook gently for 10 minutes. Remove the truffles, leaving the juices in the pan. Add to the juices 1 tablespoon ($1\frac{1}{4}$) of madeira, stir well then add the stock. Cook gently for a few minutes, return the truffles to the pan and add the remaining madeira. Keep the sauce hot but do not allow it to boil.

PORT WINE SAUCE FOR WILD FOWL

To 1 glass of port add the strained juice of half a lemon, 3 sliced shallots or the equivalent in onions, a pinch of cayenne pepper and 1 tablespoon ($1\frac{1}{4}$) of game gravy. Bring this to the boil, cook for 5 minutes and strain into a sauceboat.

SAUCE POULETTE (French)

For chicken or tame rabbit.

1 oz. (2 tablespoons) butter
1 oz. ($2\frac{1}{2}$ tablespoons) flour
2 cups ($2\frac{1}{2}$) chicken stock
salt, pepper
2 sprigs parsley

2 egg yolks, beaten
juice $\frac{1}{2}$ lemon
1 tablespoon ($1\frac{1}{4}$) finely chopped
   parsley

Heat half the butter, add the flour and stir well; let the mixture brown and gradually pour in the stock, stirring continuously. Add the salt, pepper and parsley. Bring slowly to the boil, still stirring, then lower the heat and simmer for 30 minutes. Take from the stove and discard the parsley. Gradually beat in the egg yolks and return the pan to the heat for a few minutes, still stirring. Take again from the heat, add the remaining butter, blend and add the lemon juice and chopped parsley. Serve hot.

PRUNE SAUCE

For venison, rabbit and hare.

1 lb. prunes
brown sugar to taste
rum or brandy to taste

Soak the prunes in water or strained tea overnight then cook in the same liquid until soft; strain them and rub through a sieve. Return them to the pan, add the sugar and rum and reheat.

REMOULADE SAUCE

Recipes for this sauce vary.

1. Mayonnaise to which is added, very much to taste, French mustard, anchovy essence, chopped gherkins, capers and chopped parsley.

2. French housewives put 1 or 2 tablespoonfuls of French mustard into a bowl and then stir into it enough oil to make a sauce. To this is added salt and pepper, some vinegar and then chopped hard-boiled eggs, capers, parsley and fresh herbs.

SAUCE TARTARE

For grilled chicken and grouse.

2 egg yolks
1 onion, chopped
2 shallots, chopped
a little parsley and tarragon,
  chopped
a few capers
1 teaspoon ($1\frac{1}{4}$) each tarragon vine-
  gar and plain vinegar
1 tablespoon ($1\frac{1}{4}$) olive oil
dry mustard

Cook the egg yolks until hard, then mash and dissolve in a small quantity of water. Mix the next 4 ingredients with the egg yolks and, when blended, add the vinegar, beat well, then add by degrees the olive oil and mustard.

TOMATO SAUCE

6 ripe tomatoes
1 oz. (2 tablespoons) butter
1 teaspoon ($1\frac{1}{4}$) sugar
1 onion, quartered
1 clove
1 tablespoon ($1\frac{1}{4}$) stock or water
salt, pepper

Chop the tomatoes, heat the butter in a pan, add all the remaining ingredients and bring gently to the boil. Stir occasionally and cook until the tomatoes are very soft. Strain and reheat. Garlic may be added to taste.

TRUFFLE SAUCE

2–3 truffles
6 large mushrooms
½–1 clove garlic
1 teaspoon (1¼) each chopped
   parsley and chives

1 teaspoon (1¼) olive oil
1 teaspoon (1¼) flour
¼ cup (⅓) each water and dry white
   wine
salt and freshly milled pepper

Chop the truffles, mushrooms, garlic, parsley and chives and pound together to make a paste. Add the oil and then heat in a small pan over a low heat. Sprinkle in the flour and stir until this is blended; add the water, wine, salt and pepper, stirring all the while. Cook gently, still stirring, for at least 15 minutes, until the sauce is smooth and thick.

SAUCE VENAISON

This is *sauce poivrade* to which ½ cup (⅔) of redcurrant jelly and the same quantity of fresh cream are added.

SAUCE GRAND VENEUR (French)

This is a *sauce poivrade* to which is added either some gooseberry jelly or venison essence and at the last moment, some of the blood from the animal and fresh cream. The blood is not absolutely essential although usual, especially when serving the sauce with hare. If adding the blood, do this slowly rotating the pan to swirl it into the mixture. The sauce should not be cooked after adding the blood. Diced truffles may also be added to this very *haute cuisine* sauce.

SAUCE FOR VENISON

In a small pan mix together 2 tablespoons (2½) of port, a small piece of bruised cinnamon stick, some thin lemon rind and just under a cup (1¼) of redcurrant jelly. Boil for 5 minutes and strain into a hot sauceboat.

PLAIN WHITE SAUCE (VELOUTÉ)

The stock used in this recipe should be either chicken, game or veal. If a paler *velouté* is required a little thick cream may be added.

1 oz. (2 tablespoons) butter
1 oz. (¼ cup) flour

½ pint (1¼ cups) stock
salt, pepper

Heat half the butter in a pan, add the flour and stir well. Cook for 1 minute. Gradually add the liquid, stirring continuously to prevent lumpiness. Cook 10 minutes, adding the remainder of the butter cut into small pieces. Add the salt and pepper and beat thoroughly. It is difficult to give exact quantities of liquid as it is absorbed according to the quality of the flour, but the above quantities will make a sauce of medium thickness.

STUFFING FOR POULTRY AND GAME

Stuffings are important. Erroneously called by some 'dressing', they are used mainly to give added flavour to poultry and game (meat, fish and vegetables as well). As far as poultry and game are concerned, stuffing is also used to upholster the bird and to keep it in its natural shape when being roasted. And, not unimportant, stuffing makes the bird go further at table.

The kind of stuffing used depends on the kind of bird being stuffed. Birds, being hollow, dry out while roasting and therefore stuffings are a sort of internal basting, to give off steam which will then permeate the flesh and fat to be absorbed by suction through the fibres to the meat on the outside. With this in mind it is therefore easy to understand why we often rub birds with butter or other fat before stuffing and roasting.

In general stuffings are known as 'wet' or 'dry'. Bread is one of the most commonly used stuffing ingredients, followed among the starchy items by mashed potatoes, cooked chestnuts and rice. On the Continent and in Scandinavia, there is a preference for fruit stuffings. Many of these are delicious and include such items as apples, prunes, cranberries, apricots and, of course for duck, oranges. Standard stuffings for Britain and the United States are veal and sausage or sage and onions.

When deciding on a stuffing for poultry and game, give some thought to the problem. Large birds which are going to get long, slow cooking need suet or a slow absorbent fat to assist with greasing the bird. Small birds with a roasting time of up to 20 minutes need butter or other soft fat.

The richer or oilier the bird, usually the simpler and fruitier its stuffing. Such stuffings are those which include apples, prunes and apricots. White meated birds, i.e., chicken, capon or turkey, can have such a stuffing as oyster, sausage and other rich mixtures.

Generally speaking wild duck, teal, grouse and similar game birds are left unstuffed, although there are recipes which do use a stuffing and there are several stuffings suitable for them.

Sometimes ingredients for stuffings are fried in fat before using, at other times not. In general it is better to leave certain ingredients, such as herbs, parsley, celery, even garlic and shallots, unfried but chopped. In this way they retain their bite.

To stuff a bird, fill both the neck and the body cavity, remembering not to pack it in too hard for almost all stuffings expand while cooking. Over-stuffing might lead to the stuffing becoming a soggy mass or bursting the flesh of the bird. Draw the skin of the neck back and fasten it neatly with skewers or string. Sew up the opening underneath the rump. If there is any of the stuffing left over, bake it in a greased pan; it can be used as a garnish or as a second-helping supply.

Although it is not possible to gauge exactly the quantity of stuffing required for birds of various kinds, as a general guide 1 cup ($1\frac{1}{4}$) of stuffing for each pound of weight should be sufficient. Do not tightly pack the cavities.

APRICOT AND RICE STUFFING (American)

For turkey, goose, duck, guinea fowl or chicken. This quantity is sufficient for a large chicken; increase for larger birds.

¼ lb. dried apricots, chopped

1½ cups (scant 2) cooked long
   grain rice

2 tablespoons (2½) melted butter

2 tablespoons (2½) each finely
   chopped parsley, onion and chives

½ cup (⅔) finely chopped celery tops

salt, pepper

a good pinch each dried thyme,
   mace and grated nutmeg

Mix all these ingredients together in a bowl. Refrigerate for 1 hour before stuffing into the chosen bird.

ANCHOVY AND CAPER STUFFING (Continental)

For poultry.

6 anchovy fillets, mashed

1 tablespoon (1¼) capers

1 lb. beef

giblets

2–3 bread rolls, soaked in milk
   and squeezed dry

4 oz. (½ cup) butter

3 egg yolks

a few tablespoons soft breadcrumbs

dash freshly grated nutmeg

4 egg whites, stiffly beaten

Put the beef with the giblets and the bread rolls twice through the finest blade of a grinder. Beat the butter until soft. Mix all the ingredients together (except the egg whites) and when the mixture is thoroughly blended add the egg whites, folding them in with some care.

APPLE STUFFING

For duck or goose.

½ lb. (1¼ cups) peeled and chopped
   tart apples

1 oz. (2 tablespoons) butter

1 thick slice onion

½ cup (⅔) chopped celery

3–4 carrots, grated

1 cup (1¼) soft breadcrumbs

salt, pepper

Heat the butter in a shallow pan, add the onion and brown it. Add the remaining ingredients and mix thoroughly. Cook until well heated then stuff the bird in the usual way. This quantity is sufficient for 1 duck; increase the quantities for a goose. The duck liver may also be added, chopped and fried with the onion.

APPLE AND PRUNE STUFFING

For goose and duck.

1–2 tart apples, pared and chopped

½ lb. prunes, soaked

1 oz. (2 tablespoons) butter

1 medium-sized onion, chopped

1–2 sticks celery, diced

salt

Drain the prunes, discard the stones and chop. Heat the butter, fry the onion until soft, add the remaining ingredients and blend.

ARTICHOKE STUFFING

For poultry.

1 can artichoke bottoms, chopped
½ cup (⅔) olive oil
1 medium-sized onion, chopped
1 clove garlic, mashed
salt, pepper

thyme and marjoram, to taste
nutmeg, cloves and mace, to taste
1 cup (1¼) ground lean cooked ham
1 lb. stale bread, crustless
madeira to taste

Heat the oil in a shallow pan until very hot, add the onion and garlic and when they are soft and just beginning to change colour add the artichoke bottoms, salt, pepper, thyme, marjoram, nutmeg, cloves and mace. Mix well and cook for 3–5 minutes, then add the ham. Stir. Crumble the bread, stir this into the mixture and add madeira to moisten. Take from the heat, cool, then add ½ cup (⅔) or more of madeira, depending on taste and the texture of the stuffing.

BANANA AND CHESTNUT STUFFING

For goose or turkey.

6–8 bananas, depending on size,
   chopped
2 cups (2½) soft cooked chestnuts,
   chopped
1 cup (1¼) soft breadcrumbs

salt, pepper
fresh herbs to taste
4 oz. (½ cup) butter, just melted
2 eggs, beaten

Mix together all the ingredients except the eggs. When blended add the eggs to bind the mixture. A little strained lime or lemon juice or dry white wine may be added to advantage.

BREAD STUFFING

For pigeons.

2 bread rolls
1 cup (1¼) hot milk
1 oz. (2 tablespoons) butter
parsley, finely chopped

2 small mushrooms, chopped
salt, pepper
2 egg yolks, beaten

Slice the rolls, soak them in the milk and when quite soft squeeze dry. Heat the butter, and to it add the parsley, mushrooms, salt, pepper and bread. Simmer 15 minutes. Take from the pan, add the egg yolks and, stirring all the time, continue cooking for 2–3 minutes.

MASHED CHESTNUT STUFFING

This stuffing is sufficient to fill half an average-sized turkey; the other half of it should be filled with a meatier stuffing.

3 lb. chestnuts
1½ cups (2) stock or water
1 bay leaf
a dash salt, pepper
2–3 oz. (4–6 tablespoons) butter

dash sugar
1½ cups (scant 2) soft breadcrumbs
1 egg, well beaten
a little red wine

Score the chestnuts lightly and cook in boiling water for 20 minutes or until the outer and inner skins peel off easily. Put them with the stock, bay leaf, salt and pepper into a pan and cook until they are soft enough to mash. Rub through a sieve, add butter, sugar, breadcrumbs and the egg. Mix well and add enough wine to give flavour to the mixture.

WHOLE CHESTNUT STUFFING

For turkey.

Put 3–4 lb. of cooked and peeled chestnuts into a pan adding a little butter, salt, pepper and enough wine to prevent burning. Cook until the chestnuts are soft but not too broken.

BREADCRUMB STUFFING

For chicken.

1 cup (1¼) breadcrumbs
1 oz. (2 tablespoons) butter
1 small onion, finely chopped
2 teaspoons (2½) finely chopped
   parsley

salt, pepper
2 tablespoons (2½) seedless and
   chopped raisins
milk

Heat the butter, add the onion and cook gently until this is soft. Add the crumbs, parsley, salt and pepper and mix well. Add the raisins, stir well and add enough milk to bind it all. This stuffing should be rather dry.

CELERY STUFFING

For poultry.

1 small head celery
milk or white wine
½ cup (⅔) almonds
butter
1½ cups (2¼) soft breadcrumbs

2 hard-cooked eggs
2 oz. (¼ cup) suet or butter
salt, pepper, nutmeg
1 clove garlic, crushed

Wash and finely chop the celery and cook it in as little milk as possible until tender. Blanch and then roast the almonds in a little butter. Mix with the breadcrumbs. Chop the eggs and suet. Mix all these ingredients together, including the celery and its liquid, for the stuffing should be moist. Add the seasoning, garlic and more liquid if required. Chopped lean ham may also be added.

CHIPOLATA STUFFING

For turkey.

Mix 24 chipolata sausages with a similar quantity of roasted and peeled chestnuts, baby onions (if these are not available, take larger onions and coarsely chop them), some carrots cut into balls the size of small olives, the turkey liver and finely chopped parsley. The quantity of onion and carrots is as required and if the turkey is extra large, use more chipolata sausages.

DUCK STUFFING (British)

1 duck liver and 2 chicken livers
3 tablespoons (3¾) chopped fried
  mushrooms
2 tablespoons (2½) lean bacon,
  finely chopped and lightly fried
1 small onion, blanched and finely
  chopped

1 tablespoon (1¼) finely chopped
  parsley
1 cup (1¼) soft white breadcrumbs
salt, pepper
1–2 eggs, well beaten

Mix the first 7 ingredients together and bind with the eggs. A little brandy may be added as well to moisten the mixture.

EGG STUFFING

This recipe is a modern rendering of a medieval English recipe. The quantity is sufficient for a small chicken.

3 hard-cooked egg yolks
1 good bunch parsley
1 oz. (3 tablespoons) cleaned
  currants

½ teaspoon (⅔) mixed spice
½ oz. (1 tablespoon) butter
1 egg, well beaten

Chop the parsley very finely and thoroughly mix with all the remaining ingredients. Increase quantities for larger birds.

HERB FORCEMEAT

3 cups (3¾) soft breadcrumbs
¾ cup (1) shredded suet
2–3 slices lean bacon or ham, diced
1 tablespoon (1¼) finely chopped
  parsley

mixed herbs to taste, fresh or dried
salt, pepper
2 eggs, well beaten

Mix the breadcrumbs with the suet until thoroughly blended. Add the ham, parsley, mixed herbs, salt and pepper; bind with the eggs.

For the above quantity of breadcrumbs, about 2 tablespoons (2½) of finely chopped fresh herbs or 2 teaspoons (2½) of dried herbs would be good.

STUFFING FOR HARE

This is an adaptation of Meg Dods recipe, reputed author of *The Cook and Housewife's Manual* (1826).

½ lb. stale white bread
port or claret
4 oz. (½ cup) butter or chopped
   beef suet
a little parsley, minced

a little shallot, minced
1 teaspoon (1¼) lemon rind, grated
salt, cayenne pepper
1 anchovy fillet
1 egg yolk, beaten

Grate the bread into crumbs and soak in enough port to thoroughly moisten. Add the butter, parsley, shallot, rind, salt, pepper and anchovy fillet. When thoroughly blended, bind with the egg yolk. If the liver of the hare is in a sound condition, it may be parboiled, chopped and added to the stuffing.

OYSTER FORCEMEAT

1 cup (1¼) soft breadcrumbs
1 oz. (¼ cup) shredded suet
12 fresh prepared or 1 small can
   oysters

salt, pepper
2–3 tablespoons (2½–3¾) cream
2 eggs, well beaten

Mix the breadcrumbs with the suet, then add the liquid from the oysters (whether fresh or canned). Add salt, pepper, cream and the oysters. Mix these ingredients thoroughly and add the beaten eggs. Pour into the top of a double boiler and cook over hot water for 5 minutes. Leave until cold, then use.

FORCEMEAT BALLS

For a hare.

Forcemeat or stuffing is a seasoning for flavouring meat, poultry or game, usually being introduced into the cavity, pocket or crevice in the bird or piece of meat before it is cooked. Where this is not possible, as in the case of jugged hare, the stuffing is made up into small balls, coated with egg and breadcrumbs and fried separately to accompany the dish.

liver, heart and kidneys of hare
1 cup (1¼) soft white breadcrumbs
2 tablespoons (2½) shredded suet
2 tablespoons (2½) chopped parsley
2 tablespoons (2½) minced onion

salt, pepper
2 eggs, well beaten
dry breadcrumbs or flour for
   coating
fat for frying

Lightly cook the liver, heart and kidneys in slightly salted water; drain and finely chop or grind. Add the soft breadcrumbs, suet, parsley and onion and season generously. Bind with half the egg, shape into small balls (6 or 8 according to the size required), roll in the remaining egg and then coat in breadcrumbs or flour. Fry in hot fat until brown all round. Alternatively, the balls may be baked in a hot oven in a little butter or dripping for about 15–20 minutes. In this case, baste them often.

GREEN OLIVE STUFFING (American)

For a 12 lb. turkey.

4 oz. (1 cup) stuffed green olives
4 oz. (½ cup) butter
1 medium-sized onion, chopped
handful celery leaves, chopped
1 small clove garlic, crushed
3–4 sprigs parsley, finely chopped
1 small slice cooked lean ham, diced

1 small sweet pepper, diced
salt, pepper
dash marjoram, ground cloves and
    grated nutmeg
white wine
5 cups (6¼) soft breadcrumbs

Melt the butter in a small pan, add the onion, celery leaves and garlic. Fry over a moderate heat for 5 minutes, stirring well. Take from the stove and add the parsley, ham, sweet pepper, olives, salt, pepper and spices; mix well. Add enough wine to the crumbs to thoroughly moisten them, then squeeze dry and blend into the rest of the ingredients. This stuffing in a lesser quantity can also be used for chicken, duck or goose.

OYSTER STUFFING

A Victorian stuffing for boiled chicken.

12 plump oysters, bearded and
    chopped
¼ lb. (1½ cups) soft breadcrumbs
½ teaspoon (⅔) each salt, black
    pepper and powdered mace
pinch cayenne pepper

2 oz (¼ cup) unsalted butter
rind small lemon grated
1 tablespoon (1¼) finely chopped
    parsley
1 egg yolk, well beaten

Mix the crumbs, salt, black and cayenne peppers and mace. Add the butter, lemon rind and parsley. When this is completely blended, add the oysters and bind with the egg yolk and a little of the oyster liquid.

PRUNES AND FOIE GRAS STUFFING

This quantity is sufficient to stuff a 9–10 lb. goose.

3 lb. prunes
¼ lb. foie gras
1 cup (1¼) white wine
1½ cups (scant 2) strained stock
1 tablespoon (1¼) butter
1 goose liver, finely chopped

2 tablespoons (2½) finely chopped
    shallots or spring (green) onions
½ cup (⅔) port wine
salt, pepper
pinch each ground allspice and dried
    thyme
2–3 tablespoons (2½–3¾) soft bread-
    crumbs

Soak the prunes in warm water or weak tea until soft. Remove the stones and cook the prunes in the wine and stock until they are just tender, 10 to 15 minutes should be enough. Drain them and reserve the liquid. Heat the butter in a shallow pan and sauté the goose liver and the shallots for 2–3 minutes. Turn this mixture into a bowl. Cook the port wine for 3 minutes in the same pan, scraping round the sides of the pan; stir this into the liver mixture. Mix the *foie gras* with salt, pepper, allspice and thyme, and then blend into the ingredients in the bowl. Add enough of the breadcrumbs to make the filling firm but not stiff. Taste for seasoning then stuff this filling into the prunes and reshape them. Stuff the prunes into the goose. The liquid in which the prunes were soaked is added to the pan as basting liquid when roasting the goose.

POTATO STUFFING

For goose.

4 large potatoes	1 small onion, minced
2 oz. (¼ cup) butter	1 goose liver, ground
1 large sprig parsley, finely chopped	1–2 cold fried sausages (optional)
salt, pepper, grated nutmeg, to taste	

Wash and peel the potatoes and cut them into very small pieces. Put these into a pan with the butter, parsley, salt, pepper, nutmeg and onion. Cover closely and cook gently until they are almost cooked, shaking the pan from time to time to prevent sticking. Add the ground liver and continue cooking for 2 minutes. If using the sausages, skin and cut them into small pieces and add with the liver.

RICE STUFFING

For turkey.

Mix thoroughly 1 lb. of cooked long grain rice with some finely chopped fried onions, the turkey liver (chopped), finely chopped walnuts, salt and pepper. Except for the rice, the quantities used in this recipe are as required. I favour a fair quantity of onion and plenty of walnuts, although instead of walnuts, chopped oysters or chopped cooked or canned celery or currants and pine nuts may be used. This is basically a pilau-type stuffing in which the rice is simply a foundation for other flavours.

WILD RICE STUFFING (American)

This stuffing is for game birds and guinea-fowl.

Wild rice is a native of the United States and is found in fresh water and brackish swamps from New England to Texas and North Dakota. Long a staple food of the American Indians, wild rice has been gaining favour as an American delicacy and is now marketed and transported all over the United States. It has many local names, many of which are Indian. In Texas wild rice is known as duck rice, North Carolina calls it 'wild oats', Wisconsin 'fool oats' etc. In general wild rice is cooked as white or brown rice but it takes longer. It is still, even in the United States, an expensive commodity, in England its price makes it almost prohibitive.

1½ cups (scant 2) wild rice
½ cup (⅔) oil
1 large onion, minced
½ cup (⅔) chopped celery
3¼ cups (4) strained stock

½ cup (⅔) chopped button mushrooms
½ cup (⅔) minced sweet pepper
1 tablespoon (1¼) finely chopped
   parsley
salt, pepper

Wash the rice and drain it thoroughly. Heat the oil, add the onion and sauté this until it begins to take on colour, stirring all the while. Add the celery. Stir well, cook for a few minutes, then add the rice. Stir again, add the stock and the remaining ingredients. Mix well, lower the heat and cook for about 30 minutes. This quantity is sufficient for an average-sized turkey.

FRUIT STUFFING

For poultry.

This is a German and Danish stuffing which is simply pared and chopped apples mixed with stoned raisins. Quantities depend on the size of the bird to be stuffed and the proportion of apples to raisins is to taste, although half and half is usual.

To the fruit may be added chopped onions, soft breadcrumbs, salt, pepper, garlic, herbs and spices in proportions which also are entirely to taste.

SAGE AND ONION STUFFING

This quantity will stuff 1 large duck or 2 small ones.

1 teaspoon (1¼) finely chopped
   fresh sage
2 onions, finely chopped
2 oz. (¼ cup) butter

¼ lb. (1½ cups) breadcrumbs
salt, pepper
1 egg yolk, well beaten

Heat the butter, add the onions and simmer them for 30 minutes, stirring from time to time. Take from the pan, mix with the breadcrumbs, sage, salt and pepper and bind with the egg yolk.

TURKEY LIVER AND HEART STUFFING

For turkey.

turkey liver and heart
few slices streaky bacon
6 small onions, coarsely chopped
½ cup (⅔) finely chopped parsley
4 eggs, beaten

5 cups (6¼) white breadcrumbs
¼ teaspoon (⅓) each thyme and
   marjoram
salt, pepper, dash paprika

Chop the liver and heart, bacon, onions and parsley together. Mix with the eggs, breadcrumbs, herbs and seasonings. The stuffing should be of a loose, rather light consistency, so another 1–2 beaten eggs may be added if required.

SAUSAGE AND SWEET POTATO STUFFING

For turkey or large capon.

1 lb. sausage meat
2 medium-sized onions, minced
2 cups (2½) finely chopped
   celery tops
2 cups (2½) stale soft breadcrumbs

3 cups (3¾) hot, mashed sweet potato
3–4 mushrooms, chopped
salt, black pepper
pinch grated nutmeg, thyme and
   ground cloves

Heat a thick pan and fry the sausage meat until lightly browned, breaking it up as it cooks. Take the sausage meat from the pan. In the left-over fat fry the onions and celery tops for a short while. Add the breadcrumbs and sweet potato, mushrooms, salt, pepper and spices. Mix thoroughly, return the sausage meat to the pan, mix well again and reheat. Cool before using.

TRUFFLE STUFFING

For game birds.

6–8 slices truffles, canned or fresh
1 goose liver, chopped

1 tablespoon (1¼) meat glaze (see
   page 243)
brandy and madeira

Mix the first three ingredients, adding brandy and madeira to taste. Failing goose liver, use *foie gras*.

Pies

Pies have been a favourite food in Britain since time immemorial. Children recited ditties to them and poets have written odes to pies. We are not quite sure when children first began to chant 'Simple Simon met a pieman Going to the Fair' or 'Four and twenty blackbirds, Baked in a pie'; or even 'Little Jack Horner sat in a corner, Eating a Christmas pie'; which was most likely a mince pie. In these and other rhymes live the pies of Britain.

Pies probably started as a simple method of wrapping up meat or a bird in a crust of flour and water to retain their flavour and juices. Obviously the pastry although not intended for eating absorbed enough of the juices to become succulent; also in the baking it became crisp, so soon people were eating the pastry as well.

From such simple beginnings there developed the extraordinary medieval pies which were sculptured monuments of pastry. Old writings make mention of pies filled with venison and shaped in the form of a lion; and small ones to look like pheasants, so perfect they appeared to be alive.

The cooks of the Elizabethan and Stuart days went even farther in the development of monstrous pies, and 'surprise pies' were the fashion. Surprise would seem to have been an understatement; some were shocks. The pies, enormous, would let forth a flight of birds when opened, or spew forth frogs, squirrels, even hares and foxes. These creatures scared the ladies who jumped and squealed in fright. Naturally, adds one account, the birds and other animals were not baked in the pies but added afterwards. There is a famous story of a dwarf, Jeffrey Hudson, being thus encased in an immense pie and served to amuse the bored King Charles I and his Queen. The pie was served cold (which one would hope) and the dwarf so amused the Queen she made him her court jester.

Most British and Americans are fond of pies, whether sweet or savoury, and the Americans have made a tradition for themselves with the splendour of their sweet pies. I looked up the origin of the name. The *Shorter Oxford English Dictionary* gives the word as a dish of meat, fowl or fish or vegetables enclosed in or covered with a layer of paste and baked. It also conjectures that the name pie might have come from magpie, the bird sometimes known as a pie which collects miscellaneous objects.

In the United States the word has a wider connotation. *Webster's Dictionary* tells us it is a meat dish baked with a biscuit or pastry crust, or a pastry crust dessert with various fillings, and finally and somewhat curiously for me, a layer cake split horizontally and filled with custard cream or jam.

At the time of Chaucer, hawking pies through the streets was one of London's most important itinerant trades and each district had its favourite 'penny pieman', probably thus nicknamed because he cried: 'Penny pies, all hot, hot, hot'. But these lost their popularity with the introduction of the cookshops. An ordinance of the cooks and pastelers (piemakers) fixed the price to be charged for the 'best capon baked in pastry' at eightpence. In 1578 Stowe, the analyst, wrote of London cookshops: 'the cooks cried hot ribs of beef, pies well baked'. The names of Pudding Lane and Pie Corner are derived from the eating houses so much patronised by the 'gluttonous' Londoners.

With any mention of food, we are fairly certain to find a reference to Samuel Pepys. We know he dined on 5 June, 1662, at noon and did eat among other dishes 'the umbles baked in a pie, and all well done'. He obviously was not concerned with the social status of the umbles pie, which was once given to the huntsmen and beaters while the lord and his household dined on venison pasty or pie.

Blackbirds might well have been a joke, although there are recipes for blackbird pie as well as rook and other country bird pies. Perusing seventeenth-century recipes produced pages of pie recipes, all of which called for vast quantities of ingredients as well as variety in birds. These birds, such as woodcock, swan, pheasant, sea duck, capon and young rooks, were generously flavoured with truffles, mushrooms, pickled bilberries, artichoke bottoms, sweetbreads, hard-cooked eggs etc. Filling corners of the pies were larks, thrushes, ortolans, pigeons and other small birds galore.

Certain areas were renowned for their pies. Cornwall had a reputation for good pies and so did Yorkshire. In the latter county pies with an extra thick crust were made in the eighteenth century, so they could be sent to London and withstand the jolting of the conveyance. Such pies were filled with a boned turkey, stuffed with a boned goose, and into this a boned chicken, finally a hare, pigeon, partridge, quail or other small birds. The filling was so arranged that it looked like one large turkey. It was seasoned with salt, pepper and grated nutmeg and the corners of the pie were filled with boned small birds and, of course, chunks of butter to keep the filling succulent.

The French have their pie tradition, although their passion is more restrained than the British. The original French *pâté de foie gras en terrine* was a pie and not an emasculated *pâté* sold in a can. One famous French pie, called *L'oreiller de la Belle Aurore*, was made in the shape of a pillow and dedicated to Madame Claude-Aurore Recamier. It contained partridges, duck, chicken, half a saddle of hare, veal, pork, truffles, bone marrow and mushrooms. In a modified form it has become one of France's classical pie recipes.

In the nineteenth century Britain became famed for the elegance of its game pies, and they were to be found on the sideboards of every large country house at breakfast. It was not considered then at all odd to eat a pie at breakfast, either in Britain or the United States. When Emerson was once asked whether he minded eating pie for breakfast, he is said to have replied, 'Why not, what are pies made for?'

Today we eat fewer pies and certainly make fewer game pies than in earlier times.

Some people feel that pastry is fattening, but they could of course put aside the crust. There are those (I am not among them) who claim the crust is unimportant. I feel that the pastry which has covered the filling has become succulent and crisp as it has baked and is surely important to the success of any pie.

CHICKEN PIE (A Devonshire dish)

6 servings:

1 large or 2 small chickens	**salt, pepper**
parsley, thyme, marjoram	**grated lemon rind to taste**
½ lb. ham or bacon	**puff pastry, about ¾ lb.**
2 hard-cooked eggs	**1 egg yolk**

Divide the chicken into neat, very small pieces, cut off the legs and wings at the first joint and cook these in water for 1 hour with the back bones, neck and gizzard and a little parsley, thyme and marjoram. Remove the chicken pieces and strain and reserve the stock. Parboil the chicken liver and chop it finely. Cut the ham into small pieces and slice the eggs. Arrange all the chicken pieces, ham and eggs in alternate layers and repeat until the ingredients are finished. Season, add the chopped liver and lemon rind and pour in enough stock to three-quarters fill the dish. Cover with a lid and bake in a slow oven for 3½ hours. Take from the oven and leave until almost cold. Cover with puff pastry, brush with the egg yolk and bake in a hot oven until the pastry is a golden brown. This pie is equally good served hot or cold.

If using ready-cut chicken pieces for the pie and no stock is available, use water or canned chicken stock but put some chopped fresh herbs and lemon amidst the ingredients.

CHICKEN AND MUSHROOM PIE

6 servings:

1 large chicken or its equivalent in pieces	**½ lb. mushrooms (if large, slice thickly)**
½ cup (⅔) olive oil	**6 hard-cooked eggs**
2 large onions, quartered	**½ cup (⅔) white wine**
mixed fresh herbs	**¾ lb. short or puff pastry**
salt, pepper	**1 egg yolk, beaten**
4–6 slices streaky bacon	

Cut the chicken into very small pieces. Heat the oil and in it brown the pieces of chicken. Take these from the pan and drop into another larger pan. Fry the onions in the same oil until lightly browned and add these to the chicken. Add the herbs, salt, pepper, the chicken giblets, neck etc. and sufficient water to cover. Cook gently until the chicken flesh is so tender that it falls off the bone. Trim the bacon, cut each slice into half and fry in the oil. Take from the pan and fry the mushrooms until tender. Take the chicken pieces and onions from the pan. Strain the stock. Cool. Strip off the chicken flesh from the bone. Put a layer of the chicken meat in the bottom of a medium-sized pie-dish and a layer of mushrooms and bacon and repeat these layers until all is finished. Now add the hard-cooked eggs, pushing them well down. Add the white wine and enough of the stock to almost cover the chicken.

Roll out the pastry. Line the edges of the pie-dish with a thin band of pastry and cover the top with the rest. Decorate with leaves and twirls of left-over pastry and brush with egg yolk. Bake in a moderate oven until the pastry is a golden brown. Serve either hot or cold.

STOCK-FOR GAME PIE

In this recipe it is immaterial whether British or American cups are used since the amounts are approximate.

Break up the carcass and the bones of any game bird and put into a pan with 4 or 5 cups of water. Bring to the boil, then skim. Add some vegetables such as peeled and coarsely chopped carrot and turnip and a stick of chopped celery, fresh herbs or a bouquet garni to taste. Bring this to a gentle boil and let it just boil for about 1 hour. Add salt and pepper; skim, strain and use as required.

GUINEA-FOWL PIE

6 servings:

1 plump guinea-fowl	3 slices truffle
butter	game stock
1 goose liver or small can of foie gras	1 lb. short pastry
	armagnac or brandy
4 oz. ($\frac{1}{2}$ cup) pork fat	1 egg yolk, well beaten

Bone the guinea fowl and cut it into portions. Heat a little butter and gently fry the pieces of fowl for about 15 minutes or just long enough to partially cook them. Prepare a stuffing with the goose liver by mashing and then blending it with the pork fat, truffles and a little game stock. Line a pie-dish with short pastry and spread it with the goose liver mixture. Add the pieces of guinea-fowl and moisten them with the armagnac. Cover the top with short crust, seal carefully and brush with the egg yolk. Bake in a moderate oven for 1 to $2\frac{1}{2}$ hours. Turn out the pie and serve with any favourite vegetables and a sauceboat of gravy.

RABBIT PIE - 1

6 servings:

1-2 young rabbits	$\frac{1}{4}$ lb. streaky bacon, sliced
1 onion, sliced	4 hard-cooked eggs, sliced
parsley, chopped	$\frac{3}{4}$ lb. rough puff pastry
salt, pepper	1 egg yolk, beaten

Wash the rabbit(s), dry on a cloth and chop into pieces as small as possible (the butcher will usually do this). Split the head into two and put it into a pan with the rabbit kidney, onion, parsley, salt, pepper and water to cover. Cook slowly for 1 hour, then strain. Place a layer of rabbit pieces in a pie-dish, add salt and pepper, some chopped parsley, a layer of bacon and one of egg and continue this until all the ingredients are used up. Add enough of the rabbit stock to three-quarters fill the pie-dish, cover and bake for 1 hour or until the rabbit is tender. Roll out the pastry. Take the rabbit from the oven and cool it. Put a pie funnel in the centre of the dish. Cover the top of the pie with the pastry. Decorate the top with leaves and whorls of left-over pastry and brush with beaten egg yolk. Cook in a moderately hot oven for about 30 minutes or until the pastry is a golden colour.

For those who do not like the look of rabbit, it is probably better to strip off the flesh from the bone and arrange this in layers. It also makes for simpler eating as the bones are somewhat of a nuisance.

RABBIT PIE – 2

4–5 servings:

There are no set quantities for this country recipe.

Chop 2 tender young rabbits into as many neat joints as possible (see page 177). Lay the pieces in lukewarm water or milk and leave for 1 hour. Drain and dry them. Put the pieces of rabbit into a large pie-dish, the inferior pieces at the bottom. Mix with them some bits of fat bacon. Sprinkle a mixture of salt, pepper and powdered mace (all to taste) over the rabbit. A little minced onion may be added, if liked. Barely cover the rabbit with cold stock or water. Cover with a plate or foil and bake the rabbit in a moderate oven until just tender. Take the pie from the oven and let it cool. When cool, cover it with rough puff pastry in the ordinary way, making a hole in the centre. Decorate it with leaves of left-over pastry, brush with beaten egg yolk and bake in a hot oven until the pastry is a golden brown. Serve the pie either hot or cold.

Some country cooks peel and slice potatoes and lay them in the bottom of the dish before they put in the rabbit.

HARE PIE

8 servings:

1 hare	butter
1 hambone	1 lb. herb forcemeat (see page 220)
savoury herbs	streaky bacon, sliced
grated nutmeg to taste	1 teaspoon ($1\frac{1}{4}$) redcurrant jelly
salt, pepper	$\frac{1}{4}$ cup ($\frac{1}{3}$) port
$\frac{1}{2}$ cup ($\frac{2}{3}$) red wine	1 egg yolk, beaten
$1\frac{1}{2}$ lb. short pastry	

Cut the hare into convenient pieces, chopping off all unnecessary bones. Put these bones with the head, kidneys, heart etc. into a pan with the hambone, herbs, nutmeg, salt, pepper, wine and plenty of water. Bring to a gentle boil, lower the heat and simmer for 2 hours. Make a rich short pastry. Butter a deep pie dish and line it with the pastry, saving sufficient for the cover. Heat enough butter to fry the pieces of hare for 15 minutes. Put them aside to cool. Line the pie-dish with the forcemeat, spreading it over the pastry. Add the pieces of hare in layers with 1 or 2 slices of bacon between each layer. Strain the stock, take 2 cups ($2\frac{1}{2}$) of it, mix it with the redcurrant jelly and port and pour it into the pie-dish. Cover the pie with the remaining pastry, decorate it with the bits of left-over pastry in the form of leaves and brush it with egg yolk. Bake in a moderate oven for 3 hours. If the pastry starts to brown too soon, cover the pie with greaseproof paper.

PIGEON PIE

For those who object to bones, I suggest that the pigeons are parboiled and the flesh stripped off them. In which case, 4 pigeons are better than 3. I also prefer to use home-cooked boiled ham; a small cooked hock does excellently in this pie.

6 servings:

3 pigeons
juice 1 lemon
softened butter
salt, pepper
1 lb. rump steak
flour

$\frac{1}{4}$ lb. ham, sliced
4 hard-boiled eggs, sliced
stock
$\frac{3}{4}$ lb. puff or flaky pastry
1 egg yolk, beaten

Clean the pigeons, cut each in half lengthwise; rub them with lemon juice then with softened butter and sprinkle with salt and pepper. Cut the steak into 12 pieces and toss it in flour. Fill a large pie-dish with layers of steak, pigeon and ham in this order. Arrange slices of hard-cooked eggs over the top. Half fill with the stock. Cover with the pastry. Decorate the top with bits of left-over pastry in the form of leaves and whorls, then brush it with the beaten egg yolk. Bake in the centre of a hot oven for 30 minutes then reduce the heat to fairly hot and continue cooking for a further 20 minutes. Cover with greaseproof paper and continue cooking for another 70 minutes. Serve hot.

ORTOLAN PIE WITH TRUFFLES AND CHAMPAGNE

1 ortolan per person

ortolans
truffles
salt, pepper

champagne
puff pastry

Ortolans should be plucked and cooked undrawn. It is also correct to leave the heads on, but I think for a pie the heads can be removed.

Place a small piece of truffle in the trail of each ortolan. Put the birds into a round or oval earthenware or pottery pie-dish and make sure they fit exactly. Sprinkle lightly with salt and pepper, and just cover with champagne. Roll out enough puff pastry to completely cover the dish. Decorate the top with pastry leaves, prick the pastry here and there to let out the steam and bake in a moderate oven 30–35 minutes.

A YORKSHIRE CHRISTMAS PYE

From 'The Lady's Companion' published in 1753.

'Let the Wall and Bottom of your Pye be a very thick crust; bone a Turkey, a Goose, a Fowl, a Partridge, and a Pigeon, season them all very well, take Half an Ounce of Mace, Half an Ounce of Nutmegs, a Quarter of an Ounce of Cloves, and Half an Ounce of Black Pepper, all beat fine together, two large Spoonfuls of Salt, and then mix them together. Open the Fowls all down the Back, and bone them; first the Pigeon, then the Partridge, then the Fowl, then the Goose, and then the Turkey, which must be large; season them all well first, and lay them in the Crust, so as it will look only like a whole Turkey; then have a Hare ready cased and wiped with a clean Cloth. Cut it to Pieces, that is, joint it; season it, and lay it as close as you can on one Side; on the other Side Woodcock, more Game, and what sort of Wild Fowl you can get. Season them well, and lay them close; put at least four Pounds of Butter into the Pye, then lay on your Lid, which must be a very thick one, and let it be well baked. It must have a very hot Oven, and will take at least four Hours.

'This Pye will take a Bushel of Flour. These Pies are often sent to London in a Box as Presents; therefore the Walls must be well built.'

MOORFOWL PIE

A Victorian recipe, simple, but with no precise list of ingredients. I feel it is best left like this.

'Pick and clean as many moorfowl as you require and truss them as chickens are done for boiling. Take the giblets, heads and necks, put them in a small stew-pan, cover them with boiling water, add salt and Jamaica pepper, or any trimming of meat of any kind, boil it for an hour and strain. Mix some pepper and salt, roll a small bit of butter in it and put a small piece in each bird. Lay them neatly in the dish, with the yolks of three hard-boiled eggs, put in the stock you have strained, add a glass of port wine, cover with puff paste, and bake an hour and a half in a quick oven.'

For making all of these game pies, other than the raised pies, I prefer to use a deep earthenware pie-dish, nowadays back in fashion, and not expensive.

PARTRIDGE PIE

Pigeons may be cooked in the same way.

6 servings:

3 partridges
salt, cayenne pepper
powdered mace
butter
¾ lb. puff or flaky pastry
streaky bacon or ham, sliced

½ lb. veal, thinly sliced
½ lb. mushrooms, chopped
2 tablespoons (2½) finely chopped parsley
1 cup (1¼) stock
egg yolk, lightly beaten

Divide the partridges into halves, sprinkle with salt, cayenne pepper and a little powdered mace. Heat a little butter and fry the pieces of partridge until they are equally and lightly browned all over. Line the sides of a shallow pie-dish with pastry, then with a layer of bacon, then add the partridges, veal, mushrooms and parsley. Add the stock, cover with the remaining pastry, brush with egg yolk and bake for 30 minutes in a hot oven, reduce the heat to moderately hot. Continue baking another 20 minutes, then cover with greaseproof paper and continue cooking for a further 50 minutes.

PILLAR OF RICE (A Suffolk pie)

The ingredients and quantities in this recipe are 'to taste' for it is a method of using up cold game and poultry.

cooked rice, enough to make a high-domed crust for the pie
cooked game, rabbit, pigeon, duck or poultry, all boned, using only the flesh

cold stock or gravy, preferably game or poultry
salt, pepper
breadcrumbs
butter

Fill the pie-dish with whatever cold game and poultry meats available and pour over this just enough well-seasoned cold stock to thoroughly moisten the meat. Bake in a moderate oven until the meat is hot. Cover this with a thick layer of cooked rice, neatly domed. Sprinkle lightly with breadcrumbs and over this dot with slivers of butter. Bake in a hot oven until the top is browned. Serve with peas or sliced green beans.

RAISED PIE

It is essential to work quickly when making a raised pie and, contrary to all other methods of pastry making, keep everything warm. Therefore the utensils and ingredients must be warmed before using and even while shaping, mixing and moulding, the pastry must be kept warm; otherwise it will become brittle and difficult to handle. However, if the pastry is too warm it becomes too soft and not sufficiently stiff to support its own weight when raised. Raised pies are served cold and the contents should be rather solid when cut.

10–12 servings:

2 lb. game meat of any kind, ground
2 lb. (8 cups) plain flour
salt, pepper
8 oz. (1 cup) butter
½ cup (⅔) hot water
2 egg yolks, lightly beaten

½ lb. each veal and fresh pork, ground
12 small mushrooms, peeled and sliced
egg, beaten
stock

Sift the flour into a warm large mixing bowl adding a pinch of salt. Melt the butter in a saucepan, add the water and bring the mixture to the boil. Pour this at once into the flour, add the egg yolks and mix rapidly with a wooden spoon to a firm paste. Knead with the hands (warm) until smooth. Put one-third of this aside, covered and in a warm bowl and in a warm place. As quickly as possible roll out the remainder of the paste and line a high raised-pie mould. Mould it well into the dish, working quickly. Line the bottom with a mixture of some of the veal and pork, add a sprinkling of mushrooms, on top of this a layer of game, then another of veal etc. until the mould is full. Each layer should be well seasoned with salt and pepper. Roll out the paste which was put aside and cover the top of the pie with this. Make a hole in the centre, brush with beaten egg and surround this with a wreath of pastry 'leaves'. Place a pastry rose on the top of the vent and bake in a moderate oven for 3 hours, taking care that the pastry does not become too brown but is a rich fawn colour when done. It can be covered with greaseproof paper. Take it from the oven and leave in the tin until quite cold. When almost cold take off the rose and fill the pie with a very strong stock which will jell when cold. Take care not to add too much or it will go through the pastry. Replace the rose and leave the pie until it is quite cold. Keeping it in the mould prevents the pastry from becoming too hard when filling the pie with stock. To serve take the pie from the mould and garnish with watercress.

This recipe is one of many. More ground veal and pork or even bacon may be added. Strips of tongue or ham and hard-cooked eggs, masked with finely chopped parsley and seasoned with salt and pepper, or the tiniest of button mushrooms, pistachios and truffle, some *foie gras* and cockscombs may be included as may any birds such as larks, quail, ortolans and plovers, all of which help the pie to stand high in its mould.

Game pie was much used as a side dish for wedding breakfasts, balls, suppers and picnics. It is one of the most perfect of pies for game lovers.

GROUSE PIE

When grouse are not obtainable, pigeons may be used instead.

4–6 servings:

2 grouse	**2 onions, chopped**
1 lb. rump steak	**1 cup (1¼) stock made from trim-**
butter	**mings**
salt, pepper	**½ lb. puff or flaky pastry**
½ lb. mushrooms, chopped	**1 egg yolk, lightly beaten**

Thinly slice the steak. Cut the grouse into neat joints. Heat a little butter and lightly fry the pieces of grouse until brown. Line the bottom of a pie-dish with the steak, sprinkle with salt and pepper and cover with the mushrooms and onions, add the pieces of grouse and the stock, then cover with pastry. Decorate the pie with pastry leaves and brush with egg yolk. Bake in a brisk oven for 1 hour. Serve hot. Make the stock from the trimmings of the steak, the grouse, mushrooms and onions.

WOODCOCK PIE – 1

This is a dish, I fear, for only the very lucky sportsman who is able to shoot woodcock, for they are seldom on sale. My recipe is Victorian and I will give it as it came to me.

'Line the edges of a dish with good puff pastry. Put a slice of lean veal well seasoned with pepper, salt and pounded mace at the bottom and on this place a slice of ham. Pluck 4 woodcock carefully so as not to injure the tender flesh. Do not open them but season with salt, pepper and mace and cover them with layers of bacon. Pack closely into the dish and fill up the empty spaces with hard-boiled hens or plovers' eggs. Pour over them a pint of strong beef gravy, so strong that it will jell when cold, and cover the dish with pastry. Brush it with egg, ornament it and place in the centre 2 or 3 of the feet, nicely cleaned. Bake the pie in a well-heated oven until the pastry is done. Time to bake the pie, an hour or more. A woodcock pie is considered a rare delicacy though it is rather an expensive one.'

WOODCOCK PIE—2

This is a slightly more down to earth pie.

In this recipe the pie-dish is lined with bacon, then sliced calves' liver. The prepared woodcock are packed into the centre, breast downwards and then surrounded by ham, forcemeat and seasoned with salt, pepper and finely chopped fresh herbs. This is covered either with thin slices of steak or with more calves' liver and stock or gravy is added and the whole covered with puff pastry. It is baked for an hour or more, the first 20 minutes in a hot oven to let the pastry rise, then in a moderate oven to cook the remaining ingredients. If the pastry seems to be getting too brown, cover with paper. Hard-cooked eggs may also be added to the other ingredients in this pie which can be eaten hot or cold.

Soups

Not all our poultry and game birds or our furred and antlered animals produce flesh fit for roasting or otherwise cooking in the usual ways. Those birds shot well past their first flush of youth could surely find honour and glory as a subtle soup and verily a fitting end. The carcasses and bones of those birds and animals which have been cooked and the best of their flesh consumed, can also be consigned to the stockpot.

Those of our farm-yard birds which are not as tender or as well flavoured as they should be, are best poached, steamed or boiled, and the resultant liquid turned into a soup. The flesh of the bird can be used in several ways, i.e. creamed and filled into *vol-au-vent* cases. The bones can be returned to the broth in which the chicken was cooked and thus fortified. Also the wings, feet and giblets of the birds go toward making rich and succulent soups. It would seem that without either much trouble or expense, most of us could have good poultry stock most of the time.

If a game stock requires clarifying, do this with raw game or rabbit meat. For a white stock (with poultry), put the bones etc., into the stockpot without further ado; but if a darker stock is required, brown the bones first.

When cooking a chicken whole in a stockpot, wrap it first in muslin or cheese-cloth. This makes it easier to bring out and also keeps the shape of the bird.

Chicken Stock or Broth. This can be made either with an aged fowl or from the inferior parts of the bird, i.e., wings, feet, giblets, neck or the carcass or bones of a cooked chicken. If using a carcass, use only enough water to cover; for a whole uncooked bird, use 3–4 pints ($3\frac{3}{4}$–5); for the feet etc., about 4 cups (5).

For an uncooked bird, roast it for 20 minutes before putting it into cold water; this brings out its flavour, and the flesh makes better eating later, if to be used. Add salt and no pepper, but 2 or 3 slices of fresh ginger, a mild onion, 1 stick (no more) of celery. Bring it to a slow boil, then simmer for 2 hours. Take the bird from the pot, strain the stock and leave it to cool and chill overnight. Skim off any fat and use as required. A pork bone can be added to the pot at the same time as the chicken. The Chinese cooks consider pork and chicken are interchangable for this purpose and indeed in all chicken and pork dishes.

TURKEY SOUP – 1

Goose left-overs can be used in the same manner.

1 turkey carcass	celery to taste, chopped
3 quarts (15 cups) water	salt, pepper
2 bay leaves	$\frac{1}{2}$ lb. mushrooms or equivalent
bouquet garni	dried mushrooms
4 tablespoons (5) butter	1 lb. puréed chestnuts
2 tablespoons ($2\frac{1}{2}$) flour	4 tablespoons (5) madeira

Break up the carcass, strip off any remaining meat and put this aside. Put the bones into a pan, add the water, bay leaves and bouquet garni. Bring this to a gentle boil, lower the heat and simmer for 3 hours. Strain. Heat half the butter in the same pan, add the flour and stir this to a light brown *roux*. Gradually stir in 2 quarts (10 cups) of the stock and bring this to the boil, stirring most of the time. Add the celery, salt and pepper and continue cooking for 20 minutes. In the meantime heat the remaining butter and lightly fry the mushrooms; if fresh they should be chopped. Add these to the soup with the chestnut purée and stir well. Dice the bits of turkey meat and drop these into the soup. Let this simmer until required, also add any turkey gravy or dressing available. Just before serving, add the madeira, stir well and serve hot.

TURKEY SOUP – 2

6 servings:

left-over turkey bones	2 tablespoons ($2\frac{1}{2}$) grated carrot
ham and veal bones	2 tablespoons ($2\frac{1}{2}$) tomato or mush-
8 cups (10) water	room ketchup
1 onion, chopped	$\frac{1}{2}$ cup ($\frac{2}{3}$) whipped cream
bunch savoury herbs	parsley, finely chopped

Put the turkey, ham and veal bones into a pan with the water; add the onion and herbs. Bring to a gentle boil, lower the heat and cook gently for 2–3 hours. Strain, cool, then remove the layer of fat from the top. Return the stock to the pan, reheat, add the carrot and the tomato ketchup, stir this well and cook gently for 20 minutes. Just before serving stir in the whipped cream and sprinkle parsley on top of each serving.

CREAM OF GIBLET SOUP

8–10 servings:

4 chicken giblets	2 quarts (10 cups) boiling water
2 oz. ($\frac{1}{4}$ cup) butter	a little fresh thyme
1 medium-sized onion, finely	salt, pepper
chopped	3 hard-cooked eggs, coarsely
1 each carrot and turnip, chopped	chopped
2 tablespoons ($2\frac{1}{2}$) flour	croûtons or fingers of hot toast

Wash the giblets quickly but thoroughly in cold water. Pat them dry. Heat half the butter in a pan, add the onion, carrot, turnip and cook until tender, stirring often. Add the giblets (not the livers), cook these for 3–4 minutes then sprinkle with half the flour. Stir thoroughly until blended. Add the water and thyme and bring to the boil, lower the heat and continue cooking gently for 2 hours or until the giblets are quite tender. Strain the soup and let it become quite cold. Skim off all the fat. Return the soup to the pan. Rub the chicken livers through a fine sieve and add to the soup. Heat the remaining butter in a small pan, add the remaining flour and cook this to a brown *roux*. Stir it into the soup. Bring to boiling point, add salt and pepper, stir and add the eggs. Serve with croûtons or toast. Instead of the full quantity of water, half and half chicken stock and water may be used.

CHICKEN SOUP (Malaysian)

6–8 servings:

1 small chicken or chicken pieces	garnish:
1 medium-sized onion, coarsely chopped	1–2 hard-cooked eggs, sliced shredded carrot
2 cloves garlic, chopped	leeks or spring (green) onions,
salt, pepper	thinly sliced
a small piece fresh ginger, minced	paprika
$\frac{1}{4}$ teaspoon ($\frac{1}{3}$) chilli powder	game chips (see page 206)
1 tablespoon ($1\frac{1}{4}$) soy sauce	

Put the chicken into a large pan with 8 cups (10) of cold water and add the onion, garlic, salt, pepper, ginger and chilli powder. Cook over a moderate heat until the chicken is tender. Take the chicken from the pan, strip the flesh from the bones and cut it into thin strips, almost shredding it. Strain the stock, return it to the pan, add the soy sauce and reheat. To serve the soup first put some shredded chicken into each bowl, add the garnishes, except the game chips, a little in each plate. Pour the boiling soup over the top, add the chips and serve at once.

DUCK SOUP

8–10 servings:

1–2 duck carcasses and any odd pieces of duck meat	salt
celery to taste, chopped	6 peppercorns
2–3 onions, coarsely chopped	1 good sprig parsley, coarsely chopped
1–2 cloves garlic	$\frac{1}{2}$ lb. mushrooms, peeled and
1 bay leaf	chopped
2–3 carrots, coarsely chopped	sherry or madeira

Put all the ingredients, except the mushrooms and sherry, into a large pan with plenty of water; bring to the boil, lower the heat and simmer for 3 hours. Strain, cool and chill overnight in a refrigerator. The next day scrape off the fat from the soup. Pour the stock into a pan, add the mushrooms and cook these until tender. Serve the soup very hot flavoured with sherry or madeira, and, when in season, add watercress as a garnish. Instead of mushrooms, the soup may be garnished with small cooked turnip balls or flavoured with white wine instead of sherry or madeira.

GAME STOCK

6 servings:

1 old pheasant or 2 old partridges
2 oz. ($\frac{1}{4}$ cup) butter
3–4 mushrooms, sliced
1 each onion and carrot, chopped
1 stick celery, chopped

6 pints (7$\frac{1}{2}$) white stock or water
salt
12 peppercorns
bouquet garni

Draw and clean the birds (if not already prepared) and cut into pieces. Heat the butter in a pan, add the pieces of bird and the vegetables and simmer covered for about 20 minutes. Add the liquid, let this come to the boil, lower the heat, skim well, add salt, peppercorns and the bouquet garni. Let this simmer for about 3 hours; strain well, remove all fat and set aside for use.

A good stock can also be made by using the carcass of any cooked game and odd bits of the flesh.

GAME SOUP

6 servings:

bones from any game
8 cups (10) water or stock
1 onion, chopped
1 turnip, chopped
1–2 sticks celery, chopped

2 slices bacon, chopped
$\frac{1}{2}$ cup ($\frac{2}{3}$) red wine or dark beer
$\frac{1}{4}$ cup ($\frac{1}{3}$) tomato juice
salt, pepper

Break up the bones and bake them in a dry pan in a moderate oven until they are brown. Place them in a large pan, add the remaining ingredients, bring to a gentle boil and simmer for 3 hours. Correct the seasoning and strain.

The above ingredients are approximate, more liquid may be used, depending on how many bones there are.

CLEAR GAME SOUP

There are no set quantities for this recipe.

remains of any game
1 each onion, carrot and turnip
2–3 cloves
1–2 bay leaves

a little mace
salt, pepper
small quantity raw meat

Put all the ingredients except the raw meat into a pot and cover with plenty of stock or water or a combination of both. Bring gently to the boil, lower the heat and simmer for 2 hours. Strain and return to the pan. Bring again to the boil, add the raw meat and boil up again. Only an ounce or so of the meat is required for claryifying. Strain through a cloth. If the soup is not sufficiently clear, repeat the clarifying process, i.e. boiling it up with raw meat. The soup may be flavoured with sherry or madeira after being clarified.

Garnish with croûtons or with thin strips of omelette or game royale (see page 241).

GAME SOUP WITH BURGUNDY

8–10 servings:

1 **elderly wild duck or pheasant**	2 **quarts (10 cups) chicken stock or**
flour	**water**
4 **oz. ($\frac{1}{2}$ cup) unsalted butter**	1 **cup (1$\frac{1}{4}$) cooked rice**
2 **onions, chopped**	2 **cups (2$\frac{1}{2}$) red burgundy**
1–2 **cloves garlic**	1 **lb. small mushrooms, sliced**
carrot and celery to taste, chopped	**salt, pepper**
	marjoram, thyme and basil, to taste

Cut the duck into small pieces and lightly roll these in flour. Heat the butter and fry the meat until brown adding at the same time the onions, garlic, carrot and celery. When all these ingredients are just browned add the chicken stock and rice. Stir and cook gently for 15 minutes. Add the burgundy, mushrooms, salt, pepper and herbs, bring to a gentle boil and cook until the meat is tender. Take the pieces of duck from the pan, cool and pull off all the meat from the bones. Cut it into shreds. Rub the soup through a sieve and return it to the pan. Add the shredded meat and reheat. Serve hot with croûtons. If fresh mushrooms are not available, either omit or use dried.

HUNTER'S SOUP (Polish)

6–8 servings:

2 **lb. small game birds or 1 lb.**	1 **bay leaf**
venison meat, rabbit or forepaws	**peppercorns and salt**
of a hare or a mixture of all	1 **tablespoon (1$\frac{1}{4}$) flour**
3 **oz. (6 tablespoons) butter**	1 **cup (1$\frac{1}{4}$) dry white wine**
1 **large onion, finely chopped**	2 **egg yolks**
1 **each carrot, parsnip and leek**	1 **cup (1$\frac{1}{4}$) cream**
1 **small head celery**	

Cut whatever meat is being used into small pieces. Heat two-thirds of the butter, add the onion and the pieces of meat and fry these until lightly browned. In the meantime wash, trim and dice the vegetables; add these to the pan with the bay leaf, peppercorns and salt. Continue gently frying until the meat is tender, adding a very little water to prevent burning. Take the meat from the pan, cool and put through a liquidizer or meat grinder. Return the bones to the pan, add 8 cups (10) of water and continue cooking over a low heat for another hour. Strain and mix the stock with the ground meat. Return this to the heat and bring slowly to the boil. Mix the flour with the remaining butter to a paste and gradually dilute this with some of the stock, stirring all the time. Add the wine, pour this mixture into the hot soup and bring it to the boil, still stirring. Beat the egg yolks, add these to the cream, thoroughly blend and then slowly pour it into the hot soup, not allowing the soup to boil and stirring all the time to prevent curdling. Serve with croûtons.

STEAMED PIGEON SOUP (Chinese)

4–6 servings:

2–4 pigeons
4 dried Chinese mushrooms
1 lb. winter melon or marrow
small piece fresh ginger, sliced

2 tablespoons (2½) Chinese wine
1 tablespoon (1¼) light soy sauce
salt
a little cooked ham, cut into strips

Soak the mushrooms for 30 minutes and slice thinly. Pare the winter melon and cut the flesh into rounds or cubes. Split the pigeons open along the backbone. Place the pigeons and the winter melon in a large pan. Add the mushrooms, ginger, wine, soy, salt and water to cover well. Simmer for 2½–3 hours. Remove the pigeons, pull the flesh from the bones and return it to the pan. Serve with the ham as a garnish.

The flavour of this soup is extremely delicate. Failing Chinese wine, use a fine dry sherry.

VENISON SOUP

8–10 servings:

2 lb. stewing venison
1 lb. venison scraps
3–4 sticks celery
2–3 sprigs parsley
2 each carrots and onions

1 clove garlic
1 teaspoon (1¼) salt
6 peppercorns
6 pints (7½) water

Put all these ingredients into a large pan, bring to the boil, lower the heat and simmer for 3–4 hours, by which time the liquid will be reduced by two-thirds. Skim off as much fat as possible and pour the soup first through a fine sieve and then through a cheese-cloth. Cool and chill. Skim off the layer of fat which will have formed on the top and return the soup to the pan. Reheat to serve.

This soup may be flavoured with sherry or madeira and garnished with croûtons.

GAME ROYALE

Garnish for a clear soup.

2 oz. (¼ cup) cooked game
1½ teaspoons (scant 2) demi-glaze
3 tablespoons (3¾) clear meat or
    game stock

2 egg yolks and 1 whole egg, lightly
    beaten
1 teaspoon (1¼) flour
salt

Pound the meat to a fine pulp, add to this the demi-glaze and clear stock. Add the eggs, flour and salt and beat until smooth. Pour this mixture into a buttered mould and cook in a double boiler about 45 minutes or until set. Allow it to become very cold then cut into fancy shapes.

If demi-glaze is not available, use a little meat extract or glaze (see page 244), or a little brandy. It is simply to add flavour to a good but somewhat bland garnish.

GROUSE SOUP

There comes a time in the year when elderly grouse are cheap but fit only for making into soup.

8 servings:

2 grouse	1–2 onions, sliced
2 carrots, sliced	2 quarts (10 cups) cold water
1 small head celery, chopped	salt, peppercorns
sweet fresh herbs, if available	1 lump sugar

The birds should be thoroughly cleaned, drawn and jointed. Put all the pieces into a large pan, add the remaining ingredients, except the sugar, bring to a gentle boil then lower the heat and simmer for 2 hours. Leave until the next day, preferably in an earthenware bowl in a cold place. Skim off all surplus fat and strain the stock through muslin. Bring the soup to the boil, test for seasoning, add more salt if required and the sugar. A small glass of claret will not come amiss in this soup.

HARE SOUP

8 servings:

hare giblets and left-over pieces of uncooked hare	12 peppercorns
	1 blade mace
$\frac{1}{2}$ lb. lean bacon	bouquet garni
4 oz. ($\frac{1}{2}$ cup) butter	2 quarts (10 cups) stock
2 onions, peeled and coarsely chopped	2 oz. ($\frac{1}{2}$ cup) flour
	1 cup ($1\frac{1}{4}$) port wine
4 shallots, peeled	salt

Dice the bacon. Heat half the butter, add the hare and bacon and fry until a light brown. Add the onions, shallots, peppercorns, mace, bouquet garni and finally the stock. Bring gently to the boil, lower the heat and simmer for 3 hours. Skim often during cooking. Strain. Heat the remaining butter in another pan, add the flour and stir to a *roux*. Add the strained stock, stir until it comes to the boil, add the port and salt and simmer for a further 20 minutes. In the meantime dice any of the edible meat and return it to the soup. Serve hot.

Miscellaneous

ASPIC JELLY – from gelatine

Powdered gelatines vary considerably in quality and strength so carefully check any instructions which are given with the gelatine being used.

2 egg whites and 2 egg shells
1 lemon
4 cups (5) strained stock
1½ envelopes gelatine
¼ cup (⅓) tarragon vinegar

2–3 sticks celery
chervil and tarragon to taste
10 peppercorns
1 teaspoon (1¼) salt

Whisk the egg whites slightly and wash the shells. Peel the lemon rind as thinly as possible, squeeze the lemon and strain the juice. Put all the ingredients into a pan, whisk over the heat until boiling, then simmer very gently for about 20 minutes. (If the stock has already once naturally jellied, use less gelatine.) Skim off the thick layer of froth which forms and discard the lemon rind, egg shells, celery and herbs. Strain through a jelly bag or fine cloth and let it drip slowly into a bowl. If it is still not sufficiently clear, strain again through a fine cloth.

This aspic is used mainly for lining and garnishing moulds. If too stiff it may be diluted with a little water, sherry or brandy when additional flavour is desired. If stock is not available, use instead 2 veal or chicken bouillon cubes; crumble these into the other ingredients and add 1 each onion and carrot to the pan.

MEAT GLAZE-1

This is made by boiling down stock until it is so reduced that it becomes a hard jelly when it is cold. As much as 5 pints (12½ cups) of stock will reduce to 1½ cups (2) of glaze. It can be stored. One teaspoon (1¼) stirred into a sauce or a soup will give a boost of flavour which it might otherwise lack. A meat glaze dissolved in water may be used instead of stock. It is useful to have in the larder and is of a finer flavour than commercial meat extracts or bouillon cubes.

Strain 4 pints (10 cups) of stock and make sure it is free from grease or fat. Bring it to the boil in a pan, then lower the heat and simmer until it has reduced by half. Strain it through a fine sieve into another pan and continue cooking until it is reduced to a syrup which thinly coats the spoon. Watch it carefully at this stage to make sure it does not burn. Strain into a jar. When it is cold and has become a jelly, cover and put into a refrigerator. It can also be deep frozen.

A meat glaze will keep for weeks in the refrigerator. Should it develop a few spots of mould, take it from the jar, gently skim off the mould, then simmer the glaze, adding a spoonful of water, until it is again reduced to a thick syrup.

MEAT GLAZE – 2 (Quick method)

Instead of using gravy a good strained stock flavoured with meat extract may be used.

½ cup (⅔) thick meat gravy salt
1 teaspoon (1¼) gelatine

Take the gravy from the pan in which meat or game has been roasted. Skim off surplus fat. Dissolve the gelatine in 1 tablespoon (1¼) water. Stir over steam (in the top of a double boiler) until the gelatine is thoroughly dissolved. Stir this into the gravy and add salt if required.

GAME GRAVY

This makes about 1 cup (1¼) of gravy.

1 oz. (2 tablespoons) unsalted salt, cayenne pepper to taste
    butter pinch powdered mace
1 tablespoon (1¼) flour 1 tablespoon (1¼) lemon juice
1 cup (1¼) strained giblet stock ½ cup (⅔) sherry
½ teaspoon (⅔) prepared mustard

Heat the butter, stir in the flour and mix to a *roux*. Gradually add the stock, seasoning, mace and lemon juice. Stir well and cook over a moderate heat for 20 minutes. Add the sherry, stir and serve the gravy hot in a gravy boat.

POULTRY OR GAME IN ASPIC

For this recipe any type of cold, cooked poultry or game meat may be used, all of one kind or mixed.

8–10 servings:

1–2 lb. cooked cold poultry or garnish:
    game meat black or green grapes, stoned and
2 tablespoons (2 envelopes)   halved
    gelatine green or black olives, sliced
4 cups (5) clear stock truffles, chopped
salt, pepper

To make the aspic dissolve the gelatine in the stock, strain through a cloth, taste for seasoning then cool until it begins to thicken. Slice the meat, pull off the skin and arrange the pieces on a tray. Brush each piece with the aspic, top with a little garnish and cover this with aspic. Let this set in a cool place, then add a little more aspic a small spoonful at a time until the required quantity of aspic is reached. Leave the tray in a cold place until the aspic sets completely. Pour the remaining aspic into a shallow bowl and let this set. When ready to serve, cut the plain aspic into dice. Carefully take the pieces of aspic-covered meat from the tray and arrange them on a serving platter, garnish with the diced aspic and with any remaining garnish, sliced cucumber and tomatoes, watercress or chopped lettuce, more grapes and olives; it is all a matter of personal taste. What is important is that the stock must be perfectly clear to make aspic.

FUMET OF GAME

A *fumet* is the name given to a number of different liquids used to give flavour or body to both stocks and sauces.

1 game carcass, chopped	1 bay leaf
1 oz. (2 tablespoons) butter	1 sprig thyme
2 slices bacon, diced	$\frac{1}{2}$ cup ($\frac{2}{3}$) white wine
1 small onion, sliced	4 cups (5) stock
1 very small carrot, sliced	

Put the butter into a pan; when it is melted add the carcass and the bacon. Fry these together for a few minutes then add the vegetables and herbs. Fry for a further few minutes, add the wine and cook for 10 minutes. Stir in the stock, cook for 30 minutes, skim well and strain.

POTTED GROUSE, PIGEONS, PARTRIDGES, WOODCOCK ETC.

This is based on an early eighteenth-century Worcestershire recipe.

Servings according to the quantity of game used :

game	salt, pepper
cloves, mace, nutmeg	butter

Clean the chosen birds thoroughly and wipe them dry. Season them well inside and out with the spices, salt and pepper. Put them breast downwards into an earthenware jar, cover them well with butter, closely cover the jar so that it is airtight and bake them in a slow oven for an hour or more, according to their age. Lift them from the jar and drain well. Let the butter get cold then scrape it from the thick sediment which will be found underneath. Bring the butter again to the boil, strain and use it to cover the game. Cut all the meat from the bones while still warm, keeping the meat pieces as large as possible, i.e. fillets. Place these closely together either into a potting dish or a pie dish, packing the pieces in layers. Over each layer pour a very little of the boiled butter, but be quite sure that no gravy is added. Press the layers down well. When everything is cold cover with the remaining boiled butter. The potted game will keep for a month or more in a cold dry place. When required for use, scrape all the butter off the top, stand the dish for a few seconds in hot water but not too long and the potted meat will turn out whole in the shape of the dish and can be cut across in slices. The butter left over can be put aside until some is required for basting meat or game in some other form.

POTTED GAME

This can be prepared with hare, grouse, partridge, pigeon or with rabbit combined with any of these ingredients.

1 lb. cooked hare meat without bones
salt, black pepper

cayenne pepper, mace
12 oz. (1½ cups) butter

Pound the meat well and season it with salt, black pepper, cayenne and a very little mace (ground cloves or allspice may be used instead). Clarify the butter (see page 205), combine most of this with the pounded hare and fill into small pots. When quite cold, add a little more clarified butter to cover and again leave until cold. The potted hare can be served in its little pots or turned out and sliced.

Serve with toast and butter or with a green salad, tomatoes and cucumber.

Instead of pounding the meat it may be put into a liquidizer (blender) or passed through a mouli grater.

EGGS

Before the domesticity of the hen, when eggs laid by wild birds were among the first foods of man, primitive man saw eggs as symbols of fertility. He believed that the universe was born from the Great World or Mother Egg.

Eggs are one of the most useful of the staple foods since they form a complete food in themselves, and no other food product has such wide and varied uses. They are a valuable source of vitamins A and B, also a fair quantity of D. They are low in calories and can be used at almost any meal.

It is often believed that the brown egg is fresher and finer flavoured than the white. This is not so. They may look prettier, but the colour of the shell outside bears no relation to the egg inside, nor even any fixed relation to the chicken species which laid it. In other words, the shell colour is no criterion of quality.

The colour of the yolk, however, is determined by the hen's diet. A hen fed with plenty of green stuff will produce eggs with a darkish yellow yolk, while one fed with castor oil in its diet, offers us a pale yellow yolk rich in vitamin A. For a good egg, the yolk should be well centred in the white and in a nicely rounded form. The membrane surrounding it should be firm and not break too easily.

Among the more general edible eggs are the following:

Bantam Eggs. These eggs are small with a thin shell and make an 'elegant decoration for a salad', according to Miss Eliza Acton, Mrs Beeton's famous rival. They take 6 minutes to hard-cook, 2½ to 3 minutes to poach.

Duck Eggs. These are somewhat oilier than hen eggs and have received rather short shrift from many culinary writers. When using duck eggs, care must be taken to see they are thoroughly cooked since they are more likely to be infected with bacteria due to their being laid in damp conditions which are not always clean. They are not recommended for light boiling or poaching, but can be used for hard-cooking and in general cooking. Cakes made with duck eggs are often lighter than those made with hen eggs.

Emu Eggs. These are used in Australia. Before using, it is advisable to break the egg into a bowl and leave it for several hours, overnight if preferred. Skim off the layer of oil which forms on the top like a thin skin. An excellent omelette can be made with 3 tablespoons ($3\frac{3}{4}$) of emu egg, beaten well with a pinch of salt, 1 tablespoon ($1\frac{1}{4}$) flour, and 2 tablespoons ($2\frac{1}{2}$) cream.

Guinea-fowl Eggs. Small and prettily-shaped eggs usually a pale or deep fawn colour. They are much esteemed by connoisseurs as they are rich and make excellent eating. They used to be served quite often instead of plover eggs, hard-cooked and sent to the table in the typical bed of moss, as were plover eggs. They can also be poached; for this allow 2–3 minutes.

Ostrich Eggs. These are used in some country districts of South Africa; each one is equal to about 24 hen eggs. The best way to reach the contents is to bore a hole at each end. The white and yolk can be shaken out into a bowl but must be used within 24 hours. Ostrich eggs are rich and if used in place of hen eggs, a little milk or water should be added in the proportion of 1 tablespoon ($1\frac{1}{4}$) to 4 tablespoons (5) of beaten egg. Two tablespoons ($2\frac{1}{2}$) of this equals 1 hen egg.

Penguin Eggs. These should be hard-cooked. The white becomes hard but remains translucent. They have a strong fishy flavour and are usually mashed with anchovy to disguise this. They need boiling for 30 minutes.

Plover Eggs. These used to be a great April delicacy in Britain, and were a joy to which gastronomes looked forward. It is, however, legally forbidden to take the eggs from the nest.

If you live in the country, you may still 'find' plovers' eggs and enjoy them, although you may neither sell them nor buy them. They need barely five minutes simmering in all-but-boiling water to be sufficiently hard-boiled.

If you have no facility for gathering plovers' eggs yourself, you must needs be content with gulls' eggs, similar in shape but a little larger than the plovers', and also slightly greener or bluer in colour.

Traditionally plovers' eggs are served hard-cooked and arranged as they are laid, in a rosette, points to the middle, in a nest of moss.

Quail Eggs. These are slightly smaller than plover eggs and a great delicacy, with a velvety creaminess. They are usually served hard-cooked and should be put into cold water and cooked gently for 20 minutes. Some people like to faintly colour them with beetroot juice and serve them with a bowl of green and black olives, mixed to be served with cocktails or hors d'oeuvre.

Seagull Eggs. Still a seasonal industry in some areas, but nothing like the days long ago when they were collected from the cliff face and lowered in baskets to waiting boats. They have a fishy flavour and at one time were served after a dish of herrings to help disguise their flavour. However, mashed with bloater or anchovy paste, and spread on toast they can be pleasant eating.

Swan Eggs. These are much more delicate than either their size or the tendency of the swan to eat fish, might imply. They are usually hard-cooked and the white remains transparent. They take 20 minutes to boil and should be turned a couple of times while cooking. Swan eggs can be poached; allow 5 minutes cooking time.

Turkey Eggs. These are large but delicate in flavour, and can be used in any of the many ways of cooking eggs, i.e. for breakfast, in cakes, puddings and especially for making sauces. For poaching turkey eggs, allow 4 minutes for soft boiling and 6 minutes to obtain a firm white.

Glossary

BAMBOO PARTRIDGE. A name given somewhat haphazardly to a species of small game birds, native to Asia. They are also called Chinese partridge and can be prepared in the manner as pigeons.

BARD, TO. To bard is to cover the breasts of poultry, game birds and other type of game with thin strips of streaky bacon or larding. It is especially necessary when roasting small dry birds such as snipe, woodcock, quail etc., which need to be roasted in a hot oven in the least possible time. This process gives extra succulence to the flesh and obviates the continuous basting which would otherwise be required. The slices of bacon usually completely enclose the small birds and when vine leaves are also used the bacon or larding covers these.

BARNACLE GOOSE. A medium-sized wild goose, a bird of passage, allied to the brent or brant which breeds in Greenland, Spitsbergen and Russia but which is a common winter visitor to Europe. It is white-faced with a lavender-grey body streaked with black and white, and legend has it that this goose was born from barnacles adhering to trees reached by the sea at high tide. Feeding extensively on marine life, the flesh of this bird is edible but has a somewhat fishy flavour and is not very digestible. It is popular for the table when obtainable and is prepared in the same manner as for grey lag goose.

BILBERRY. Also called blueberry, huckleberry and whortleberry. A dark blue berry slightly bitter-sweet with a tender skin and just enough tart flavour to give distinction to the fruit. They grow on a small shrub in somewhat cold climes. Apart from being sold fresh, they are marketed in tins and bottles as well as being frozen. They can be made into an excellent sauce for game dishes.

BONE, TO. To strip meat from the bones of a bird or animal without destroying its shape more than is absolutely necessary. Boning a bird is an art and time consuming. It can be done (see page 20) but it is the job for a professional and the best way to learn it is to persuade a professional to let you watch him at work.

BOUQUET GARNI. The classic bouquet garni consists of 3 sprigs of parsley, 1 of thyme and a bay leaf tied together. The thyme and the bay leaf should be in the middle of the bunch, the parsley protecting the smaller leaves. Marjoram is sometimes added to a bouquet garni. This method of adding herbs to any dish is excellent as they do not float in small particles among the other ingredients, yet they impart a subtle flavour to the food being cooked. They may be tied up in a piece of muslin. The English equivalent is faggot but the word has gone out of fashion.

BRAISE, TO. This means to cook food, i.e. poultry, fish, meat or vegetables, on a bed of fried root vegetables, called in French a *mirepoix*, with just enough liquid, usually stock or water, to barely cover the *mirepoix*. The result is a combination of stewing, steaming and pot roasting. From time to time the food being braised must be basted in its own liquid. The pan must be kept covered all the time. Usually the meat or poultry to be braised is first browned in fat and sometimes under a hot grill (broiler). The juices from the braising pan are used when serving the dish, either as it is or thickened with a *roux* or *beurre manié*. The *mirepoix* vegetables although somewhat over-cooked and often brown can be served as a garnish as their flavour is excellent. Failing this, they can be puréed and made into a soup or thick sauce. Braising is usually applied to tough poultry and game or cuts of meats.

BREAD, TO. This means to coat food with a layer of breadcrumbs. Usually one cup (1¼) of crumbs will be required to coat 1 lb. of meat or fish.

BROTH. The liquid in which poultry, game, meat and vegetables have been cooked.

BROWN, TO. In culinary parlance this means to heat butter or other fat until hot and to cook whatever food is required in this until brown.

BRUSH TURKEY. Also known as the scrub turkey, this large gallinaceous bird inhabits wooded areas of eastern Australia. It is not in fact a turkey, belonging to the Megapodiidae, but it is roasted in exactly the same way.

BRUSH WITH BUTTER. Melt the butter and then stroke it over the food as required with a brush. Other fat can be so used.

BUTTER, TO, or GREASE. This is to rub a pan with softened butter to keep food from sticking.

CHASSEUR, À LA. The French culinary term for game or poultry cooked in white wine with mushrooms and shallots.

CHOP, TO. To cut into very small pieces.

COLONIAL GOOSE. Not a goose at all but an Australian way of stuffing and roasting a leg of mutton. Formerly the meat was roasted in a camp oven which, it was claimed, possessed the virtue of making any mutton as tender as lamb.

COOK UNTIL TENDER. A term employed by cookery writers to accommodate the vagaries of cooking. Different cooking utensils, fuels, temperatures, age and size of the food being cooked, all make an absolute definition impossible. What we are saying is, timings are average; take care and test from time to time as a double check. Poultry is 'done' (see this section) when the joints move easily and the juices run freely.

COVER, TO. Water to cover means to just submerge the food being cooked. This amount varies according to the size of the pan and the shape of the food under discussion etc.

CROÛTONS. These are small cubes of bread which have been browned by frying in fat or baking. They can be prepared in advance, stored in a closed tin and thus kept in a cool place for at least 2 weeks.

DEEP FAT. Enough fat, when melted, to completely submerge the food to be fried in it.

DEVIL, TO. This means to apply a highly seasoned paste to meat, fish or poultry before grilling or frying. Sometimes the paste is applied directly, and other times mixed with breadcrumbs. It is particularly good with poultry, and at one time devilled turkey and chicken bones were a regular feature of household cooking as well as appearing on restaurant menus. The French culinary term is *diable*.

DICE, TO. To chop into very small cubes.

DRAIN, TO. To place fried food on absorbent paper. The fat drains off on to the paper.

DRAW, TO. To remove the innards and fatty deposits from the inside of a bird.

DRESSED WEIGHT. When referring to poultry, this is the weight after the bird has been plucked but before it has been drawn etc.

DRESS, TO. In poultry and game it means plucking, singeing and cleaning the birds before trussing. Nowadays dressing is usually done by the poulterer.

DRIPPINGS. These are the fats and juices which excude from poultry and game while cooking.

DRUMSTICK. The lower portion of a bird's leg.

DUCK PRESS. A device used to extract the juices from duck carcasses.

FAISANDAGE. Derived from *faisan*, pheasant, this is the French term for red meat which is high or gamey.

FLAMBER. 1. This means to remove hairs from poultry and game by singeing.
   2. To set warmed alcohol alight and, while it is still flaming, pour it over food. The alcohol burns out but its flavour remains, enhanced by the slight singeing.
   Only good quality alcohol will ignite properly.

FOWL. In present-day usage, an edible bird, more particularly applied to a chicken which is suitable only for boiling or steaming.

FROTHING. A very old practice of dredging roast meats or poultry with flour and salt just before taking them from the oven and then applying a fierce heat to the bird or roast so that it appears encased in a crisp froth. This is seldom done today in British or American cooking, but one frequently finds such instructions in Continental cookery books as well as in old British ones.

GALANTINE. This was originally a cold preparation of boned, stuffed and pressed chicken served in its own jelly. Nowadays galantines are made from young turkey, guinea-fowl, Nantes duckling, pigeon and game birds such as pheasant, partridge and grouse, in addition to the original chicken. Veal and fish are also prepared in this way.

The term galantine by itself implies galantine of poultry; if meat or fish are used this must be indicated.

GAME. Under this designation are all wild animals and birds (other than domestic) which are used for human consumption.

GAME SHEARS. Extra strong shears or scissors designed to cut through bone and used to divide fowl, and more particularly game, into halves or small portions.

GARNISH, TO. To decorate, more or less as one chooses, although the best garnishes add flavour as well as decoration to a dish.

GIBLETS. The edible entrails of poultry and game, namely the heart, liver, gizzard, neck and on occasion the feet, which are stewed separately to provide stock for gravy or soup. It is important to remove the gall bladder if it is still attached to the liver and to ensure that it remains unbroken or the giblets will be discoloured and given an unpleasant flavour by the bitter gall juice. Livers may be used as stuffing and for *pâtés* and other savouries, among them an Italian polenta dish which is served with chicken livers.

GLAZE, TO. This means to make glossy, i.e. by coating with aspic, a glaze chaudfroid sauce etc.

HANG, TO. To suspend game by its feet or a bird by the head in a cool place for several days before it is plucked, skinned, drawn etc. See HANGING (page 95).

HEATHCOCK. The male of the black grouse, also called, in Devon, heathpoult.

HOOSIER. Indiana is the Hoosier State and hoosier fried chicken is chicken jointed, browned in hot fat and then simmered at a lower heat, covered, for about 20 minutes. They are then given a final 10 minutes, uncovered, on raised heat to re-crisp them. There are many regional variations both in cooking and serving.

HOWTOWDIE. Scots for pullet, possibly related to the old French *hutadeau*. 'Stoved howtowdie with drappig eggs' is a stuffed chicken pot-roasted with button onions, herbs and spices. Eggs are poached in gravy or broth and placed around the bird on the carving dish, each on a bed of spinach.

JUG. A game stew, especially of hare (see page 168).

JULIENNE. To cut food, usually vegetables, into thin sticks the size of kitchen matches.

JUNGLE FOWL. The popular name of more than one species of those birds from which our domestic fowl is supposed to be descended.

JUNIPER. There are several species of juniper but the berries which are used in flavouring are blue and grow on a waist-high bush found over the entire northern hemisphere. The berries vary in flavour, those growing in the Mediterranean areas having more flavour than those found in the north. The berries are used to flavour gins and other spirits; and, in the kitchen, are added to marinades, stews, ragoûts, game and poultry dishes, as well as to pork, sauerkraut, cabbage etc. They should be crushed before being used and they marry well with thyme, fennel, bay, marjoram, garlic, spices, wine and spirits.

LARD, TO. To lace or cover poultry, game or meat with narrow ribbons of fat using a larding needle to get the fat into the interior of the meat. Lacking a larding needle, the fat can be tied on to the meat and as it melts it will baste the meat.

LARDOONS. These are the thin ribbons of pork used when larding.

MARINADE. See page 202.

MERRYTHOUGHT. Fanciful name for the furcula between the neck and the breastbone of poultry, also called the wishbone. Both names refer to the custom of two persons making a wish and pulling the bone. The holder of the larger broken portion will, it is said, be granted his wish.

MINCE, TO. To cut into very small pieces. In the United States finely chopped food is described as minced, although in Britain this usually refers to food put through a grinder.

OIL SAC. A small gland at the base of the chicken's tail which should always be removed before the bird is cooked. Probably the butcher will do it but otherwise it should be carefully cut out without breaking it.

OYSTER OF CHICKEN. Two oyster-shaped pieces of meat on the back of a fowl, situated in the bone cavities on the lower part of the carcass and the only good meat on the back.

PARSON'S NOSE. Also called Pope's Nose. The extreme tail-end portion of a fowl, and considered by many to be delicious.

PEMMICAN. A food devised by the North American Indians which would remain edible for long periods so that it could be used in times of war and on long journeys. They cut venison or buffalo meat into strips, dried it in the sun, pounded it to a paste with fat and mixed this with wild berries. The mixture was formed into cakes which were packed tightly into rawhide bags. In more recent times a similar concoction has been used on Arctic expeditions, using beef and raisins, as this provides a food of maximum nutritional value which requires the minimum of space while travelling.

PURÉE, TO. To push food through a sieve or beat it until it is like a thick cream.

REDUCING. This means just what it implies, to reduce or concentrate liquid by rapid boiling.

RUB WITH GARLIC, TO. Peel a large clove of garlic, cut it into half and rub the cut side of the garlic across the food concerned.

SADDLE. This is the upper back portion of the animal carcass, including the loins. As far as game is concerned, the term applies mainly to hare and venison.

SAUTÉ, TO. To fry in a small amount of fat, i.e. only enough to prevent the food sticking to the pan.

SCORE, TO. To cut gashes or lines into the surface of food. To score fat on meat means to slit or notch the outside rim.

SEASONED FLOUR. This is simply flour into which has been mixed salt and pepper.

SHRED, TO. To cut or grate into thin strips, thinner than julienne (which see).

SIMMER, TO. To cook gently in liquid just below boiling point. Simmering brings out flavour and tenderizes meat. Water is simmering when tiny bubbles dance on the top but are not actually breaking the surface.

SINGE. To pass a flame over a chicken or other bird to burn off the fine hairs left after plucking. A gas taper or a wooden spill gives the least smoke.

SOUR CREAM. This does not mean cream which has turned sour but a definite product sold as sour cream. Fresh cream can be soured by the action of lemon juice if necessary. To 2 cups (2½) of warmed fresh (sweet) cream add 2 tablespoons (2½) of strained lemon juice. Leave for 15 minutes and it will be ready for use.

STEAM, TO. To cook above water. The food is held either in the top of a steamer, which is perforated, or on a rack, but it must be protected from touching the surrounding water in which it is cooking.

TAPPIT-HEN. 1. The Scottish name for a hen with a crest or top-knot. 2. A pewter drinking vessel having a lid with a knob.

TRUFFLE. The underground fruit of a fungi. They grow in the earth in the vicinity of certain trees. The two best kinds of truffles are the Italian white truffles from Piedmont and Alba, and the French black or Périgord truffles. The flavour varies according to locality, some truffles being better flavoured than others, and are correspondingly more expensive. Truffles look like ungainly potatoes and are seasonal. Their perfume is strong, unique and delicious and must be smelt to be understood. Its flavour is somewhat peppery and not important for it is the odour of the truffle which causes the gourmet to salivate. In Italy white truffles are thinly sliced and often added to a dish after it has been cooked. In France truffles are used when cooking the dish. Truffles are not cheap, even in their places of origin.

TRUSS. To fix the wings and legs of a bird to its carcass by means of twine or skewers and to tie as a bundle.

UMBLES. The edible entrails of any mammal, but chiefly of the deer.

Vintage Chart

Year	CLARET	BURGUNDY	WHITE BURGUNDY	SAUTERNES	RHONE	RHINE	MOSELLE	CHAMPAGNE	PORT	LOIRE
1945	7	6	–	6	7	–	–	5	7	–
1946	1	1	–	2	5	–	–	–	–	–
1947	5	6	–	6	6	–	–	6	7	–
1948	5	5	–	5	4	–	–	–	7	–
1949	6	5	–	5	7	–	–	6	–	–
1950	5	3	–	6	6	–	–	–	6	–
1951	0	1	–	2	4	–	–	–	–	–
1952	6	5	5	6	6	5	4	7	4	–
1953	6	5	4	5	6	7	6	6	–	–
1954	4	3	1	2	7	2	2	–	6	–
1955	6	5	4	6	6	5	4	6	7	–
1956	0	1	1	2	5	1	1	–	–	–
1957	5	5	5	4	7	4	4	–	5	–
1958	4	3	4	4	5	5	5	–	6	–
1959	6	7	6	6	6	7	7	7	–	6
1960	4	1	1	3	6	2	2	–	7	2
1961	7	7	7	5	7	5	4	7	–	5
1962	6	5	6	6	6	3	3	6	5	4
1963	1	4	3	2	5	3	2	–	7	1
1964	6	7	7	5	6	6	7	7	–	7
1965	0	1	2	2	5	1	1	–	4	1
1966	6	7	7	6	6	6	6	–	7	5
1967	5	5	7	5	6	5	4	–	6	6
1968	1	1	1	0	5	1	1	–	–	3

0=no good　　　7=the best

Comparative Cookery Measures

It is not simple to convert with absolute accuracy measurements for the kitchen. Generally speaking, absolute accuracy is not required, except when making cakes or pastries. Throughout this book both British and American measurements have been used and, as far as possible, ingredients have been measured in cups and tablespoons for easy conversion.

Fortunately for the cook, British and American solid weights are equivalent; but this does not always mean that the British housewife can readily understand American measurements or *vice versa*. In the United States the average housewife has her set of measuring spoons and cups. In Britain this is never so general, although most housewives do have a measuring cup or jug.

The British measuring cup used in this book is the British Standard Institute's Cup which gives a ½-pint measure, the equivalent to 10 fluid ounces (it is the size of the average British breakfastcup or tumbler). The American standard cup is equal to the American ½ pint, which is equivalent to 8 fluid ounces.

All spoon measurements are level unless otherwise specified.

Throughout this book British measurements are given first; the American equivalent follows, where necessary, in brackets.

CONVERSION OF METRIC MEASURES INTO BRITISH AND AMERICAN MEASURES

Exact measurements are, of course, not possible, and if applied in the kitchen would require all housewife-cooks to be also mathematicians, which most of us are not. The best, therefore, is the nearest approximate.

EXACT MEASUREMENTS

1 kilogram (kg)	=	2.2 lb.
1 litre (1.)	=	1.8 pints

1 lb.	=	0.5 kg. or 500 grams	1 gallon	=	4.5 litres
8 oz.	=	240 grams	1 quart	=	1.125 litres ($1\frac{1}{8}$ litres)
4 oz.	=	120 grams	1 pint	=	0.5 litres
1 oz.	=	30 grams	$\frac{1}{2}$ pint	=	0.25 litres
			$\frac{1}{4}$ pint	=	0.125 litres ($\frac{1}{8}$ litre)

OVEN TEMPERATURE CHART

In this book oven heats are described as 'slow', 'moderate', 'hot' etc. The following chart gives the corresponding temperature and oven settings both for gas and electricity as used in most modern cookers.

ELECTRIC OVEN SETTING, APPROXIMATE TEMPERATURE	GAS THERMOSTAT	OVEN DESCRIPTION
250°F. (121°C.)	$\frac{1}{4}$	very cool
275°F. (135°C.)	$\frac{1}{2}$	,,
300°F. (149°C.)	1, 2	cool
325°F. (163°C.)	3	warm
350°F. (177°C.)	4	moderate
375°F. (191°C.)	5	fairly hot
400°F. (204°C.)	6	,,
425°F. (218°C.)	7	hot
450°F. (232°C.)	8	very hot
475°F. (246°C.)	9	

Index

The International
Wine and Food Society

The International Wine and Food Society **was** founded in 1933 by André L. Simon, C.B.E., **as a** world-wide non-profit-making society.

The first of its various aims has been to bring together and serve all who believe that a right understanding of wine and food is an essential part of personal contentment and health; and that an intelligent approach to the pleasures and problems of the table offers far greater rewards than the mere satisfaction of appetite.

For information about the Society,
apply to the Secretary,
Marble Arch House,
44 Edgware Road, London, W2